Donated by CLI Prison Alliance
Box 97095 Raleigh NC 27624
Write us a letter today!
Enroll in the CLI Bible study

This publication is provided by:

Freedom in Jesus Prison Ministries

www.fijm.org

info@fijm.org

Diving Deeper
A Daily Leap into a Life More Abundant

Daily Discipleship Field Guide

Stephen E. Canup

Author of <u>Jail-House Religion: From Park Avenue...to Park Bench...to Prison</u>

Special thanks to Rev. Don Castleberry

Founder, Freedom in Jesus Prison Ministries

ACKNOWLEDGEMENTS

Everyone needs a mature spiritual mentor and trusted accountability partner. I love and appreciate Don Castleberry for fulfilling this role for me. His trust, time and commitment to me have been invaluable. He and his wife, Donna, have become some of my very best friends.

Rev. Don Castleberry is the Founder of Freedom in Jesus Prison Ministries. Learn more about this anointed prison ministry at www. fijm.org; or, write to Freedom in Jesus Prison Ministries, P.O. Box 939, Levelland, TX 79336. You may e-mail us at info@fijm.org

Special thanks to Kevin Rhoads, Dream Taxi Media + Marketing, for the cover design. For more creative and marketing assistance, contact Kevin Rhoads: kevin@creativeguy.com

Additional thanks to Slate Group, Lubbock, TX, for assistance in creative design and lay-out. Special appreciation goes to Angella Jordan, Account Representative, Slate Group, Lubbock, TX. For more information on Slate Group services, contact Angella Jordan: ajordan@slategroup.com

Appreciation is also expressed for printing services at Perfection Press. For information contact Robert Riggs, rriggs@ printedtoperfection.com

Diving Deeper

A Daily Leap into a Life More Abundant

Daily Discipleship Field Guide

Table of Contents

INTRODUCTION

In Matthew 28:18, the last command Jesus gave His followers was to "go and make disciples". A "disciple" is a "disciplined learner". A church member is not necessarily a "disciple".

This **"Discipleship Field Guide"** is for anyone who wants to become a more "disciplined learner" by growing in knowledge of the Scriptures, and by being led by the Spirit to apply the Word to every life situation.

The Bible gives us guidance as to the attributes of a disciple:

- Disciples are proven by their fruit (John 15:8).
- Disciples are proven by their love for one another (John 13:34-35).
- Disciples are hated by the world (John 15:18-19).
- Disciples are persecuted by those who do not know God (John 15:20-21).
- Disciples should be like their teacher (Luke 6:40).
- Disciples should obey their teacher (Luke 6:46).[1]

Jesus came to restore us to relationship with our Father. The Holy Spirit is our Teacher, Counselor, Friend, Helper and Guide. The practice of committing a block of time daily with Him is a key to growing in relationship with our Heavenly Father.

This book helps the believer establish the discipline of spending time daily in the Word, and with the Holy Spirit. Seeking God earnestly every day results in personal spiritual growth and rewards (Hebrews 11:6).

<u>Diving Deeper</u> demonstrates how to obtain freedom from every form of bondage. I was bound in prisons of my own making – addictions, pride, depression, anger, bi-polar illness, un-forgiveness, shame, regret, etc. – long before I was incarcerated behind the steel bars and razor wire of a penal institution. The Truth I found in Jesus and His Word by His Holy Spirit set me free long before I was released to the free world.

You too can obtain positive measurable results in your life through the daily, personal application of Scripture; and, the personal empowerment of the presence of the Holy Spirit. Paul closes his second letter to the Corinthians by stressing the importance of the presence, communion, sharing together, and fellowship with the Holy Spirit:

"The grace (favor and spiritual blessing) of the Lord Jesus Christ and the love of God and the presence and fellowship (the communion and sharing together, and participation) in the Holy Spirit be with you all. Amen (so be it)." (2 Corinthians 13:14, AMP)

Join me today in Diving Deeper… let's take a daily leap into a life more abundant!!!

[1]Chip Brogden, www.chipbrogden.com , from his teaching on the Gospel of John.

1

Transformation

THE "OLD MAN"

Six Months before Prison (2007)

Stephen Canup

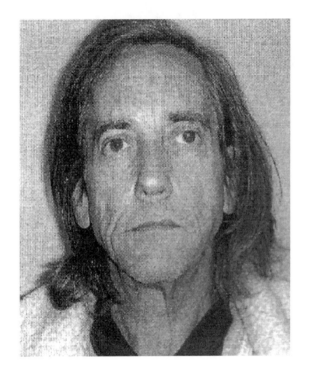

Guilty and Condemned by Sin to Death
Romans 6:23 "For the wages of sin is death…

Guilty of these sins against God, others and self:

Addictions to drugs, alcohol, sex, pornography, praise of men, work.

Pride	Judgment	Thievery
Worry	Self-hate	Adultery
Fear	Resentment	Sexual identity
Depression	Regret	Confusion
Hopelessness	Anger	Lying
Anxiety	Covetousness	Conceit
Profanity	Depravity	Intellectualism
Fornication	Reprobation	Humanism
Lustful desires	Un-forgiveness	Shame
Perversion	Immorality	Remorse
Idolatry	Self-abuse	Guilt
Selfishness	Bitterness	Offense

The sinful and cursed life I was living before prison resulted in me being:

- Homeless, living on the streets of Nashville, TN, for 3 years prior to prison.
- Unemployed for 7 years prior to incarceration.
- Broke after having filed for bankruptcy twice.
- Destitute with all my earthly possessions contained in 1 hanging garment bag in the prison's property room awaiting the day of my release.
- Desolate having abandoned all family and friends, leaving me lonely and utterly forsaken.
- Depressed so deeply by these life conditions that I had attempted suicide several times.
- Hopeless and absolutely convinced nothing would ever change or get better in any way.

THE "NEW MAN"

One Year after Prison (2012)

Stephen Canup

A Free Man - Alive in Christ

...but the gift of God is eternal life in Christ Jesus our Lord." Romans 6:23

"I have been crucified with Christ and I no longer live, but Christ lives in me. The life I now live in the body, I live by faith in the Son of God, who loved me and gave himself for me." (Gal. 2:20)

"Therefore if any is (ingrafted) in Christ, the Messiah, he is (a new creature altogether), a new creation; the old (previous moral and spiritual condition) has passed away. Behold, the fresh and new has come!" (II Cor. 5:17, AMP)

"So if the Son sets you free, you will be free indeed" (John 8:36)

The new life in Christ that began in prison in 2009 has brought many blessings. As of 2019, some of these abundant life realities include:

- My spiritual re-birth April 20, 2009!!!
- Restored relationships with every family member.
- A mentor and accountability partner, Don Castleberry, who speaks the truth in love.
- President of Freedom in Jesus Prison Ministries, as well as Board Member.
- Author of <u>Jail-House Religion: From Park Avenue…to Park Bench…to Prison</u> (240,000 copies in print as of 2019).
- Author of <u>Diving Deeper: A Daily Leap into a Life More Abundant</u>.
- Acceptance instead of rejection.
- Joy and hope instead of depression and hopelessness.
- Purpose and passion to help set others free.
- Peace, boldness and confidence instead of anxiety and fear.
- The righteousness of Christ Jesus instead of perversion and depravity.
- Love and compassion for others instead of selfishness and self-hate.
- Freedom from addictions to alcohol, drugs, pornography, smoking and gambling.
- A tongue of blessings and respect instead of pride, criticism and profanity.
- A tender, new heart rather than the old heart of stone.
- Re-made to be a cheerful giver of tithes and offerings.
- A beautiful, three-bedroom, two bath home provided rent-free except for utilities.
- Two late-model vehicles were given to me in great condition with low mileage.
- A house full of good furniture, and a closet full of good clothes.
- Debt-free, with also some money in savings.
- A renewed mind free of all the bad effects of addictions and depression.
- Good health.
- Mature Christians I can call for prayer or advice anytime about anything.
- Licensed and ordained in 2012 as a minister of the Gospel of Jesus Christ.

Diving Deeper

Daily Discipleship Field Guide

January 1

JAIL-HOUSE RELIGION

Luke 19:10
"...for the Son of Man has come to seek and to save that which was lost."

The religious leaders of the day wanted to know why Jesus ate with and ministered to "sinners". Where are plenty of us lost sinners? Locked up in prison. Jesus is seeking to save us!

In here we are sober and in our right minds. We are "still". If we listen, we can hear Him here!

Isn't this the time and place that makes the most sense to cry out to God?

Can someone really find God in a jail or prison? Is God close enough to us here to hear our sincere cry? Can we really be heard by Him as we commit, or re-dedicate, our hearts to walk with Christ? Can He actually use a convict, who turns his life around, to advance the cause of His Kingdom?

"Jail-House Religion", a term we have all heard in a negative light, does not have to be a cheap imitation. Rather, it can be "the real thing". God CAN change you forever, but you must LET Him! You must WANT to be changed. It begins with absolute surrender and submission to His Will for you.

TODAY'S CHALLENGE:

Are you ready to surrender to God? Tell our Heavenly Father you are ready to submit your life, and your own will, to His plan for you. Trust Him one day at a time to lead you into His future by His Holy Spirit.

Begin today.

Dive Deeper: Study Luke 19.

January 2

SEEK THE LORD

God tells us if we seek Him (look hard for Him), we will find Him! It does not matter where we are, how old we are, what our problems are – if we seek Him, He will be found by us.

Is. 55:6-7 - *"Seek the Lord while He may be found: Call on Him while He is near. Let the wicked forsake his way and the evil man his thoughts. Let him turn to the Lord, and he will have mercy on him, and to our God, for He will freely pardon."*

Jer. 29:11-14 - *"For I know the plans I have for you, declares the Lord, plans to prosper you and not to harm you, plans to give you hope and a future. Then you will call upon me and come and pray to me and I will listen to you. You will seek me and find me when you seek me with all your heart. I will be found by you, declares the Lord, and will bring you back from captivity…"*

In other words, when we seek God with all of our heart we will find Him – even when we are locked up.

You'll never have more time to earnestly seek God than you do right now.

TODAY'S CHALLENGE:

Tell the Father you desire to find Him. Ask Him to give you a hunger and a thirst for Him and His Word. Ask the Holy Spirit to teach you how to diligently seek God.

Dive Deeper: Study Jeremiah 29:1-14; Isaiah 55.

January 3

CAN GOD USE YOU?

2 Samuel 12:9
(God said to David) *"Why have you despised the commandment of the LORD, to do evil in His sight? You have killed Uriah the Hittite with the sword; you have taken his wife to be your wife..."*

Throughout the entire Bible, time after time, we find God using some of the most unlikely people to accomplish His will to advance His Kingdom. He has used murderers, adulterers, thieves, lowly shepherds, hated tax collectors; and, a lot of them had, at one time or another, been in some form of confinement or captivity.

But these men repented, committed their lives to God, and cried out to Him from their own miserable circumstances. People like Peter, Paul, Samson, James, John the Baptist, Joseph, and Jeremiah had been incarcerated just like us. Leaders like Moses, David, and Jacob – who were once murderers, adulterers and thieves - were used mightily once they called on God and turned their lives back to Him. Even Jesus was arrested and put on trial.

God does not care about your record. Unlike men, God does not discriminate against the down-trodden, the lowly, the forgotten – we who are labeled as felons, prisoners, convicts and inmates.

Yes, God can use even me and you.

TODAY'S CHALLENGE:

Confess your sins to God. He already knows anyway. As you truly humble yourself before Him, thank Him for His forgiveness found in Jesus Christ alone. Be real. Have an honest talk with Him.

Ask God to use you in His Kingdom.

Dive Deeper: Study 2 Samuel chapters 11 & 12; Psalm 51.

January 4

GOD LOVES PRISONERS

God must have a special love and attention reserved for people like us – prisoners, convicts, inmates, and captives. In fact, Strong's Concordance listed over 340 verses where the word "prison", "prisoner", "captive" or "captivity" is a key word.

Here are some examples:

Psalm 102:19-20 – *"The Lord looked down...from Heaven...to hear the groans of the prisoners..."*

Psalm 69:33 – *"The Lord... does not despise His captive people..."*

Psalm 146:7 – *"The Lord sets prisoners free."*

Zechariah 9:11-12 – *"I will free your prisoners from the waterless pit...O prisoners of hope; even now I announce that I will restore twice as much to you."*

Matthew 25:36 – *Jesus said, "...I was in prison and you came and visited me."*

Also, in one of His first talks in the synagogue, Jesus quoted:

Isaiah 61:1 *"...the Lord has anointed me to preach good news to the poor. He has sent me to bind up the broken-hearted, to proclaim freedom for the captives and release from darkness for the prisoners..."*

God has compassion for those in bondage. He listens. He wants to set them free! Even though you may be incarcerated, you can in fact be free. I was in several prisons of my own making long before I ever heard a succession of steel doors slam behind me. Going to prison set me free forever after God found me and saved me right there on my prison bunk.

TODAY'S CHALLENGE:

Tell the Father you want true freedom through Jesus by His Holy Spirit. Be free on the inside.

Dive Deeper: Study Isaiah 61; Zechariah 9.

January 5

RESCUE ME

God has plenty of experience pulling people up out of their own miry, dark, damp, deep pit. David, a man after God's own heart, must have known exactly what it was like:

Psalm 69:14-15 *"Rescue me from the mire, do not let me sink; deliver me from those who hate me, from the deep waters. Do not let the floodwaters engulf me or the depths swallow me up or the pit close its mouth over me."*

Psalm 40:1-2 *"I waited patiently for the Lord; He turned to me and heard my cry. He lifted me out of the slimy pit, out of the mud and mire..."*

Before I went to prison, I lived for years in hopelessness and despair. Having been previously diagnosed as bi-polar, I lived in an almost constant state of suicidal depression. Homeless and helpless, I thought nothing would ever get better in any way. Frozen in fear of what might happen if I ever tried to climb out, I sunk lower and lower into what I was sure was a bottomless black hole pit.

When I finally admitted I could not help myself, and turned to Him in true humility, God was ready, willing and able to step in, reach down and pull me out.

Can you see yourself sinking? Are you bogged down? Are you finally ready to stop trying to save yourself? Cry out for help.

TODAY'S CHALLENGE:

Reach out to God. Call on the Name of Jesus. He will give you Peace. He will rescue you.

Let Him.

Dive Deeper: Study Psalm 40; Psalm 69.

January 6

STOP LISTENING TO OTHERS

Mark 5:40
"And they ridiculed Him (Jesus)..."

Luke 23:11
"Then Herod, with his men of war, treated Him with contempt and mocked Him..."

Many inmates taunt Christians with stuff like, "You weren't reading your Bible on the street"; or, "You weren't going to church or chapel services before they locked you up"; or, "Man, that's just that old jail-house religion, it will wear off pretty soon. It's not real. It's just the same old fake stuff we've seen before." I heard all that too.

In one respect they were right. I don't know about you, but if I had been caught up in God's Word instead of my addictions, I wouldn't have ended up in prison. If I had been going to church every week instead of going out to beg, borrow or steal enough to get my next hit, I wouldn't have ended up here. Are you sick and tired of places like this?

After I got saved in prison and while I was still locked up, I began to see that the people ridiculing Christians were the ones who were satisfied with their circumstances. They already figured they were coming back. They did nothing to change. Making fun of others gave them the excuse they wanted to reject God.

Do you want to be a better person for your family? Do you realize your need for Jesus? Do you want to change?

TODAY'S CHALLENGE:

Stop listening to people who do not have the courage to change.

Follow hard after God.

Dive Deeper: Study Mark 5; Luke 23 & 24.

January 7

THE REAL THING

Romans 12:2
"and do not be conformed to this world, but be transformed by the renewing of your mind, that you may prove what is that good and acceptable and perfect will of God."

"Jail-House Religion" can either be "the real thing", or, "a cheap imitation". All of us have seen imitation, "knock-off" products – fake Nike tennis shoes, imitation Air-Jordan's, fake designer handbags like Gucci, etc. You can tell the fakes over time, maybe not so much at first, but over time the imitation breaks down, falls apart and gets thrown away. We don't use it anymore. It becomes clear why it was so cheap to begin with.

Unlike when we might have been tricked into buying a fake "knock-off", in our new relationship with God we determine through our own actions, habits and beliefs, whether we get "the real thing" or "a cheap imitation".

Finally, I wanted "the real thing". God got my attention. I wanted the rest of my life to be the opposite of my past. I did not want to come back to prison.

We must decide to stop conforming to the world around us. For too long we have cared too much about what others say. Instead, we should care what God says. We must desire to be transformed by His Word.

TODAY'S CHALLENGE:

Tell God the Father you truly want the real thing. Tell Him you're not playing anymore, and that you are ready to let Him transform you.

Get real with God. God will get real with you.

Dive Deeper: Study Romans 12.

January 8

THE ONLY WAY

John 14:6
"Jesus said to him, 'I am the way, the truth, and the life. No one comes to the Father except through Me.'"

They say insanity is doing the same old thing over and over again, but expecting different results.

Similar to "The Prodigal Son" in Luke 15:17-20, when I finally "came to my senses" after my first ten months of incarceration, I wanted to go home to my Father. I returned to Him.

I decided I was going to do things differently, so I could be different, and so I could finally make a difference in the lives of my family, and in my community.

The only way this can happen is through a personal relationship with Jesus Christ as Savior and Lord! Each of us must make our own decision. Have you made this decision? Have you decided to go "all in and all out" for Jesus?

There is no better time to cry out for God. He will hear you. His Word says you are special to Him. He will help you. He loves you wherever, and however, and whoever you are now. You do not have to "change" before you find Jesus. He will change you if you let Him. Just go to Him. He will take care of the rest.

TODAY'S CHALLENGE:

Tell God the Father you believe, and confess, that Jesus is the only way to Him. Ask the Holy Spirit to reveal Jesus to you.

Stop running from God. Get up, dust yourself off, and go home.

Dive Deeper: Study John 14; Luke 15.

January 9

REPENT

Matthew 3:3
"In those days John the Baptist came preaching in the wilderness of Judea, and saying, 'Repent, for the kingdom of heaven is at hand!'"

True repentance must happen to see or enter the Kingdom of God.

The Bible says to "repent and believe the gospel", "repent and be saved", "repent and be baptized", and, "unless you repent you will likewise perish".

Repentance is a 180-degree turn away from sin and towards God. It is like making a u-turn on a highway. To repent is to change your mind to agree with God about sin, and make a heart-felt decision to change.

There must be a day that you are sick and tired of being sick and tired, and make a determined choice to follow hard after God rather than continuing on the same old path where the enemy waits to steal, kill and destroy your life. In one direction is death and darkness. In the other direction lies Life and Light.

When true repentance has taken place you will see positive changes in the way you think, talk and act. Others will see and hear something different from you. Repentance is about change.

If you have not truly repented, you are not saved.

TODAY'S CHALLENGE:

Ask yourself if you have ever truly repented. Ask the Holy Spirit to convict you of the truth about this in your life. Tell the Father you are ready to abandon your past and your previous path.

Make a u-turn.

Dive Deeper: Study Matthew 3.

January 10

SURRENDER

Isaiah 64:8
"But now, O Lord, you are our Father; we are the clay, and you are our potter; we are all the work of your hand."

Before I was saved in prison, I wanted to change my life but was powerless to do so. I learned that I could not change me. If I could have changed me I would have done so long before I was addicted, depressed, suicidal, homeless, lonely, lost, and eventually incarcerated! Is this also true of you? Have you tried to change yourself?

I tried to change myself an endless number of times but failed every time. So it was really great news to me that God did not expect me to change myself! Really. He only wanted me to allow His Holy Spirit to possess me, be willing daily to allow Him to lead me in the right way, and try my best to be instantly obedient to His promptings.

When we willingly surrender to God the Holy Spirit in us, and daily submit to be led by His Spirit instead of being led by our "flesh", He will begin His work of sanctification in us! In other words, when we surrender to the Spirit, and submit to His leadership moment by moment, He will change us. We are not responsible for changing ourselves.

TODAY'S CHALLENGE:

Ask the Holy Spirit to help you learn to surrender daily to His leadership. Decide today to submit to God in every way, every day.

Let Him change you. Stop trying to change yourself.

Dive Deeper: Study Isaiah 64.

January 11

SUBMISSION

Romans 9:20
"But who are you, O man, to answer back to God? Will what is molded say to its molder, 'Why have you made me like this?'"

The best picture of submission is one of clay in a potter's hands. The potter transforms the clay from a shapeless handful of ugly mud into an exquisite object of beautiful art. The potter is totally in charge of the transformation, and the end-product is determined in large part by his patience and skill. As followers of Jesus, we can be sure we have the best Master Potter!

Sometimes God allows extreme circumstances, like prison or other hardships of life, to get our attention. Often these may come as a consequence of poor choices made by ourselves or others, but they are best viewed as opportunities for positive change. To be transformed, a piece of clay must be soft so it will yield. We must consciously and willingly submit to God.

We may not understand why God made us the way He did, or what He is trying to teach us in the midst of our trials and circumstances. However, we must trust Him to mold us into a vessel of honor He can use and work through to positively impact others.

TODAY'S CHALLENGE:

Will you submit to the Hand of the Potter? Prayerfully put yourself in His Hands daily and patiently allow Him to form you. As you willingly submit to the hardening fire of trials and circumstances, trust Him today to make a beautiful vessel.

The Potter knows what He is making.

Dive Deeper: Study Romans 9.

January 12

THE POTTER'S CLAY

Jeremiah 18:1-6

"This is the word that came to Jeremiah from the Lord: ² "Go down to the potter's house, and there I will give you my message." ³ So I went down to the potter's house, and I saw him working at the wheel. ⁴ But the pot he was shaping from the clay was marred in his hands; so the potter formed it into another pot, shaping it as seemed best to him. ⁵ Then the word of the Lord came to me. ⁶ He said, "Can I not do with you, Israel, as this potter does?" declares the Lord. "Like clay in the hand of the potter, so are you in my hand, Israel."

Regardless of how bad a mess we have made of our lives, and how far we may have run away from God, we are never so broken or so lost in the world that God cannot find us, joyfully accept our returning to Him (Luke 15:32), make us a new creation (2 Corinthians. 5:17) and establish His plan for our lives (Jeremiah. 29:11-14a).

However, we must be *gratefully humble, prayerfully submissive and faithfully obedient.*

In *humility* we must recognize we cannot re-make ourselves and be *grateful* He can. In *submission* we must *prayerfully* put ourselves in His hands and patiently allow Him to form us, and subject us to the hardening fire of trials and circumstances. We must be always *faithful* in *obedience* to follow His instructions so that we will experience the best of His intentions as He accomplishes His will through us, forming us into the image of His Son, Jesus (Romans. 8:29).

TODAY'S CHALLENGE:

Stay on the Potter's wheel. He is still working.

Dive Deeper: Study Luke 15:11-24, 32; Jeremiah 18; 2 Corinthians 5:17; Romans 8:29; Jeremiah 29:11-14a.

January 13

REASONS TO SURRENDER

Job 10:8-9
"Your hands fashioned and made me, and now you have destroyed me altogether. Remember that you have made me like clay; and will you return me to the dust?"

As a former inmate, I can relate to the term "surrender". ☺ Back then, I remember surrendering before being taken into custody for incarceration. I was forced to comply with their commands, and follow their lead. I was a captive. Do you remember?

However, now that we have accepted what the Father has provided for us in salvation, we surrender completely to the Lordship of Jesus, and to the Potter's hands for our benefit – in fact, for our freedom rather than our captivity or incarceration. As a new creation in Christ, we willingly comply with His commands. We desire to follow the leading of the Holy Spirit.

God has every right to demand that we give Him our all. He made us. We are under His authority whether we choose to submit to it or not. It is in our best interest to willingly surrender. He saved us. He has a vision of a perfectly completed vessel ready for His use, and we are better off when we allow Him to make of us what He wants.

TODAY'S CHALLENGE:

Someone once said, "Ask God, Who gave Himself completely to you, to help you give yourself completely to Him." Simply say, "Yes, Lord" when He speaks to you through His Holy Spirit.

Surrender fully to God. You will be glad you did.

Dive Deeper: Study Job 9 & 10.

January 14

PRESENT YOURSELF

Romans 12:1
"I appeal to you therefore, brothers, by the mercies of God, to present your bodies as a living sacrifice, holy and acceptable to God, which is your spiritual worship."

My full surrender to the justice system required that I submit myself to their rules and their way of doing things. Before I was "born again" in prison, I was not always willing and compliant to their demands. I did not have a good attitude and I had little respect for authority. Doing time was hard. Can you relate?

However, once I began to understand God's Word, I knew I should respect positions of authority because God has placed them there. I began to submit and comply. Doing my time got easier.

As Christians, we are urged by the Apostle Paul to sacrifice our self-will, and willingly present our lives to God. We fully surrender to Him. In respecting His ultimate authority, we position ourselves to allow His Holy Spirit to gradually sanctify our lives so that we become ever more pleasing, holy and acceptable to our Father.

Jesus said we should worship the Father in spirit and in truth. Our hearts must truly desire to live sacrificially to and for Him.

TODAY'S CHALLENGE:

Real worship of God results as we live our lives with eternity firmly in mind. That is, we are increasingly concerned with obedience, holiness, and self-sacrifice so that we become more pleasing to our Father. We become less concerned with pleasing others.

Present your life daily to God.

Dive Deeper: Study Romans 11:33 – 13:6.

January 15

RENEW YOUR MIND

Romans 12:2
"Do not be conformed to this world, but be transformed by the renewal of your mind, that by testing you may discern what is the will of God, what is good and acceptable and perfect."

Before going to prison, much of my life was centered around desiring to be accepted in and by "the world". I wanted to "fit in". I was convinced I had to "go along to get along."

I never felt God had any plan for my life, although I remember many times wishing that I knew what He wanted, and why I was here on this earth. I had a strong internal desire to "make a difference" in this world, but I did not know how.

As I began to study the Word, I realized "the world" has plenty of ways to distract us from God's mission for our lives. For the most part, the ways of life in "the world" are opposed to the ways of abundant, eternal life in the Kingdom of God.

As we allow God's Love and His Word to renew our minds; our way of thinking, talking and living will position us to know and receive God's Will – His perfect, pleasing and acceptable plan for our lives.

TODAY'S CHALLENGE:

Ask the Father what His perfect Will is for you today. Start by telling Him you want to live less in "the world" and more in His Kingdom. It really is a choice you make minute by minute.

Stop conforming. Be transformed.

Dive Deeper: Study 1 Peter 2:9-12; 2 Corinthians 6:14-18; Romans 8:5-8; James 1:26-27.

January 16

A NEW ATTITUDE

Ephesians 4:22-23
"You were taught, with regard to your former way of life, to put off your old self, which is being corrupted by its deceitful desires; to be made new in the attitude of your minds..."

When we begin the process of transformation in renewing our mind by the Word of God, we are often besieged with old ways of thinking from our former way of life. The influences of "the world, the flesh and the devil" continue to try to direct our thoughts, words, and actions.

These negative attitudes are prevalent in prison. Surrounded by constant talk of past offenses, present trials, and future plans for "getting up", it is sometimes difficult to think positively about our own situation. We can easily be discouraged if we don't separate ourselves from the crowd.

Paul instructs us to consciously remind ourselves that our old man is dead and our new man is alive in Christ Jesus. We can choose to ignore the enemy's deceitful attempts to appeal to our old man's fleshly desires.

We must adopt a new attitude toward life – one based solidly on the wisdom, hope, peace and love found in the truth of God's Word.

TODAY'S CHALLENGE:

Begin today to make positive choices to divorce yourself from the type of thinking that has been destroying your life and has now landed you in prison. Separate yourself from those who are still thinking and talking like you did before you were saved.

Adopt a new attitude. Be made new.

Dive Deeper: Study Ephesians 4.

January 17

THINK ABOUT THIS

Philippians 4:8-9
"Finally, brothers and sisters, whatever is true, whatever is noble, whatever is right, whatever is pure, whatever is lovely, whatever is admirable—if anything is excellent or praiseworthy—think about such things... And the God of peace will be with you."

"Garbage in. Garbage out."

In the early days of computer programming, this familiar expression was often used to caution programmers to be certain they were entering good, reliable data into the system. In the same way, what we allow to enter our mind through our eyes and ears directly affects what we think about, what we say and how we act.

Do you have problems with lustful thoughts, impure daydreams, hateful speech, and wrong actions? In prison, it is hard not to give in to such but we must be proactive in fighting and winning this battle.

Paul tells us to program our minds with thoughts that are true, noble, right, pure, lovely, admirable, excellent, and praiseworthy. Make sure you are putting the right data into your own powerful, personal computer – your mind.

What kinds of reading material do you have? What types of television programming occupies your time? Examine the topics you talk about and the conversations to which you listen.

TODAY'S CHALLENGE:

As Joyce Meyers says, we must "think about what we are thinking about!" The battlefield really is in your mind. Ask the Father to help you examine the type of input your eyes and ears receive into your brain.

There is a good reason we put on the helmet of salvation. It guards our minds. Think about this.

Dive Deeper: Philippians 4.

January 18

SET YOUR MINDS

Colossians 3:2-3
"Set your minds on things above, not on earthly things. ³ For you died, and your life is now hidden with Christ in God."

Wrong "mindsets" are available in abundance in prison. To counter this, we must "set our minds".

We are encouraged in the Word to "set our minds" on things above, not on earthly things so prevalent around us. Another version says to "set our hearts". I believe right mindsets affect our heart – our deepest core of being.

Setting our minds and hearts on things above can be done by adopting Heaven's priorities and rejecting worldly influences and demands. We concentrate on things of eternal importance instead of temporarily insignificant distractions and temptations. As Christians, our real home is where Jesus is. The Word says we are seated with him in Heavenly places.

When you think of your old man as dead, and realize you are now alive in Christ Jesus, you will have as little desire for worldly things as a corpse has – none. Admittedly, this is not achieved overnight, especially in prison. It is a process requiring practice and perseverance.

Observe the world around you through God's lens of love and holiness.

TODAY'S CHALLENGE:

Ask God the Father to help you view and evaluate everything from a heavenly and eternal perspective. Decide to try your best today to see things through His eyes. Ask Him to love others through you today by His Holy Spirit in you.

Overcome wrong mindsets by setting your mind on things above.

Dive Deeper: Study Colossians 3:1 – 4:6.

January 19

CAPTURE WRONG THOUGHTS

2 Corinthians 10:5
"We demolish arguments and every pretension that sets itself up against the knowledge of God, and we take captive every thought to make it obedient to Christ."

In prison, there are plenty of arguments, false teachings, unrighteousness and spiritual strongholds that are diametrically opposed to the principles and truth of Jesus Christ. How do we demolish them? How do we overcome?

The only weapons capable are not the normal worldly ones we are familiar with; rather, we have the authority of the Name of Jesus, the power of His Blood, the word of our own testimony, and the powerful spiritual gifts exercised by the Holy Spirit in us.

Weapons are useless unless they are used. In our warfare, God is our Commander in Chief, and even our thoughts should be submitted to His leadership. We must quickly arrest any thoughts that try to overpower us, and immediately yield them up to Christ.

When we are exposed to ideas or opportunities that might lead to wrong desires or actions, we are faced with a choice. Will we go along with the world and its way of doing things; or, will we choose to exercise our Kingdom authority?

TODAY'S CHALLENGE:

Admit to God our Father any inappropriate thoughts, fantasies or desires that are not consistent with a life in Christ. Tell Him you want to make better choices today, and ask Him to help you by His Holy Spirit.

Be determined to reject any unwholesome thoughts. Capture them and submit them quickly to the Light of Christ.

Dive Deeper: Study 2 Corinthians 10.

January 20

SUBMIT FIRST, THEN RESIST

James 4:7-8
"Submit yourselves, then, to God. Resist the devil, and he will flee from you. Come near to God and he will come near to you..."

While I was in prison, people often told me to "resist the devil and he will flee". Certainly, there are many opportunities daily where we are faced with temptations. Resisting them in our own power often does not work. Why?

Incomplete verses taken out of context lose their power to set us free. First, we are told above to submit to God. Then, we resist. Satan is required to flee from the power of God the Father and the authority of Jesus. He does not have to leave if we are operating in our own power and authority rather than that exercised through us by God the Holy Spirit.

Next, we are instructed to draw near to God. As we draw ever nearer to Him, He comes closer to us. When we humbly submit to God and draw near to Him, He gives us everything we need to successfully resist temptation, and be victorious in every situation of life.

The devil can't read my thoughts, but when he hears me verbally submit to God, he has to flee.

TODAY'S CHALLENGE:

Today, be sure to submit first to God every situation and temptation the enemy throws at you. Let yourself hear you turn to God in submission and gratitude that He has already defeated your adversary, the devil.

Submit first, then resist.

Dive Deeper: Study James 4; 1 Peter 5:8-9; Ephesians 6:10-18.

January 21

WHILE WE WERE STILL SINNERS

Romans 5:8
"But God demonstrates his own love for us in this: While we were still sinners, Christ died for us."

In the poor spiritual and emotional state I lived for so long prior to being born again in prison, I believed that I had "gone too far and done too much" for God to forgive me. I was overcome with guilt, regret, remorse and shame. Have you ever felt this way?

I read in a booklet by RBC Ministries, "The Forgiveness of God", that "If we believe our emotions, we may feel we have gone too far. Our self-contempt seems deserved. But there's hope. God wants us to believe in His ability to forgive sins we cannot forget." Our Heavenly Father is angry at sin, but "His anger is not a denial of His love...The truth is that His love is equal to His anger, and because of His love He found a way to show mercy." He sent His Son, Jesus.

It was great news to me when I learned that my sin was forgiven. My guilt was removed. By one Man, once and for all!

I could never be "good enough" to be saved; Jesus died for me even while I was still a horrible sinner. That's good news!

TODAY'S CHALLENGE:

Ask the Father to help you receive His great Gift. Tell Him you are grateful that Jesus paid for all your sin – past, present and future. Jesus took away your sin. All of it. Forever.

Choose today to believe and receive.

Dive Deeper: Study Romans 5; 1 John 4:9-10.

January 22

JUSTIFIED BY HIS BLOOD

Romans 5:9
"Since we have now been justified by his blood, how much more shall we be saved from God's wrath through him!"

I have heard the word "justified" explained as "just-as-if-I'd" never sinned.

The Blood of Jesus is so powerful that God the Father sees me through the lens of Christ's finished work as being pure, spotless and holy. He treats me as if I had never sinned. How incredibly marvelous is that?

In the booklet I previously referred to by RBC Ministries, "The Forgiveness of God", they wrote that "the moment we trust Christ as Savior, we are given immunity from punishment. The issue is settled: Our case is closed and God will not open the files of our guilt again. Just as the courts of earth honor the principle of double jeopardy, heaven will not judge twice those whose sins have been punished in Christ. We will not be tried again for the sins He bore in our place."

Having been in numerous court settings I can relate to the concept of double jeopardy. Can't you?

God is much more just and merciful than any earthly judge. Jesus has already taken the punishment I deserved. He has finished my sentence. My time is discharged. I can go free.

TODAY'S CHALLENGE:

Talk to the Father about how grateful you are to be seen by Him as a son who has been forgiven. Think about the high price Jesus paid so that this could be true for you.

You are justified. Take a deep breath and receive it.

Dive Deeper: Study Romans 3:21 - 5:11.

January 23

JESUS WAS MADE TO BE SIN

2 Corinthians 5:21
"God made him who had no sin to be sin for us, so that in him we might become the righteousness of God."

Jesus was made sin with our sinfulness, so that we could be made righteous with His righteousness. The Father declares as righteous all those who appeal to the death of Christ as payment for their sin. No sin is excluded. We are saved by grace alone through faith alone in Jesus Christ alone.

There is nothing in the entire universe more powerful than the Blood of Jesus that takes away our sin. When we do not deny the Spirit - and thereby accept by faith what Jesus did for us - there is no sin (and no sinner) beyond God's love and forgiveness.

My many sins were taken away! This was a "break-through" realization for me. I knew I could start over. I found present and eternal hope, and freedom in Jesus, when I accepted the Father's forgiveness! Have you finally and fully accepted His mercy, love and forgiveness?

In Christ Jesus, I have the very righteousness He has. I can stand before the Father unashamed and free from condemnation as if I had never sinned. So can you! God does not discriminate. What He does for one He will do for all!

TODAY'S CHALLENGE:

Thank God the Father for accepting you as righteous because you are in Christ Jesus. Let the Holy Spirit change you today so you can more fully realize the incredible power of righteousness.

Dive Deeper: Study 2 Corinthians 5; Isaiah 52:13 – 53:12.

January 24

FORGET THE PAST

Philippians 3:13-14
"Brothers and sisters, I do not consider myself yet to have taken hold of it. But one thing I do: Forgetting what is behind and straining toward what is ahead, I press on toward the goal to win the prize for which God has called me heavenward in Christ Jesus."

After I truly accepted the Father's forgiveness, He began to show me the importance of forgiving myself, so that my past would stay in the past. That way, I could be unburdened of the guilt, shame, regret, remorse and embarrassment I had been carrying for so long. When I finally put my past behind me, I began to trust God one day at a time with my future.

Our past can keep us imprisoned even after we get released. We must decide to put the past in the past and leave it there. Paul emphasized how important it was by saying "one thing" - as if it is the most important thing. Then, as he forgets what is behind, he works hard at focusing on that day's race, trusting God that He will take care of the future outcome.

God is omnipresent, that is, everywhere present all the time. If the enemy can keep us ashamed and regretful about our past, we cannot enjoy relationship in the present with our Father.

TODAY'S CHALLENGE:

Ask God the Father to help you get on with your new life in Christ. Allow the Holy Spirit to help you make the decision to bury your past.

Otherwise, your past will bury you.

Dive Deeper: Study Philippians 3:1 – 4:1.

January 25

DO NOT DWELL ON THE PAST

Isaiah 43:18
"Forget the former things; do not dwell on the past. See, I am doing a new thing! Now it springs up; do you not perceive it?"

After I had been in prison long enough to be free of all the physical effects of my addictions, I began to think more clearly. I was honest with myself and God. I realized I hated myself for what I had done to ruin my life. I never blamed anyone else – only me – for the poor choices I made, one after another, that eventually led me to prison. Maybe you feel this way now.

I had broken relationships with, and pushed away, all my friends and family. Having been homeless for most of the three years leading up to my incarceration, I was left with no material possessions other than what was zipped-up inside a single, hanging garment bag in the prison's property room. I was convinced there was no hope of anything ever getting better. I thought my future could never be any better than my past.

God was ready to do a new thing in my life, but I couldn't see it if I kept looking at my past. He did not reveal all His plans for me at once. It would have blown my mind!

TODAY'S CHALLENGE:

Tell God the Father you are willing to quit looking at your past. Ask Him to lead you by His Spirit one day at a time into the future He has planned for you. Trust Him to do it.

Do not dwell on the past.

Dive Deeper: Study Isaiah 43.

January 26

GOD DECLARES NEW THINGS

Isaiah 42:9
"See, the former things have taken place, and new things I declare, before they spring into being I announce them to you."

I will never forget the first glimmer of hope I experienced as I began to accept the Father's forgiveness of me and the removal of all my sin – past, present and future.

I had never experienced the peace, emotional freedom and mental release I felt when He showed me I must forgive myself, so I could trust Him and move forward as the "new creature" He made me when I was "born again". I had to make a deliberate and determined choice to "let the past be the past".

It was clear to me that God had forgiven me, but I couldn't forgive myself. Did you ever feel this way?

We must believe that our Father is no longer holding our past against us. He wants us to realize we can't do anything to change the past, but if we trust Him, He will declare new things for our future. As we seek Him diligently daily, He will reveal each new part of His plan for us at just the right time. So, we walk by faith, not by sight.

TODAY'S CHALLENGE:

Ask God the Father to forgive you for holding unforgivingness towards yourself. Thank Him that the Blood of Jesus is so powerful as to take away all your sins. Today, let the Holy Spirit show you new things that the Father has declared.

Forgive yourself. Move on.

Dive Deeper: Study Isaiah 42.

January 27

DON'T LOOK BACK

Luke 9:62
"Jesus replied, 'No one who puts a hand to the plow and looks back is fit for service in the kingdom of God.'"

When a farmer is plowing his field, he can't make a straight row if he is looking back. He must keep focused on a point in front of him. In the same way, Jesus says we are not able to function effectively in His Kingdom if we are looking back over our shoulder at our past.

I finally realized there is absolutely nothing I could do about the past. Guilt, shame, regret, remorse and embarrassment had overwhelmed me for far too long. It had paralyzed me with fear, anxiety and depression, all of which kept me from moving forward. I was stuck. I decided that, more than anything else, I needed and wanted to trust God with my future.

I accepted the truth of His Word that He no longer held my past against me. He showed me I too had to stop holding my past against myself. I needed to accept His forgiveness, forgive myself, and move on. Are you stuck? Have you forgiven yourself?

If we aren't focused on the path ahead we will still be impacted by the crookedness of our past.

TODAY'S CHALLENGE:

Tell God the Father you want to be effective in His Kingdom, and that you will focus on what He has for you today. When the devil reminds you of your past, remind him of his future!

Get un-stuck. Stop looking back.

Dive Deeper: Study Luke 9.

January 28

HUMBLY SEEK FORGIVENESS

James 4:6
"God opposes the proud but shows favor to the humble."

Often times we do not want to admit we were wrong. This is usually because of our pride. God hates pride, and opposes those who insist on walking in it. If we hold onto it, we set ourselves up for a destructive fall.

In my sin, I had in one way or another offended all my family and friends. I had pushed or driven everyone away. As I began to learn about forgiveness, I sensed that I needed to get past my pride so that I could humble myself to ask forgiveness from the ones I had offended who I could go ahead and contact from inside prison. At first, it was my two older brothers and my younger sister. I felt a burden begin to lift off of me as I wrote and mailed those first letters asking for forgiveness.

It was a great experience to hear my name called at "mail call" for the first time in the ten months that I had then been incarcerated. My two brothers quickly answered me, and let me know they were not holding anything against me. They both expressed their regret for where I was and why I was there, but they also both asked if they could do anything to help me.

God showed me that it might just be possible to receive forgiveness from others if I would just humbly ask.

TODAY'S CHALLENGE:

Ask the Father to show you who you might contact to humbly ask to forgive you.

Put your pride aside.

Dive Deeper: Study James 4; Isaiah 57:15; Isaiah 66:1-2; Psalm 51:17; Matthew 5:3.

January 29

BE KIND AND COMPASSIONATE

Ephesians 4:32
"Be kind and compassionate to one another, forgiving each other, just as in Christ God forgave you."

Yesterday we learned that pride often keeps us from humbling ourselves and asking others to forgive us for whatever we did to hurt or offend them. If you do this from your heart, do not be concerned that they might not be quick to forgive. You will have done your part. It may take them a while to do theirs.

If you handled it with God, and have humbly asked them for their forgiveness, let God work on their hearts that they might eventually come around to forgiving you. You will have cleaned up your side of it.

While it is very important, whenever possible, that we humble ourselves and ask forgiveness from those we have hurt, we must use good judgment about this. Above all, we must always try to be loving, kind, and compassionate.

If the person you sinned against does not know what you did, it may not always be wise to tell them since it might then hurt them very deeply. However, it is most important that we get right with God the Father by confessing to Him what we did wrong to the other person, and resolving not to behave that way again. Ask the Holy Spirit to guide you.

TODAY'S CHALLENGE:

If you have unconfessed sin and broken relationships, confess them to God the Father and repent. Ask Him to give you the gift of Holy Spirit discernment as to how to proceed with others.

Be kind and compassionate.

Dive Deeper: Study Ephesians 4; Colossians 3:12-14.

January 30

FORGIVE

Colossians 3:13
"Bear with each other and forgive one another if any of you has a grievance against someone. Forgive as the Lord forgave you."

I think it is safe to say we have all been hurt by someone, and probably many times.

As I continued to study the Word during my incarceration, I learned that I needed to forgive those who had offended and hurt me throughout my life. That was difficult at first, but I made a conscious decision to forgive them. All the bad feelings, and desire to get even, that I had been carrying was hurting only me. I decided to give it all up and let it go.

What I discovered was that when we hold un-forgiveness towards someone, it causes a root of bitterness in us – a stronghold for the enemy. Like the unforgiving servant in Matthew 18:21-35, we turn ourselves over to "the tormenters" of anger, resentment, hatred, temper, and control – all of which can lead to retaliation, violence and even murder.

Since Jesus has forgiven us, we must forgive others. As we exercise patience, exhibit love, and extend forgiveness, we are exemplifying the qualities of Christ. Our best witness to others is not necessarily something we preach, rather it is a life well walked-out in Christ.

TODAY'S CHALLENGE:

Ask the Holy Spirit to bring to your remembrance the events and persons in your life where you have been hurt. Make a list, and pray to the Father about each one. Tell Him you forgive, and ask Him to heal the hurt you felt when it happened.

Ask Father God to forgive you for holding un-forgiveness.

Dive Deeper: Study Colossians 3; Ephesians 4:22-32.

January 31

FORGIVE, TO BE FORGIVEN

Matthew 6:14-15
"For if you forgive other people when they sin against you, your heavenly Father will also forgive you. But if you do not forgive others their sins, your Father will not forgive your sins."

The above verse is very sobering. It is clearly stated. If we want forgiveness from the Father, we must forgive others. There is no middle ground.

A "seed" of un-forgiveness planted in a "ground of hurt" gives us a "harvest" of pain. It grieves our spirit, torments our mind, and distresses us emotionally. All these, combined with a desire for vengeance or retaliation, hurt us - not the person who offended us. Often times they may not even realize their offense. This has been likened to drinking poison ourselves, thinking it will kill the other person!

One of the primary reasons Jesus came was so we could have forgiveness through His blood. One of the last things Jesus did was to cry out to God, asking His Father to forgive those who had spit upon Him, ridiculed Him, beat Him, mocked Him, and nailed Him to that cross. I'm sure he did not "feel" like forgiving them, yet that's what He chose to do, and prayed to His Father in like manner. We must also be willing to forgive and pray for those who have harmed us. Aren't there people you too should choose to forgive?

TODAY'S CHALLENGE:

In spite of your feelings, make a choice to forgive those who have hurt you. Ask the Father to help you by His Holy Spirit.

Forgive, to be forgiven.

Dive Deeper: Study Matthew 6; Mark 11:20-25.

February 1

BE FREE

John 8:36
"So if the Son sets you free, you will be free indeed."

Jesus took all our burdens on Himself so we could be free to live and walk in the abundantly blessed life He planned for us.

Many people in "the free world" are in self-imposed, self-constructed prisons. Whether we are in an actual prison behind razor wire, or not, people everywhere struggle with "addictions" that negatively impact their lives - such as pride, selfishness, depression, anger, pornography, alcohol, prescription medicines, illegal drugs and many others. We may have been enslaved by them for many years. I know I was certainly in a prison of my own making many years before I was actually incarcerated.

Oftentimes, we indulge in addictive behavior to try to fill the emptiness we feel inside, and/or to avoid thinking about and dealing with the root causes of the addictions. At first, dealing with the underlying issues is emotionally painful, and our natural tendency is to avoid pain, even when something good like freedom awaits us on the other side. But the Word of God is clear that Jesus took all our pain, shame, guilt and sin on Himself when He hung on the Cross.

The enemy of your soul wants to keep you in bondage. Remember, he is the father of lies.

TODAY'S CHALLENGE:

Ask your Heavenly Father to help you fully understand and appreciate all Jesus accomplished for you at the Cross. Request your Helper, the Holy Spirit, to give you discernment to reject the lies of the enemy.

Be free.

Dive Deeper: Study John 8.

February 2

HOLD TO HIS TEACHING

John 8:31-32
"To the Jews who had believed him, Jesus said, "If you hold to my teaching, you are really my disciples. Then you will know the truth, and the truth will set you free."

Most of us are familiar with the last part of John 8:31-32, "you shall know the truth and the truth will set you free". Almost all of us who have been incarcerated have seen it quoted in courtrooms. In actual fact, the truth did not set me free; rather it got me locked up!

I did not realize that the freedom promised as a result from knowing the truth is dependent on the verse preceding it regarding obedience to the teachings of Jesus. If we "hold" to His teaching we are true followers - the pre-condition for "knowing the truth". Who is the Truth? Jesus (John 14:6). So that means that to the extent we know, obey and follow Jesus, the truth of His teachings will set us free! This was truly a new revelation of what had always been a very familiar verse, even to a "heathen" like I once was.

Jesus does not give us freedom to do what we want, rather our obedience to Him gives us the power to truly follow Him. The truth does not set us free, but obedience to the Truth does.

TODAY'S CHALLENGE:

Tell your Heavenly Father you want to obey as best you can today. Let Him know that you want to truly follow Jesus by following the leadership of His Holy Spirit today.

Hold to His teaching.

Dive Deeper: Study and compare John 8:31-32, 47, 51; John 9:31; John 10:22; Romans 8:14; and James 1:22-25.

February 3

FREEDOM IN THE SPIRIT

2 Corinthians 3:17
"Now the Lord is the Spirit, and where the Spirit of the Lord is, there is freedom."

I determined in 2009 to radically follow Jesus, and do my best to obey His teachings. Certainly, I was growing in the knowledge of Him as "the Truth" as I studied His Word and spent quality time in His Presence daily. Consequently, for quite some time, I had in fact realized inside me a freedom I had never experienced before, accompanied by real joy and true peace by His Holy Spirit.

The Spirit prompted me to make a list of oppressions, strongholds and addictions that I was once in bondage to, but from which I have now been set free. The list you saw earlier in this book was the result. Believe me, like Paul, I was "the chief of sinners" – it is a very long list - and I add to it as the Spirit reveals. Why have I chosen to be this embarrassingly direct and transparent with you? Because I want you to know that if God can change me so miraculously inside and out, He can change anybody! Do you want to be forever finished with being a slave to old strongholds and addictions?

Seek more of God the Holy Spirit. Be led by the Spirit. Pray in the Spirit. Walk in the Spirit.

TODAY'S CHALLENGE:

Tell your Heavenly Father you want to be free from old bondages. Take your time. Be specific.

Ask the Holy Spirit to help you stay free.

Dive Deeper: Study and compare 2 Corinthians 3:17; 1 Peter 2:16; Romans 6:7,11,18; Romans 8:1-4; Galatians 5:13; and Isaiah 61:1.

February 4

YOUR OLD MAN IS DEAD

Galatians 2:20
"I have been crucified with Christ and I no longer live, but Christ lives in me. The life I now live in the body, I live by faith in the Son of God, who loved me and gave himself for me."

The list I made of "old man" sins and bondages was very long. I am truly free of all those things and I have not been seriously tempted to return to any of them because I quickly take captive every "old man" thought the enemy brings.

I know now that those thoughts and temptations the enemy throws at me daily all belong to the "old man" who is now "dead" (Romans 6:6-7). I am a new creature (2 Corinthians. 5:17)! I do not let Satan convince me to resurrect that old, dead man! Therefore, I now experience daily the freedom and liberty of an abundant, over-flowing LIFE in Christ! I know who I am now in Him!

This is only accomplished by totally surrendering daily to the leadership of the Holy Spirit in my life. I am dead, and the life I live now is not me, but Christ living in me, by His Holy Spirit.

Jesus has liberated us to live an abundant life. Don't remain enslaved. Let Jesus set you free and choose to stay free!

TODAY'S CHALLENGE:

Thank your Heavenly Father for sending Jesus to set you free from sin and every form of bondage. Ask the Spirit of Christ, the Holy Spirit, to live in and through you.

You are new!

Dive Deeper: Study Galatians 2; Romans 6:6-7; 2 Corinthians 5:17.

February 5

TAKE THOUGHTS CAPTIVE

2 Corinthians 10:5
"...we take captive every thought to make it obedient to Christ."

One of the most important things I had to learn in order to remain free from addictions, resist temptations and overcome depression was how to "take my thoughts captive to the obedience of Christ". See 2 Corinthians 10:3-5.

As Joyce Meyers described, the battlefield is in the mind! Sometimes it may seem we fight against impossible odds. The enemy wants you to believe it is always a battle, and it is always uphill. But I want you to know that God has already provided the victory and it is relatively easy to maintain it. Do you want to know the secret?

We often hear people say "resist the devil and he will flee" (James 4:7b), but many don't realize that the enemy does not have to flee if you don't first "submit to God" (James 4:7a); and then, after resisting the devil and his demons, we must "draw near to God so that God draws near to us" (James 4:8).

So the secret I have learned is to "submit to God" first as soon as I discern the enemy's attack when he tries to plant his deceitful lies and thoughts in my mind. By submitting first to God I can successfully recognize and resist the wrong thoughts, and take them captive by rejecting them and filling my mind instead with the thoughts of God.

TODAY'S CHALLENGE:

Ask the Father to give you wisdom and power by His Holy Spirit to take wrong thoughts captive in obedience to Christ.

Submit to God!

Dive Deeper: Study 2 Corinthians 10.

February 6

SUBMIT TO GOD

James 4:7
"Submit yourselves, then, to God. Resist the devil, and he will flee from you."

How does one "submit to God"? By countering the lies, accusations and hopelessness of the enemy with the truth, acceptance and eternal hope of the Word of God. We must know what God says about us in His Word in order for us to successfully combat and take captive what the enemy says about us, or accuses us with. And when we confess God's Word about our situation we are able to "draw near to God". Doesn't this make good sense?

For example, we read in Luke 4:1-14, that Jesus Himself countered the enemy's temptations successfully when He came out of the wilderness by recognizing the devil's voice and responding to him with the Word of God. Note that the scripture Jesus utilized was very specific to the area of temptation. Jesus knew what the Word said and used it to counter the enemy. We must do likewise.

The Word operates alongside the Spirit. When we proclaim the Word we are submitting to God the Father and the Holy Spirit empowers us to resist the devil. When we know the Truth, Who is the Living Word, Jesus, we will apply His teaching to our lives, and the truth will set us free (John 8:31-32).

TODAY'S CHALLENGE:

Ask the Father to give you a hunger and thirst for His Word. Talk to your Friend and Teacher, the Holy Spirit, about showing you the specific scriptures you need to counter the lies of the enemy.

The Word is a weapon! Use it.

Dive Deeper: Study James 4; and, compare James 4:7-8; 1 Peter 5:8-9; Ephesians 6:10-18; Hebrews 10:19-22; and Jeremiah 29:13.

February 7

CONFESS THE WORD

Psalm 119:11
"I have hidden your word in my heart that I might not sin against you."

So, what is the secret to knowing the truth disclosed in the Word of God regarding His thoughts about us as "new creations in Christ"? I believe the secret is to daily confess aloud what the Word of God says about us, and to pray personalized daily prayers to ask the Father to help us apply the Word to our lives in every situation.

Let me recommend something to you. While I was still incarcerated, two different ministers encouraged me to begin the practice of agreeing daily with God about what His Word says about me, and praying powerful, personalized daily prayers over my life. I typed these up after my release, and I am enclosing them near the end of this book for your review and use.

I encourage you to repeat these daily for six months, even if you only whisper loud enough where only you hear it. "Faith comes by hearing, and hearing by the Word of God" according to Romans 10:17. These daily confessions are so very powerful because they are all directly from the Word of God. And praying the Word of God is the most powerfully effective request of the Father that you could ever possibly pray!

TODAY'S CHALLENGE:

Ask the Father to give you the mind of Christ so that you can remember and confess His Word over your life. Open your heart to His Wisdom.

Fill your heart and mouth with the Word.

Dive Deeper: Study Psalm 119.

February 8

THE WORD IS POWERFUL

Hebrews 4:12
"For the word of God is alive and active. Sharper than any double-edged sword, it penetrates even to dividing soul and spirit, joints and marrow; it judges the thoughts and attitudes of the heart."

Yesterday, I encouraged you to use the Daily Confessions and Personalized Prayers in the back of this book as part of your daily time with the Father. The Word is so very powerful! It is crucial to confess it, meditate upon it, pray it back to God, and apply it to our daily lives.

We must know what God says about us so that we can recognize and reject the lies of the enemy, taking captive every thought to the obedience of Christ. I challenge you to confess and pray these daily for an extended period. After six months, continue to recite them at least weekly thereafter. I promise you they will change the way you speak, think, pray and act.

The Word is not just a collection of words from God, it is alive, and has within it the ability to create good for our future out of the bad ruins of our past. It shines Light into the darkness that once inhabited our souls. The Word helps us love God, others and ourselves from our heart, the deepest core of being.

TODAY'S CHALLENGE:

Tell the Father how much you love and appreciate His Word. Ask the Holy Spirit to help you make wise decisions using His Word. Tell Him you want the Word to shape your life from the deepest level of your soul.

Receive the Word. Use it today.

Dive Deeper: Study and compare Hebrews 4:12; 2 Timothy 3:16-17; 2 Peter 1:19-21; Romans 15:4; Joshua 1:7-9; Psalm 1:1-3; Psalm 19:7-11; Proverbs 4:20-23; Isaiah 55:11: Jeremiah 15:16.

February 9

TURN AROUND

Luke 15:17-18
"When he came to his senses, he said, 'How many of my father's hired servants have food to spare, and here I am starving to death! I will set out and go back to my father and say to him: Father, I have sinned against heaven and against you.'"

Clearly, everything that happened in my life leading up to prison was not what God had planned and intended for me. Rather, it was the result of my slow, steady, downward spiral into utter depravity. See Romans 1:18-32. If your Bible had pictures in it, mine would be there, for this was certainly a picture of me.

God turned me over to my own perverted and misguided, selfish desires which led to a "reprobate" mind – one that can rationalize and do the most evil, despicable things and still convince itself that they are good and acceptable. I was "dead" – like a walking zombie – in my sin and self-deception.

Like the prodigal son, when I came to my senses in prison, I was empty. I had a "longing" for something more than what I had available to me in my sin, my mess. I longed to "go home". The parable of the prodigal son really got my attention. I could really identify with him. He demonstrated for me that true repentance is "brokenness", and a change of life-direction.

TODAY'S CHALLENGE:

Tell the Father you regret your past life of sin, and that you want to come home. He will welcome you with open arms!

Turn around. Go home.

Dive Deeper: Study Luke 15; and compare Luke 15:17-18; Psalm 34:18; and Psalm 51:17.

February 10

JESUS PREACHED REPENTANCE

Matthew 4:17
"From that time on Jesus began to preach, 'Repent, for the kingdom of heaven has come near.'"

In order to experience the Kingdom of God we must repent. We must agree with God that we have been going the wrong way.

I learned that repentance is not an emotion – for example, not the feeling of "I am sorry", or, "I feel bad about what I've done" – rather, it is a decision. It is like deciding to make a "U-turn" on a highway. You are then headed in the opposite direction from where you were going. Someone in true repentance does not just say, "I'm sorry I did that"; they will also live a different life demonstrating a new mind-set of "I won't do it again".

The Greek words translated as "repentance" in the New Testament mean "to think differently", "to change your mind", "to turn about in opinion", "to turn about from an intended way"; and, Webster's Dictionary defines it as "to turn from sin and resolve to reform one's life".

In order for me to return to the Father, I had to go by way of repentance. True repentance is the only way to salvation in and through Jesus Christ. Has true repentance changed your direction? Have you made a "U-turn"?

TODAY'S CHALLENGE:

Let the Father know you realize you were once heading the wrong direction away from Him. Tell Him you are forever turning from your past. When you fall on this new path, resolve to repent quickly, get up, and keep heading toward God.

Repent, so you will experience the Kingdom.

Dive Deeper: Study and compare Matthew 3:2; Mark 1:15; Luke 13:3; Acts 2:38; Acts 3:19; Acts 17:30-31; Acts 20:20-21; Acts 26:18; 2 Peter 3:9; Revelation 2:5, 16; Revelation 3:19.

February 11

DO NOT BE DECEIVED

Matthew 24:4
"Jesus answered: 'Watch out that no one deceives you.'"

When four of Jesus' closest disciples went to Him privately to ask Him what would be the signs of His Second Coming and of the "end of the age", Jesus warned them several times not to be deceived. Surely, we are even now seeing all the signs come to pass before our very eyes just as He foretold. Likewise, we are already seeing signs of the great deception.

I believe the greatest part of this deception is to try to convince the world that there are more ways to God and Heaven than just through Jesus. THAT IS A LIE. DO NOT BE DECEIVED. The only way to Father God is through the finished work of Jesus Christ of Nazareth at the cross and through His resurrection.

Many are suggesting that Jesus is just one way to Heaven, not necessarily the only way. This has reportedly come from even a few influential leaders within "Christian" circles! It is heresy to espouse this view.

Jesus told us that if it were possible, even "the elect" would be deceived (Matthew 4:24). Deception is here. Don't fall for it. It is eternally important for you to be sure you are part of "the elect".

TODAY'S CHALLENGE:

Ask the Father to give you the spirit of discernment through His Holy Spirit so that you will not be deceived. Reaffirm your desire to be included in "the elect" about which Jesus spoke.

Be watchful. Don't be deceived.

Dive Deeper: Study John 14:6; Matthew 24.

February 12

PHARISEES WERE OFFENDED

Matthew 15:12
"Then the disciples came to him and asked, 'Do you know that the Pharisees were offended when they heard this?'"

In this age of secular humanism where mankind says they determine their own fate and future, not God, we as Christians are susceptible to their attempts to convince everyone that truth is "relative" to what is going on in society, and so it changes with the times. We are urged to be tolerant of everyone for every reason. No-one must be "offended". We are told that everyone must be "included" and not "confronted" in any way about anything.

While we must certainly treat those who do not agree with us with respect, kindness and gentleness, we must be very careful not to compromise on Who we know is Truth - the Son of God, Jesus Christ. Jesus makes it very clear that He is the only way, the only truth and the only life. He assures us that no-one gets to the Father except through Him (see John 14:6).

Peter preached this truth about Jesus in Acts 4:12 when he said, "Salvation is found in no one else, for there is no other name under heaven given to mankind by which we must be saved." Isaiah quotes Jehovah, Father God, in Isaiah 43:11 as saying, "I, even I, am the Lord, and apart from me there is no savior."

TODAY'S CHALLENGE:

Ask the Father to give you wisdom and courage through His Holy Spirit so that you will be able to stand firm in the Truth, Jesus.

Pray for those who are offended.

Dive Deeper: Study Matthew 15:1 – 16:4.

February 13

JESUS IS COMING SOON

Revelation 22:12
"Jesus said, 'Look, I am coming soon! My reward is with me, and I will give to each person according to what they have done.'"

Our King of kings and Lord of lords is returning for us soon! We are seeing Biblical prophecy fulfilled before our very eyes. Pastor David Jeremiah says everything that must be fulfilled before the return of our Lord has, in fact, already happened.

The world has never been in such turmoil. Earthquakes, fires, devastating storms, terror, wars, deception and rampant sinfulness abound as never before. Persecution of Christians is prevalent and increasing dramatically.

Jesus is coming back for His people (John 14:1-3).

He is coming quickly, in an instant of time (Matthew 24:27).

Jesus is coming soon, any day now (Revelation 22:12-13).

Are you sure you're ready (Matthew 24:42-44)???

I urge you to study carefully what Jesus revealed in Matthew 24, Mark 13, and Luke 21.

Read the visions of Daniel the prophet in Daniel chapters 7, 11 and 12. Of course, John tells us about the end of the age in Revelation. After studying these passages, I am certain you will agree that surely these times in which we are living are "the last days". We are closer now than ever.

TODAY'S CHALLENGE:

Tell the Father you long for the appearing of His Son, Jesus. Ask the Holy Spirit to draw the lost to Him. Tell somebody about Jesus.

Dive Deeper: Study Revelation 21 – 22; 1 Thessalonians 4:13 – 5:11; 2 Thessalonians 2:1-17; 1 Timothy 4:1-2; and 2 Timothy 3:1-5.

February 14

LOVE COMES FROM GOD

1 John 4:7
"Dear friends, let us love one another, for love comes from God. Everyone who loves has been born of God and knows God."

Our Father God loved us so much that He sacrificed His only Son to save us from our sin and open the door for us to return to an intimate personal relationship with Him - the same closeness Adam and Eve had in the Garden of Eden. He did this even while we were all still hopelessly lost in sin.

As a recent song says, "Oh, the overwhelming, never-ending, reckless love of God!" The more we believe and receive the eternal, immeasurable love of our Father, the more we will be able to love Him and love others. Love comes from God.

Jesus commanded us to love God, and love others as we love ourselves. In fact, He commanded His followers to love each other as He loved them. If we do this, He said the world would know we are His disciples.

Love is the first and primary fruit produced in our lives by the Holy Spirit. In fact, all the other fruit brought forth by the Spirit proceeds from love. We must yield to the Spirit and remain attached to the Vine, Jesus, so His Power will flow into us and through us to others. Love is the best gift. Love conquers all.

TODAY'S CHALLENGE:

Tell the Father you are overwhelmed by his never-ending, reckless love. Thank Him for his ultimate gift of love in His Son, Jesus. Ask the Holy Spirit to produce more love in you.

Dive Deeper: Study 1 John 4.

February 15

BE BAPTIZED IN THE SPIRIT

Acts 1:5
Jesus said, "For John baptized in water, but in a few days you will be baptized in the Holy Spirit."

When I was still incarcerated I saw several Christians who were released before me leave, only to return to prison within a year or so. I had also heard of others who had been following Jesus in prison with me that, after their release, fell away from their relationship with Jesus Christ and returned to "the world". I don't know if they returned to a physical prison, but they returned to their emotional and spiritual prisons from which they had once been set free. I know most of them had every good and honest intention to keep walking with Him, but many were powerless to resist old habits, places, and people.

Since I have been released, however, I know personally many former offenders who were transformed in prison, and who are still walking in Christ many years later. They are strong soldiers in God's army. I have seen God working in the lives of their families. I have seen them continue to prosper and experience the abundant life Jesus came to give us (John 10:10). Many have their own effective ministries now. Broken relationships have been restored. Broken hearts have been healed.

The baptism of the Holy Spirit makes all the difference!

TODAY'S CHALLENGE:

Ask the Father, through Jesus, to give you more of Him, and His power to live a sanctified life, by baptizing you in His Holy Spirit.

Receive more.

Dive Deeper: Study Acts 2:1-22; and compare Luke 11:9-13, Luke 24:49; John 1:32-34.

February 16

RECEIVE THE HOLY SPIRIT

Acts 8:15-16
"When they arrived, they prayed for the new believers there that they might receive the Holy Spirit, because the Holy Spirit had not yet come on any of them; they had simply been baptized in the name of the Lord Jesus."

I firmly believe that the extra level of empowerment brought about by being baptized (immersed) in the Holy Spirit makes all the difference in enabling and empowering us to walk out our faith effectively and genuinely in prison and then, after our release, in "the free world".

When we accept the finished work of Jesus at the Cross, and confess His resurrection as the Son of God, the Holy Spirit comes to live in us. We "possess" the Spirit, and He begins His ongoing work of sanctification to steadily make our "new man" conform to the image of Christ.

However, true empowerment – God's own power – comes to us, and for us, as we totally submit to the Holy Spirit and allow Him to "possess" us - one giant step more than us merely "possessing" Him inside us. We actually are able to allow Him to "possess" us!

We are His Temple. Shouldn't we voluntarily give Him full control of His home? The Holy Spirit of God is a Gentleman. He will not force Himself upon us, but He responds to our invitation.

TODAY'S CHALLENGE:

Jesus is the Baptizer of the Holy Spirit with fire and power. Ask Him to baptize you in His Holy Spirit.

Don't stop at water baptism. Take the next step.

Diving Deeper: Study Acts 8.

February 17

TWO BAPTISMS

Acts 19:4-6
"Paul said, 'John's baptism was a baptism of repentance. He told the people to believe in the one coming after him, that is, in Jesus.' On hearing this, they were baptized in the name of the Lord Jesus. When Paul placed his hands on them, the Holy Spirit came on them, and they spoke in tongues and prophesied."

We are baptized (immersed) into water as an outward representation of the inward change in us. We are buried with Christ in baptism (our "old man" died); and, we are raised to walk in newness of life (our "new man" came alive).

But the Book of Acts makes it clear we should also desire to be baptized (immersed) into the Holy Spirit to receive the same power that resurrected Jesus from the dead – the power to walk out this new life in the way He desires for us. He in us, and us in Him!

We know the verse that says, "Greater is He that is in me than He that is in the world" (I John 4:4). So, the Holy Spirit is in us. We possess Him. But another verse we know is "I can do all things through Him who strengthens me" (Phil. 4:13). That verse is also translated as, "I can do all things through the One who empowers me within". It is the Holy Spirit that empowers us within so that we can do everything the Father desires for us to do, and assigns us to do!

But we must let Him empower us. We must let Him possess us.

TODAY'S CHALLENGE:

Seek the full empowerment of God. Receive.

Dive Deeper: Study Acts 19.

February 18

YOU WILL RECEIVE POWER

Acts 1:8
Jesus said, "But you will receive power when the Holy Spirit comes on you; and you will be my witnesses in Jerusalem, and in all Judea and Samaria, and to the ends of the earth."

When Jesus finished His work on earth and returned to the Father, the Father sent the Holy Spirit to earth for each of us. Jesus' followers at that time were instructed to wait until they were endued with power from on High before they began to carry out the ministry of Jesus.

We should do likewise; that is, we should seek the power of the Holy Spirit before we move out among the people in the name of Jesus. We need the power of the Holy Spirit. Using only our own strength, we will burn out quickly, we will not be effective, and we can even do harm to His Kingdom.

Above all, we must remember the Holy Spirit is a person, He has a personality, and He can be grieved. His purpose in coming was to teach, lead, guide, correct, protect and comfort – the Helper who would walk alongside us as well as dwell within us.

However, we must yield to Him and allow Him to do His work in us. If we refuse Him, resist Him, or grieve Him, we will restrict the work that the Father wants Him to do in our lives. He is a gift from the Father, and we need Him!

TODAY'S CHALLENGE:

Tell your Father you want to do all the work He has planned for you. Thank Him for the Helper!

You will receive power.

Dive Deeper: Study Acts 1:1-11; Luke 24:36-49; Mark 16:15-20.

February 19

WE NEED THE HOLY SPIRIT

Acts 9:17

"Then Ananias went to the house and entered it. Placing his hands on Saul, he said, 'Brother Saul, the Lord—Jesus, who appeared to you on the road as you were coming here—has sent me so that you may see again and be filled with the Holy Spirit.'"

Not only did "Saul" receive power with the Baptism of the Holy Spirit, he had his name changed to "Paul"!

Paul depended upon the power of the Holy Spirit for his life and ministry. See, for example, Romans 15:17-19; 2 Corinthians 12:9; Ephesians 3:16-21; and, Colossians 1:29. In fact, Paul warned Timothy to stay away from religious people in the last days who deny the power of God, the Holy Spirit (see 2 Timothy 3:1-7).

Jesus needed the power of the Holy Spirit too! See Matthew 3:16-17; Matthew 4:1; Luke 4:1; Luke 4:14; Luke 4:18-19; and, Acts 10:38.

If Jesus, Paul and the other Apostles needed the Holy Spirit, surely we too must have all of God, the Holy Spirit, that He will give us! HE is the "game-changer" for our walk in the Christian life.

I urge you to learn as much as you can about your Helper, Teacher, Counselor, Guide and Friend.

TODAY'S CHALLENGE:

Ask Father God to help you learn more about His Spirit of Truth, your Teacher, Helper, Guide and Friend.

You need the Holy Spirit.

Dive Deeper: Study Acts 9:1-31; Acts 26:12-18; Romans 15:17-19; 2 Corinthians 12:9; Ephesians 3:16-21; Colossians 1:29; 2 Timothy 3:1-7; Matthew 3:16-17; Matthew 4:1; Luke 4:1, 14, 18-19; Acts 10:38.

February 20

RECEIVE THE GIFT

Acts 1:4-5
Jesus said, "Do not leave Jerusalem, but wait for the gift my Father promised, which you have heard me speak about. For John baptized with water, but in a few days you will be baptized with the Holy Spirit."

We thank the Father for His gifts. He not only gave us His Son, Jesus, but He gave us His Holy Spirit. What a marvelous Father He is.

When I think about it, I realize how gullible we are to believe the enemy's lie — the lie that the Holy Spirit is not for today, that we don't need Him. If anything, the truth is we need Him even more because we are living in the last of the last days when Scripture tells us that many will be deceived.

The Holy Spirit can help us not to be deceived if we will let Him lead us, and recognize that we "host" Him as the very Presence of God in us. We need Him. We need Him in His fullness.

Have you asked the Father for Jesus to baptize you with the Holy Spirit (Luke 3:16)? If you ask the Father, He will give Him to you (Luke 11:13). Have you allowed the "rivers of living water" to flow from within you (John 7:38-39)?

Our Father desires for us to walk in all His fullness by His Holy Spirit.

TODAY'S CHALLENGE:

Tell your Heavenly Father you are grateful for the Gift He and Jesus gave you – their Holy Spirit.

Receive God's Gift.

Dive Deeper: Study Acts 1:1-11; Acts 2:1-41; Luke 3:16; Luke 11:13; John 7:38-39.

February 21

BE SANCTIFIED BY THE SPIRIT

1 Peter 1:2
"...who have been chosen according to the foreknowledge of God the Father, through the sanctifying work of the Spirit, to be obedient to Jesus Christ and sprinkled with his blood..."

It is the sanctifying work of the Spirit that allows us to be obedient to Jesus Christ (1 Peter 1:2). As obedient children we are encouraged and empowered by His Holy Spirit not to "conform to the evil desires we once had when we lived in ignorance. But just as He who called you is holy, so be holy in all you do." (1 Peter 1:14-15).

In our own strength this is impossible, but all things are possible with God the Holy Spirit doing the work of sanctification in us.

The Word tells us that "His Divine Power has given us everything we need for life and godliness" (2 Peter 1:3) and that He "teaches us to say 'No' to ungodliness and worldly passions, and to live self-controlled, upright and godly lives in this present age" (Titus 2:12). We must receive everything He has given us and be willing to say "No" to worldly temptations. He will help us if we let Him.

Near the back of this book I have included two prayers for submission I think you will find helpful. It is His job to change you. Your job is to willingly surrender, submit and be obedient to what He wants to do in His ongoing process of sanctification in you.

TODAY'S CHALLENGE:

Pray the Prayers of Submission near the back of the book.

Allow the Spirit to do His work.

Dive Deeper: Study 2 Peter 1:1-10; 1 Peter 1:13-25; Titus 2:11-14.

February 22

BE TRANSFORMED

Romans 12:2
"Do not conform to the pattern of this world, but be transformed by the renewing of your mind. Then you will be able to test and approve what God's will is—his good, pleasing and perfect will."

I am so thankful God impressed upon me to use those last 20 months of confinement as a time to grow spiritually in His Word and, thereby, to be "transformed by the renewing" of my mind (Romans 12:1-2). I quit letting my "time do me" and started "doing my time".

I quit watching TV and playing cards. Instead, the Spirit motivated me to spend that time in spiritual education and Christian life training programs sponsored by the Chaplain. Additionally, many Bible correspondence courses, frequent Chapel service attendance and intense personal Bible Study hours prepared a solid foundation for me and sowed seed in fertile ground.

I am now a living witness of the Father's grace, mercy, forgiveness and power in Christ Jesus. The Holy Spirit has never been more real to me. The differences in me are real and permanent. God has changed me from the inside out. My attitudes, thoughts, desires and speech have all drastically changed. I am truly a "new creature in Christ – old things are passed away, everything has been made new" (2 Corinthians 5:17).

TODAY'S CHALLENGE:

Ask the Father to reveal by His Holy Spirit the areas of your life where you are still conformed to the world. Be sensitive to the Spirit's leading as to how He wants you to participate with Him in renewing your mind.

Do not conform. Be transformed.

Dive Deeper: Study Romans 11:33-12:21.

February 23

DO YOUR TIME WISELY

Ephesians 5:15-17
"Be very careful, then, how you live—not as unwise but as wise, making the most of every opportunity, because the days are evil. Therefore do not be foolish, but understand what the Lord's will is."

I am often asked what kinds of things I did in prison after I got saved but before I went home. As I stated earlier, I planned every day as to how I could pursue more of God during my waking hours. I tried to separate myself as best I could from all the worldly activities going on around me such as watching TV, reading newspapers, playing cards, and the usual kinds of conversations most inmates have in prison. I'm certain you know what I'm talking about.

The verse quoted above really got my attention and I tried to apply it to my situation. We all know how much evil there is around us, especially in prison. God's will is for us to separate ourselves from it, and use our time wisely in living for Him. It would be foolish not to heed this warning, especially since we want to know what the Will of the Lord is for our lives.

Don't let your time foolishly do you. Instead, take control and do your time wisely.

TODAY'S CHALLENGE:

Ask the Father to show you by His Holy Spirit some things you can begin to implement in your daily schedule to better use your time. Ask Him to help you make the most of every opportunity.

Do your time wisely.

Dive Deeper: Study Ephesians 5.

February 24

BIBLE BOOT CAMP

2 Timothy 2:15
"Do your best to present yourself to God as one approved, a worker who does not need to be ashamed and who correctly handles the word of truth."

After I got saved in prison, I looked at the remainder of my time as a Bible Boot Camp, or even Bible College.

I tried to focus as much as possible on studying the Word, memorizing scripture verses, and attending every sort of Chaplaincy class and almost every Christian worship service available to me. I completed many Correspondence Bible Study courses, and for one of them I earned a Study Bible for satisfactorily completing the course. What a wealth of information it contained in its verse commentaries, articles, concordance, subject index and maps!

While you are still incarcerated, for however brief or lengthy a time that may be, make a decision now to use your time wisely. Further your education. Study the Word and learn how to apply it to your daily life. Seek the Father diligently with all your heart.

Cultivate an intimate, personal relationship with the Father through His Holy Spirit living in you. Choose to be led by the Spirit moment by moment, instead of being constantly influenced by fleshly desires, the world, or the devil and his demonic hosts.

TODAY'S CHALLENGE:

Tell the Father you want to know more about Him and His Living Word, Jesus. Ask Him by His Spirit to show you ways to invest your time and talents learning the Word. Ask the Holy Spirit to show you how to apply what He teaches you.

Enroll in Bible Boot Camp.

Dive Deeper: Study 2 Timothy 2.

February 25

LISTEN TO YOUR TEACHER

Job 6:24
"Teach me, and I will be quiet; show me where I have been wrong."

The Holy Spirit is your teacher and guide. He will help you. He is able to gently instruct you where you have gotten off track in the past. Be open to what He will show you about areas of needed change in your life so that He can lead you into the future God wants for you.

Pray often for wisdom, knowledge, understanding, truth, revelation, discernment, and how to apply them to your life. These are all things God wants you to have so He will give them if you ask. He has a plan and a hope-filled future for you.

There are certainly ways for you to be more active in the Kingdom even right where you are now. If you start now you will be more likely to continue good habits when you are released.

If your unit offers a faith-based housing area, apply for it. Attend every sort of Chaplaincy program and service that is offered. Read as many Christian books as possible. If your facility offers a spiritual mentorship program, apply for that too. Volunteer for your Chaplain. Get involved with the inside church. Enroll in Bible Correspondence courses.

TODAY'S CHALLENGE:

Ask the Father to forgive you for where you have been wrong in the past, and trust Him by His Spirit to reveal His better future for you. Tell the Holy Spirit you are ready to learn. Ask Him to teach you.

Listen to your Teacher.

Dive Deeper: Study Job chapters 6-7.

February 26

BE PREPARED

2 Timothy 4:2
"Preach the word; be prepared in season and out of season; correct, rebuke and encourage—with great patience and careful instruction."

God wants to use you right where you are. Many people tell me they want to "do prison ministry" when they are released. But I tell them that the most important person in prison ministry is the turned-on, committed Christian still locked up. That is the person who can see firsthand who needs help, who needs prayer, who needs encouragement – right there on the inside.

In fact, I believe if you are not already engaging in prison ministry on the inside, you won't do it effectively, if at all, on the outside.

You should become a prayer warrior by praying boldly and diligently for the lost souls around you, for the officers in your unit, for the facility's administration, and for your family. In fact, praying for your family is one of the most powerful and beneficial gifts you can give them. As I learned to pray inside prison I saw the Lord move in mighty ways that built my faith and made me want to pray more!

God is preparing you right where you are. If you fully surrender to Him in obedience He will achieve remarkable results. You are part of God's Special Forces operating behind enemy lines!

TODAY'S CHALLENGE:

Tell the Father you are fully surrendering to Him so He can minister to others through you by His Holy Spirit. Ask Him to show how you can be more effective.

Be prepared.

Dive Deeper: Study 2 Timothy 3:1 – 4:8.

February 27

WALK YOUR TALK

1 Peter 2:11-12

"Dear friends, I urge you, as foreigners and exiles, to abstain from sinful desires, which wage war against your soul. Live such good lives among the pagans that, though they accuse you of doing wrong, they may see your good deeds and glorify God on the day he visits us."

Don't expect perfection from anyone in the church. Just do the best you can to walk your talk (1 Peter 2:11-12). As you know, people are watching, and wanting to know if your commitment is real. In fact, many privately hope it is real because it would mean more hope for them that they too could be changed by a real encounter with our living Lord Jesus.

Even though they are quick to criticize anyone really trying to follow Jesus Christ, your honest attempt to live a surrendered life makes more of a positive impression than you might think. This is especially true the longer you serve Him. When you stumble, be quick to admit it and quit it. Own your mistakes and commit to do better.

If you mess up, get up, confess your sin to the Father (I John 1:9), and keep headed in the right direction. Pay no attention to snide remarks from others. At judgment day, you will be standing in front of the King alone. Focus on pleasing Him daily instead of pleasing others.

TODAY'S CHALLENGE:

Ask your Heavenly Father to give you power to more faithfully follow Jesus by His Holy Spirit. Tell Him you want to be authentic in living out your Christian witness.

Walk your talk.

Dive Deeper: Study 1 Peter 1:22 – 2:25.

February 28

PRAY FOR YOUR PRISON

Jeremiah 29:7
"Also, seek the peace and prosperity of the city to which I have carried you into exile. Pray to the Lord for it, because if it prospers, you too will prosper."

Jehovah God allowed His people to go into captivity because they had turned their backs on Him in rebellion. They had followed idols – gods made by human hands. They chose to disobey. Choices have consequences.

Although the Israelites deserved their punishment, Father God gave them specific instructions in Jeremiah 29 as to how to make the most of a bad situation. He encouraged them to settle in and begin to change their lives for the better. He wanted them to prosper even in the midst of their circumstances.

One key to their prosperity was to pray for the place which held them captive. If it prospered, they too would prosper. It is important for followers of Jesus to pray for the prison where they are captive. Never underestimate the power of prayer to change people, places and things.

Begin to pray regularly for your facility, the Wardens, official rank, correctional officers, teachers and administrative staff. These people have their own family problems, personal issues, spiritual strongholds, financial stress, and the need for more of Christ. Some are strong Christians. Many are not. Do battle on your knees in prayer. Watch God move!

TODAY'S CHALLENGE:

Ask your Heavenly Father to show you how to pray more powerfully by His Holy Spirit. Ask Him to bless and prosper the facility and everyone who works there. Be specific. Be diligent.

Pray for your prison.

Dive Deeper: Study Jeremiah 29:1-14.

February 29

LEAP FOR JOY

Psalm 28:7
"The Lord is my strength and my shield; my heart trusts in him, and he helps me. My heart leaps for joy and with my song I praise him."

Leap year only comes around every four years, but our hearts can leap for joy in praise for our Lord and Savior every day!

As we fully realize and receive our Lord as our strength and shield of protection, we will trust Him more. As we count on and receive His help, our joy and praise will naturally increase.

Every day we can declare that we choose to rejoice for the new day God has made and allowed us to share. He will use us another day! We can choose to be glad every day in spite of our circumstances. See Psalm 118:24.

James tells us to be joyful when we face trials of many kinds because trials produce perseverance and patience, which help us grow towards maturity and completion in Christ where we will lack nothing! See James 1:2-4.

Jesus instructs us that in the face of persecution we can "rejoice and be exceedingly glad, for great is your reward in Heaven." See Matthew 5:12. Also, Paul encourages us to rejoice always! He even repeats it in the same verse, "again I say rejoice." See Philippians 4:4.

TODAY'S CHALLENGE:

Ask your Heavenly Father to fill you with more joy. Tell Him you know that joy is a fruit of the Spirit, and that, in submission, you will let Him produce more of this fruit in your life.

Leap for joy!

Dive Deeper: Study Psalm 28 & 29; Psalm 118:24; James 1:2-4; Matthew 5:12; Philippians 4:4.

March 1

GOING HOME

Jeremiah 29:14
"I will be found by you," declares the Lord, "and will bring you back from captivity."

As you look forward to the day you will be released, if you are like me you may wonder if you can really follow Christ out there "in the free world". You can. But it will require daily focus and commitment.

If I were to name nine most important things to help you be consistent and faithful about your commitment to follow Christ in "the free world", they would be:

1. Join a church and attend as often as possible.
2. Restore broken relationships - and work at maintaining them once restored.
3. Separate totally and permanently from the former bad influences of certain people, places and things.
4. Faithfully maintain prayer, Bible study and private worship daily.
5. Maintain a constant, prayerful attitude of gratefulness and humility towards God.
6. Get an accountability partner and meet regularly. Having a trusted accountability partner is an important factor in maintaining a faithful walk. Don't walk alone.
7. Get actively involved in serving in an anointed ministry as a volunteer. As you invest yourself in the issues and challenges of others, the joy of the Lord will strengthen and enrich you. You will be drawn closer to the Father by the Holy Spirit, and your personal testimony will encourage others.
8. If you fall, quickly confess and truly repent. Get right back up on your Christian walk.
9. Forgive yourself. You did your time – put the past behind you and move on! You are a new creation (2 Cor. 5:17)!!

TODAY'S CHALLENGE:

Ask your Heavenly Father for wisdom in preparing for your release.

Dive Deeper: Study Jeremiah 29:4-14; Jeremiah 24:4-7.

March 2

GOING HOME: JOIN A CHURCH

Hebrews 10:24-25
"And let us consider how we may spur one another on toward love and good deeds, not giving up meeting together, as some are in the habit of doing, but encouraging one another—and all the more as you see the Day approaching."

It is very important to be a part of a body of like-minded believers, starting while you are incarcerated and continuing after your release to "the free world".

Make sure you are in a group that exalts Jesus Christ and honors the Holy Spirit.

Do not expect perfection. It has been said that the church is not a collection of saints but a hospital for sinners. Receive grace. Give grace.

Being with others who are diligently trying to walk with God is crucial. They can become like a new family for you. Learning to give and receive love is an important benefit. Banding together to achieve good work projects for the Kingdom is rewarding and fun.

Coming together regularly is refreshing, instructive and encouraging. It can be for you like a pleasant oasis in the middle of a long, dry journey through the desert.

Sitting under the regular teaching of an anointed shepherd of God should better equip you to represent Jesus every day as you go about your work and daily life. Small groups and Bible studies with your new family during the week are important too.

TODAY'S CHALLENGE:

Ask your Father to give you discernment by His Spirit to select the group of believers that will help you best honor Him in your daily life.

Dive Deeper: Study Hebrews 10.

March 3

GOING HOME: RESTORE RELATIONSHIPS

Matthew 5:23-24
"Therefore, if you are offering your gift at the altar and there remember that your brother or sister has something against you, leave your gift there in front of the altar. First go and be reconciled to them; then come and offer your gift."

Before going to prison my sin, actions and addictions destroyed relationships with my family and friends. For the first year of incarceration, I received no letters, no visits and no money on my books. Have you been in this position too? Perhaps you still are.

It is so important to do whatever you can to try to mend broken relationships. This should be started while you are still incarcerated, and must be pursued after being released.

Today's verse indicates that broken relationships hinder our relationship with God. We are being hypocritical if we claim to love God but hate others. We are not loving others if we are satisfied in letting personal relationships suffer and go unreconciled.

The most important first step is to humble ourselves, and ask forgiveness for our part in whatever the problem was that led to a bad relationship. It might take the other person a while to forgive, but being the first to reach out with the love of Christ can be a very powerful witness.

TODAY'S CHALLENGE:

Ask your Heavenly Father to show you how to identify relationships that need restoration. Request the Holy Spirit to teach you how to humbly ask forgiveness, and give you the patience to wait on Him to move on the heart of the other person.

Dive Deeper: Study Matthew 5; Ephesians 4:32; Colossians 3:13.

March 4

GOING HOME: SEPARATE YOURSELF

2 Corinthians 6:17
"Therefore, 'Come out from them and be separate, says the Lord. Touch no unclean thing and I will receive you.'"

One of the most important things we must do to stay out of prison after we have been released is to separate ourselves totally and permanently from certain people, places, and things. In fact, this process must begin while we are still incarcerated.

I have also heard it expressed this way, "we must change our playground, playthings and people with whom we used to play." Is that familiar to you?

In this passage (verses 14-18) Paul urges believers not to form binding relationships with unbelievers because it can weaken our own commitment to God's integrity, character and standards. This does not mean we are to totally isolate ourselves from unbelievers.

As believers, we should be active in our witness to unbelievers, but we must be careful not to lock ourselves into personal and business relationships with them. Imagine standing on a stool reaching down for an unbeliever. It is much easier for the enemy to use them to pull us down than it is for us to pull them up.

If we are single, all this becomes even more critical as we consider a life partner. (see 2 Corinthians 6:14). Wait on God to bring the right person.

TODAY'S CHALLENGE:

Tell your Heavenly Father you want to start life over in Christ Jesus by surrounding yourself with Godly people, pursuing the right kinds of activities, and habitually going to the right places. Ask the Holy Spirit for discernment and wisdom.

Separate yourself.

Dive Deeper: Study 2 Corinthians 6:14-18; James 4:4-5, 8-9; 1 John 2:15-17; Colossians 3:1-2; John 15:19; Romans 8:5-7; 1 Peter 1:14-17; 1 Peter 2:11-12; 1 Peter 4:4-5; 1 John 5:19, 21; Hebrews 12:14.

March 5

GOING HOME: MAINTAIN PRIVATE TIME

Mark 1:35
"Very early in the morning, while it was still dark, Jesus got up, left the house and went off to a solitary place, where he prayed."

Starting off our day in private, personal time with our Heavenly Father is so important, necessary and rewarding. If Jesus needed to spend time early with His Father, all the more so should we. I hope you are already establishing this as a personal priority right where you are.

When we have re-grounded ourselves in Christ Jesus early in the day, it is much more likely we will respond appropriately to the attacks of the enemy later on. It is all too easy to allow many other worldly commitments and distractions to keep us from spending daily time focused on heavenly priorities.

These distractions are especially challenging in the close environment of prison. Even though a place of total solitude is rare or even impossible in prison, we must choose to withdraw in a spiritual sense to a secluded place in which we are seeking God with all our heart, mind and soul.

We may need to get up earlier or stay up later to experience a little more peace and quiet. For me, doing this early in the day works best. Reading the Word, prayer and worship are important ways to spend this time.

TODAY'S CHALLENGE:

Ask your Father to show you how to dedicate and cultivate more time with Him each day. Decide to arrange your schedule to accommodate this important daily practice.

Treasure your private time with God. Maintain it faithfully.

Dive Deeper: Study Mark 1; compare today's verse with Psalm 91.

March 6

GOING HOME: BE THANKFUL AND HUMBLE

Hebrews 12:28-29

"Therefore, since we are receiving a kingdom that cannot be shaken, let us be thankful, and so worship God acceptably with reverence and awe, for our 'God is a consuming fire.'"

Thankfulness itself is a sign of humility. The Word says we are to be clothed with humility because, "God opposes the proud, but gives grace to the humble." See 1 Peter 5:5-6. If you desire more grace in your life, be more humble.

It has been said, "humility is not thinking less of yourself, it is thinking of yourself less". We give credit to God and others for our successes rather than ourselves. Realizing more fully every day that everything in our life comes from God will naturally increase our thankfulness to Him.

When our hearts are overflowing with thankfulness, the peace of Christ will rule in our hearts". See Colossians 2:6-7 and 3:15. Our Father has already made you "free on the inside" even right where you are now. Be intentional every day in counting your blessings. Name them one by one to our Father in prayer.

While you are anticipating and looking forward to being released to the free world, your heart will be filled with peace if you keep your mind focused on God in thankfulness and true humility. See Isaiah 26:3. Keep God first in your life all the rest of your days.

TODAY'S CHALLENGE:

Tell your Father how thankful you are today for all the many blessings He has given you. Take your time. Consider even the simplest things.

Take nothing for granted.

Dive Deeper: Study Hebrews 12; James 4:4-10; 1 Peter 5:5-6; Isaiah 26:3, 57:15, 66:1-2; Psalm 51:17; Matthew 5:3; Colossians 2:6-7, 3:15.

March 7

GOING HOME: BE HELD ACCOUNTABLE

Ecclesiastes 4:9-10
"Two are better than one, because they have a good return for their labor:
If either of them falls down, one can help the other up. But pity anyone
who falls and has no one to help them up."

Having a trusted accountability partner is an important factor in maintaining a faithful walk, both inside and outside of prison. This requires an attitude of respect and humility towards each other. We must commit to be transparent and honest with one another.

For many the idea of sharing personal information seems restrictive, or even an invasion of our privacy. However, the Bible says we are to confess our faults to each other, so that we may be healed. See James 5:16. I believe this primarily refers to the healing of our wounded souls.

Paul tells us to submit to one another. See Ephesians 5:21. The disciples were submitted and accountable to Jesus. Jesus was submitted and accountable to the Father. Regardless of one's position, everyone is accountable to somebody.

The enemy sees our weaknesses, and knows how to exploit them. One of his most successful strategies is to convince us to keep our failings a secret. We must not cooperate with the enemy. We can overcome him by being honest with a trusted accountability partner who will help and encourage us. It is generally agreed that accountability partners should be the same gender.

TODAY'S CHALLENGE:

Tell your Heavenly Father you desire to be held accountable to Him and to others in the Body of Christ.

Be held accountable for your thoughts, words and actions.

Dive Deeper: Study Ecclesiastes 4; Ephesians 5:21; James 5:13-16; Hebrews 10:24; Galatians 6:1-10; Matthew 25:14-30.

March 8

GOING HOME: GET INVOLVED

1 Peter 4:10
"Each of you should use whatever gift you have received to serve others, as faithful stewards of God's grace in its various forms."

I urge you to be actively involved in serving others. Jesus demonstrated servanthood in every part of his life and ministry. Being part of the Body of Christ implies you are actively involved in functions that enable others.

While I was incarcerated, I looked for ways to serve the inside church, our Chaplain, and my cellies. Putting others' needs before our own takes the focus off ourselves, and our own problems, and rightly turns our attention outward to others.

In today's verse, Peter tells us God has given each of us unique gifts, talents and abilities we should use to serve others. As stewards of God's Grace we are to generously give to others the grace we have received.

As we intentionally invest ourselves in the issues and challenges of others, the joy of the Lord strengthens and encourages us! In serving others, we are drawn closer to the Father by His Holy Spirit, and our personal testimonies give hope and encouragement to many.

I recommend you commit to being actively involved now. You will begin to see your gifts and talents in action, and you will be humbled by how wonderfully God uses even the simplest of your words or actions.

TODAY'S CHALLENGE:

Ask your Heavenly Father to show you how you can be involved in the needs and challenges of other, and commit to Him to start today.

Step outside yourself. Get involved.

Dive Deeper: Study 1 Peter 4; Romans 12:6-8; Ephesians 4:11-16; 1 Corinthians 12:27 – 13:13.

March 9

GOING HOME: CONFESS AND REPENT

1 John 1:9
"If we confess our sins, he is faithful and just and will forgive us our sins and purify us from all unrighteousness."

May I suggest it would be most helpful right now to stop and review the devotional of January 9 to learn more about true repentance.

After we have truly repented, we turn away from the life direction where we were headed and commit to consistently follow the Spirit as He leads us in the opposite direction through Christ to a deeper intimacy of personal relationship with our Father.

If we stumble, and we all sometimes do, we must quickly confess to the Father and truly repent. We cannot let the enemy keep us down or convince us we might as well go back to our old ways of life away from God.

Our Father is not mad at you when you stumble. In fact, He is mad ABOUT you! He patiently encourages us to allow His Holy Spirit to pick us up, dust us off, and get us quickly back on the right path.

True repentance brings about a commitment to no longer walk in outright rebellion and sin. A truly saved and repentant person does not make a practice of sin. See 1 John 5:18.

I like to say, "When you mess up, 'fess up! Admit it and quit it."

TODAY'S CHALLENGE:

Tell your Heavenly Father you want to please Him today. Commit to go to Him quickly and confess any and every instance of personal failure.

Be quick daily to confess and repent.

Dive Deeper: Study 1 John 1; 1 John 5:18; Romans 4:7-8; Proverbs 28:13; Psalm 32:5; Isaiah 59:1-2.

March 10

GOING HOME: FORGIVE YOURSELF

Isaiah 43:18
"Forget the former things; do not dwell on the past."

After we are truly saved, God no longer holds our past against us. We must make a positive and committed choice to stop holding our past against ourselves. God has forgiven you. Forgive yourself. Put the past in the past and keep it there.

The enemy wants us to stay bogged down in guilt, shame and embarrassment from our past. If we dwell on the past, we cannot enjoy the beautiful gift of each present day in relationship with our Ever-Present Father.

Jesus tells us that the one who looks back after putting his hand to the plow is not fit for service in the Kingdom of God. See Luke 9:62. I am certain you remember what happened to Lot's wife when she looked back. See Genesis 19:26.

Paul himself emphasized the crucial importance of this concept. His dedication and commitment came in part from this decision - *"One thing I do: Forgetting what is behind and straining toward what is ahead, I press on toward the goal to win the prize for which God has called me heavenward in Christ Jesus."* See Philippians 3:12-14.

The world, and the enemy, are unforgiving and may try to hold your past against you. You are discharging your legal debt to society, and God has already forgiven you in Christ Jesus. Forgive yourself.

TODAY'S CHALLENGE:

Ask your Heavenly Father for a deeper revelation of His unlimited love and unconditional forgiveness.

Put your past in the past. Stop looking in the rearview mirror.

Dive Deeper: Study Isaiah 43; Philippians 3:12-14; Genesis 19:26; Luke 9:60-62; Isaiah 42:9.

March 11

YOU ARE APPOINTED

1 Timothy 1:12
"I thank Christ Jesus our Lord, who has given me strength, that he considered me trustworthy, appointing me to his service."

When we truly put our past in the past, we realize God has been waiting for us to seek Him and His plan for our lives. He has appointed each and every one of us to serve Him in various unique ways.

No one is excluded. If He can use Paul, who as "Saul" was one of the worst persecutors of the early Christ-followers, He can use all of us! This fact amazes me, but I realize more every day how true it is.

When we first truly surrender our lives to God, we must learn to trust Him one day at a time to walk with us into our future. He does not reveal all His plans for us at once; if He did it would probably blow our minds! We would think we had to achieve it all ourselves, and we might succumb to the pressure we would be feeling.

But in His grace, He takes responsibility for our future asking only that we are obedient moment by moment to the leading of His Holy Spirit. Surrender daily. Listen closely to His promptings. Make a decision to be instantly obedient. He will fulfill His plan through you.

TODAY'S CHALLENGE:

Realize your Heavenly Father has a perfect plan designed specifically for you. Ask Him what He wants you to do today to participate with Him in His work for you, in you, and through you for others.

Dive Deeper: Study 1 Timothy 1; Luke 7:36-50.

March 12

GOD SHOWS MERCY

1 Timothy 1:13-14
"Even though I was once a blasphemer and a persecutor and a violent man, I was shown mercy because I acted in ignorance and unbelief. The grace of our Lord was poured out on me abundantly, along with the faith and love that are in Christ Jesus."

God is not the God of second chances. Rather, He is the God of another chance...and another chance...and another! He does not hold our past against us.

When we live in ignorance and unbelief, we are blinded to our sin. But, our Lord is patient with us, giving us many chances to respond to Him. We do many incredibly stupid, hurtful, rebellious acts before we finally respond to God's love and grace.

He is always forgiving when we repent for our failures. He pours out His mercy on us abundantly along with His love. How very precious His forgiveness is to us when we choose to believe and receive it!

His unlimited love, grace and mercy are always available to anyone who comes to Him in humility and sincerity. God the Father gives us an unlimited number of chances.

He freely gives us a measure of faith to believe Him, and His goodness draws us to repentance. Jesus paid the price for us to say, "Yes", to everything our Father is offering us.

TODAY'S CHALLENGE:

Tell your Heavenly Father you are grateful for another chance. Thank Him for not giving up on you when "the world" was ready to write you off. Ask Him to teach you how to receive His mercy!

Dive Deeper: Think about the love, mercy and forgiveness of God towards David, Peter, and Saul (Paul). Consider what might have happened if Adam and Judas had repented in humble sincerity.

March 13

JESUS CAME TO SAVE SINNERS

1 Timothy 1:15-16
"Here is a trustworthy saying that deserves full acceptance: Christ Jesus came into the world to save sinners—of whom I am the worst. But for that very reason I was shown mercy so that in me, the worst of sinners, Christ Jesus might display his immense patience as an example for those who would believe in him and receive eternal life."

One of my problems was how much I knew of my deceitful heart of stone before I came to Christ Jesus! Because I knew how very depraved and sinful I had been, it was hard to understand how He could forgive me and accept me into His family. Surely, I was one of the worst sinners.

Yet, knowing how much a sinner I was actually turned into a benefit in the sense that, even today, it makes me so very grateful for His forgiveness. What once was a hard heart has been replaced by a soft, compliant one. His Word tells us that those who have been forgiven much, love much! See Luke 7:36-50.

Have you ever really stopped to consider how much you have been forgiven? I know it is sometimes hard to believe "the Good News" when it comes to your own sinfulness, but Jesus really did die to forgive every single one of your sins!

TODAY'S CHALLENGE:

Tell your Heavenly Father you how very thankful you are for Jesus paying the price for ALL of your sins. Ask Him to give you the courage to tell someone else how grateful you are for your salvation.

Dive Deeper: Study 1 Timothy 1; Luke 7:36-50; John 21:15-22; Ezekiel 36:22-32; Ezekiel 11:19-20; Jeremiah 31:31-34.

March 14

THE HOLY SPIRIT AND FIRE

Matthew 3:11

"I baptize you in water for repentance. But after me comes one who is more powerful than I, whose sandals I am not worthy to carry. He will baptize you in the Holy Spirit and fire."

After we repent and are saved, we are instructed to follow our Lord into baptism with water. This is an outward manifestation of the inward change taking place in our lives. Paul teaches us that, symbolically, we are buried with Christ in baptism, and raised to walk in newness of life. See Romans 6:4.

Someone who is saved has the Spirit of Christ, the Holy Spirit, living in their heart. We could say the Spirit is immersed in them.

But, in addition, Jesus desires to baptize you with the Holy Spirit. He is "in you", but are you immersed "in Him"? This is a baptism that gives the believer great power to live and witness for Christ.

Many believe the "fire" John refers to in the verse above is the purifying and cleansing effects of the Holy Spirit baptism. Our old ways, like chaff from wheat, need to be burned away.

This "fire" may also refer to the ongoing process of sanctification the Holy Spirit continues to do in the life of the believer. Like silver refined in the fire, our impurities are removed.

TODAY'S CHALLENGE:

Ask your Heavenly Father to teach you more about His Holy Spirit. Tell Jesus you want more power to serve Him faithfully and witness for Him effectively.

Are you baptized in the Holy Spirit? Is His fire working in you?

Dive Deeper: Study Matthew 3:1-12; Mark 1:8; Luke 3:1-17; John 1:29-34; Acts 19:1-7; 1 Peter 1:1-2; Romans 6:4.

March 15

JESUS NEEDED THE HOLY SPIRIT

Matthew 3:16-17
"As soon as Jesus was baptized, he went up out of the water. At that moment heaven was opened, and he saw the Spirit of God descending like a dove and alighting on him. And a voice from heaven said, 'This is my Son, whom I love; with him I am well pleased.'"

The loving heart of the Father for the Son is revealed in His precious gift of the Holy Spirit! God the Father knew Jesus would need all His Power to carry out His work on Earth.

As a man, Jesus needed the Holy Spirit. So do we. The Father and the Son sent us the Holy Spirit as our Helper. See John 14:16-17. The Holy Spirit is our Friend, Counselor and Guide. He is the Spirit of Truth.

Everything Jesus did – His preaching, His healings, His suffering, His victory over sin – He did by the power of the Holy Spirit. See Acts 10:38. If Jesus could do nothing without the empowerment of the Spirit, how much more do we need the Spirit's power in our lives?

The almighty power of the Father on this earth is manifested in, and administered by, the Holy Spirit! What a wonderful mystery that He would want to dwell in us! See 1 Corinthians 3:16. Because His Spirit lives in us and we belong to God, we will desire to live a life that is pleasing to God.

TODAY'S CHALLENGE:

Ask the Father to continually refill you with His Holy Spirit, and to show you how to surrender more to the Spirit's leadership in your daily life.

Dive Deeper: Study Matthew 3; John 14:16-17; Acts 10:38; 1 Corinthians 3:16; 1 Corinthians 6:19-20.

March 16

JESUS WAS LED BY THE HOLY SPIRIT

Matthew 4:1
"Then Jesus was led by the Spirit into the wilderness to be tempted by the devil."

Immediately after the water baptism of Jesus, and the Father's audible declaration of His love and pleasure with Him, the Holy Spirit, like a dove, descended upon Jesus and led Him into the wilderness to be tempted, tested and tried by the devil.

After my salvation in prison, I looked back upon my life and realized how many times I was tempted, tested and tried by the Devil in the desert of my past. I wandered through a wilderness of my own making for most of forty years. I almost always failed the tests. Can you relate to this?

Jesus, the man, passed all His tests and trials. He did not fall for the Devil's temptation tricks. I believe the most important difference for Him was His obedience to the leading of the Holy Spirit. Similarly, we need to be led by the Spirit!

Another critical factor was how the Spirit prompted Him to respond to each of the three specific temptations we are told about in Scripture (I am certain He had many more we do not specifically know). His Spirit-led response was to answer the Devil with a scripture very specific to the area of temptation.

Likewise, we should be putting scripture deep in our heart daily so that the Holy Spirit can help us access it every time we are tempted and tested.

TODAY'S CHALLENGE:

Talk with the Father about your need and desire to be led daily by the Spirit. Tell Him you want to be instantly obedient to the Spirit's promptings. Ask Him for His help in learning scripture.

Dive Deeper: Study Matthew 4:1-17; Luke 4:1-14; Hebrews 4:12-13; Proverbs 4:20-23; Isaiah 55:10-11.

March 17

JESUS WAS FULL OF THE HOLY SPIRIT

Luke 4:14
"Jesus returned to Galilee in the power of the Spirit, and news about him spread through the whole countryside."

After the Holy Spirit helped Jesus resist all the temptations of the Devil in the desert, Jesus returned to Galilee to begin His ministry in the power of the Holy Spirit. The effectiveness of His ministry from start to finish depended upon the Holy Spirit indwelling.

We see in today's scripture how news about Jesus spread quickly. In our own strength, we will be poor imitations of Christ as we go about our own lives daily. However, people will see a real difference in us when we are full of the Holy Spirit and are following His direction moment by moment.

When I returned to "the free world" after having been saved and filled with the Holy Spirit in prison, those who had known me before could not believe the difference in me. Actually, I almost did not know myself either!

Even while I was incarcerated, my "cellies" saw God beginning His transformation in me by His Spirit. Everything about me was changing as I dedicated myself to seek God with all my heart. Having been baptized in the Spirit, I had an anointing I had never had before, and I was more empowered to minister to others.

Are you full of the Holy Spirit?

TODAY'S CHALLENGE:

Ask the Father to lead you today by His Holy Spirit. Be sensitive to His leadership. Obey His promptings as He desires to minister to others today through you.

Dive Deeper: Study Luke 4; Matthew 4:12-25.

March 18

THE SPIRIT OF THE LORD WAS ON JESUS

Luke 4:18-19
"The Spirit of the Lord is on me, because he has anointed me to proclaim good news to the poor. He has sent me to proclaim freedom for the prisoners and recovery of sight for the blind, to set the oppressed free, to proclaim the year of the Lord's favor."

After returning from the wilderness, the first public message we know about was the one we are reading today. Isn't it interesting that he selected the passage from the scroll of Isaiah that had been prophesied of Him 700 years earlier? See Isaiah 61:1-2.

Notice the first phrase. Jesus Himself recognized how important it was for Him to acknowledge the true source of His anointing and power. He knew His mission and publicly declared it.

Aren't you glad the Spirit of the Lord was on Him to proclaim freedom for the prisoners and to set the oppressed free!?!? The first time I read this in prison my heart was full of wonder and overflowing with gratitude. Do you feel it?

If we are to be successful followers of Christ, and do the type of works He did, we must realize our same source of power is His Holy Spirit. God has a plan uniquely designed for each of us. He does not want us to try to accomplish it in our own strength, but in the Spirit of the Lord.

TODAY'S CHALLENGE:

Ask the Father to show you His plan for you today right where you are. Tell Him you do not have the power within yourself, but you know His Spirit is upon you!

Dive Deeper: Study Luke 4:14-44; Isaiah 61; Acts 2:22, 32; Acts 10:37-38.

March 19

JESUS WAS ANOINTED

Acts 10:38
"...how God anointed Jesus of Nazareth with the Holy Spirit and power, and how he went around doing good and healing all who were under the power of the devil, because God was with him."

In Luke's account, Peter is relating to us in this passage the very secret of the successful ministry of Jesus – God the Father anointed His Son, Jesus, with the Holy Spirit and power! Jesus was able to do good wherever He went because God was with Him. His healing power came from the Spirit. Devils had to obey because the Spirit of the Father was always with Jesus.

Isaiah 10:27 indicates that it is the burden-removing, yoke-destroying power of the anointing that sets us free from the influence of the Devil. The anointing of the Holy Spirit upon us enables us to carry out God's purpose and plan for us. The Spirit helps us exercise the authority of Jesus over all the power of the enemy.

With all the challenges presented to us in prison, where there are plenty of people influenced by the enemy, we need every bit of help available to us! You are not alone when you serve Jesus. You always have the presence and power of God the Father in the form of His Holy Spirit!

Are you utilizing this power? Be still, and know that He is God.

TODAY'S CHALLENGE:

Thank your Heavenly Father for anointing you with His Holy Spirit! Ask Him to demonstrate His power over the enemy through you today as you surrender to the leadership of the Holy Spirit, and the Lordship of Jesus.

Dive Deeper: Study Acts 10; Acts 1:4-5, 8; Luke 24:45-49; Isaiah 10:27.

March 20

A GOOD FATHER GIVES THE BEST GIFTS

Luke 11:11-13
"Which of you fathers, if your son asks for a fish, will give him a snake instead? Or if he asks for an egg, will give him a scorpion? If you then, though you are evil, know how to give good gifts to your children, how much more will your Father in heaven give the Holy Spirit to those who ask him!"

In this passage of scripture, Jesus had just before been teaching His disciples to pray, and had emphasized to them the importance for them to ask, seek and knock! "For everyone who asks receives…" For context, see Luke 11:1-10.

As earthly fathers, we can relate to the requests of our children. Sometimes their innocence just melts your heart doesn't it? If it is within our power, and does not harm them, we will give them whatever they ask.

Our verse today probably does not refer to the indwelling of the Spirit when we are re-born since we all receive this automatically. So, many believe Jesus is talking about the baptism of the Holy Spirit that He promises His followers.

If as imperfect earthly fathers, we give good gifts to our children, how much more will our perfect and great Heavenly Father give the best gifts to His children who ask Him?

In my opinion, after salvation, the Baptism of the Holy Spirit may be the very best gift.

TODAY'S CHALLENGE:

Ask your Heavenly Father for His Holy Spirit. He desires to give you the best gifts. He knows what you need. He would never give you anything to harm you.

Receive His best gift for you.

Dive Deeper: Study Luke 11; Luke 24:49; John 14:26; John 15:26; John 16:7.

March 21

IT PAYS TO BE THIRSTY

John 7:37-39
"On the last and greatest day of the festival, Jesus stood and said in a loud voice, 'Let anyone who is thirsty come to me and drink. [38] Whoever believes in me, as Scripture has said, rivers of living water will flow from within them.' [39] By this he meant the Spirit, whom those who believed in him were later to receive. Up to that time the Spirit had not been given, since Jesus had not yet been glorified."

Thirst is a powerful motivator. Someone can live several weeks without food, but only 3-4 days without water. During the day, we find ourselves drinking liquid much more often than eating. Next to air to breathe, water is the most important ingredient to sustain life.

Jesus offers us spiritual water in the form of His Holy Spirit to sustain us and meet our most basic needs. What would our life look like if we depended on God's Very Presence, the Holy Spirit, the same way we depend on water?

This constant dependence on God is part of what Jesus meant when He said He was the vine and we are the branches. The branch is connected to the vine and the life source of the vine flows in and out of the branch to sustain life and bring forth fruit. We must stay connected, and desire the life force, to live fruitfully.

TODAY'S CHALLENGE:

Tell the Father you need and want more of Him every day. Ask Him to let you drink continuously from His Living Water. Ask and you shall receive.

It pays to be thirsty.

Dive Deeper: Study John 7; John 4:13-14; Isaiah 12:3; Isaiah 35:3-6; Isaiah 43:19-21; Revelation 21:6-7.

March 22

COME, DRINK, LIVE

Revelation 22:17
"The Spirit and the bride say, 'Come!' And let the one who hears say, 'Come' Let the one who is thirsty come; and let the one who wishes take the free gift of the water of life."

The Holy Spirit is constantly, but gently, calling us to "Come". He wants us to choose His path, listen to His voice and follow His lead. He desires to lead us to an ever-increasing level of intimacy of personal relationship with the Father.

The Bride of Christ, that is, the true body of Believers, corporately calls us to "Come" and join into meaningful fellowship together with one another and the Spirit.

Others who have heard and responded to the Spirit's call, and made this choice, urge and encourage us to "Come" and join them on the path. But, in order for us to respond, we must recognize the deep longing inside, the deep emptiness, and desire with all our heart to be filled with something permanently life-sustaining.

Do you really wish to be filled? Think about how many times you have been encouraged to go deeper in Christ, to go "all in". It is a free gift, and is yours for the taking. There is always more of God no matter how long you have been in relationship with Him. Drink deeply daily.

TODAY'S CHALLENGE:

Ask the Father to reveal to you the source of emptiness and loneliness deep inside. Tell Him you desperately want to be filled forever. Ask Him for the pure living water of His Spirit and His Word.

Come to Him. Drink deeply. Live eternally filled.

Dive Deeper: Study Revelation 22; Matthew 11:28-30; Ephesians 5:18-20.

March 23

THE COUNSELOR OF TRUTH

John 14:16-17
"And I will ask the Father, and he will give you another Counselor to help you and be with you forever— [17] the Spirit of truth. The world cannot accept him, because it neither sees him nor knows him. But you know him, for he lives with you and will be in you."

Can you imagine what the Disciples must have been thinking when Jesus told them it is better for them if He goes away? They had been with Him almost constantly for three years or more. They had been learning from Him, watching Him work powerful miracles, seeing Him demonstrate mercy, love and compassion, and hearing Him speak Truth to everyone at all times. Everything was great!

But they could only experience this in His immediate physical presence. Sometimes they were separated from Him and things did not go so well. For example, they floundered in the midst of the storm on the sea when Jesus sent them ahead to the other side.

Jesus tells them in today's scripture they will have His Spirit living inside them when He goes away, therefore, His Spirit will never leave them. They will always have His Presence.

This is unique to true disciples. "The world" does not accept Jesus, has no relationship with Him, and, therefore, cannot have His Spirit. They cannot recognize the Truth they so desperately need.

TODAY'S CHALLENGE:

Tell the Father you are thankful for having His Counselor of Truth living inside you. Ask Him to help you listen closely to His wisdom and follow His direction.

Dive Deeper: Study John 14.

March 24

RECEIVE THE GIFT OF POWER

Acts 1:4-5
"On one occasion, while he was eating with them, he gave them this command: "Do not leave Jerusalem, but wait for the gift my Father promised, which you have heard me speak about. *⁵ For John baptized with water, but in a few days you will be baptized with the Holy Spirit."*

Jesus had already told His disciples to go into "all the world" to make other disciples and represent Him and the Kingdom of God. Yet, He told them to wait. This seems contradictory at first glance.

They must have been overflowing with excitement after His Resurrection, and ready to tell the world the Good News. They had been trained for over three years in the best School of Christ ever available. They probably thought they were ready, but Jesus told them to wait.

There was still something they needed - the very best Gift from the Father that they had not yet received. Jesus knew they needed the Baptism of the Holy Spirit before they would have the Power necessary for them to fulfill what He had commanded them to do.

Often times, after our salvation and water baptism, we are excited and want to do things for the Lord and His Kingdom. But we really have no power for success on our own. Of our own selves we can do nothing, but with Him, all things are possible.

TODAY'S CHALLENGE:

Ask the Father for revelation about all His Power available to you in and through His Holy Spirit. Tell Him you want to be re-filled daily with His Spirit.

Receive the Gift of Power.

Dive Deeper: Study Acts 1:1 – 2:47.

March 25

PENTECOST POWER

Acts 2:1-4
"When the day of Pentecost came, they were all together in one place. ²Suddenly a sound like the blowing of a violent wind came from heaven and filled the whole house where they were sitting. ³ They saw what seemed to be tongues of fire that separated and came to rest on each of them. ⁴ All of them were filled with the Holy Spirit and began to speak in other tongues as the Spirit enabled them."

For ten days after His Ascension, the Disciples waited as they had been instructed by Jesus. They were told there was a Gift coming from The Father and The Son, so they stayed together in faith and unity. This must have taken a great deal of self-control and patience.

They did not yet know what would be the great reward for their obedience, but they had spent enough time with Jesus to know with certainty that it would be magnificent. They had been told of Power, and they had been taught about a Person - a Counselor, Advocate and Helper.

Then, suddenly, they saw and felt that the Power and the Person were One! The Holy Spirit came upon them in the upper room where they were assembled, and demonstrated to them individually His Power and Presence.

There is always a reward for our obedience but we too must exercise faith, patience and self-control.

TODAY'S CHALLENGE:

Ask the Father to empower you with His Presence today. Tell Him you are willingly, and obediently, waiting to receive His Gift before you start your day.

Pentecost power awaits. Receive it.

Dive Deeper: Study Acts 2.

March 26

INDWELLING SPIRIT

John 20:21-22

"Again Jesus said, 'Peace be with you! As the Father has sent me, I am sending you." *²²* *And with that he breathed on them and said, 'Receive the Holy Spirit.'"*

Soon after the Resurrection of Jesus, He appeared to His disciples. Once they recovered from what must have been great shock, their hopelessness, despair and loneliness turned to overflowing hope, joy and peace! Now they were true Believers, the first ones to personally encounter the Risen Lord.

In this moment "the Church" was born. The Body of Christ must contain the indwelling Spirit of Jesus for there to be true and abundant life. Knowing His disciples must be able to succeed in their mission long after He ascended to Heaven, Jesus empowered them with the same indwelling power He had been given – the Spirit of the Father, the Holy Spirit.

Jesus wanted to send them out with peace, so He breathed on them the very Spirit of Peace! Similar to the way the Father breathed life into Adam in the Garden by sharing His very Essence, Jesus breathed upon His disciples the supernatural life of the Third Person of the Godhead, the Holy Spirit.

For the first time, a follower of "the Way" (later to be called "Christians") was permanently indwelt by the very Spirit of the Father and the Son – the Holy Spirit. Jesus needed Him, and so do we.

TODAY'S CHALLENGE:

Thank your Heavenly Father today that the same Spirit Jesus had was also given permanently to you if you are a true Believer.

Jesus sends us out with His Peace and Power.

Dive Deeper: Study John 20; 1 Corinthians 3:16; 1 Corinthians 6:19-20; Ephesians 2:22.

March 27

COME HOLY SPIRIT

Acts 8:14-17

"When the apostles in Jerusalem heard that Samaria had accepted the word of God, they sent Peter and John to Samaria. ¹⁵ When they arrived, they prayed for the new believers there that they might receive the Holy Spirit, ¹⁶ because the Holy Spirit had not yet come on any of them; they had simply been baptized in the name of the Lord Jesus. ¹⁷ Then Peter and John placed their hands on them, and they received the Holy Spirit."

The Samaritans were treated as second-class citizens, and even worse, they were often viewed as common "dogs". For word to come to Jerusalem that even the Samaritans had accepted the Gospel must have been quite a surprise to the disciples. Two of the early Church leaders, Peter and John, were sent to meet with them.

It must have been clear to the two from Jerusalem that the believers in Samaria had not yet been baptized with "power from on high" the way Peter, John and the others had been at Pentecost, so they prayed. They must have been asking the Father if this power was for everyone who truly believed, not just the Jews.

Learning that they had indeed been baptized into the Name of our Lord Jesus, Peter and John placed their hands upon them for the Samaritans to receive the second baptism of fire and power. Once again, they saw proof that God does not discriminate.

TODAY'S CHALLENGE:

Tell the Father you want everything He has to give you. If you have not received this second baptism, ask Him. His powerful Spirit is for everyone who believes, and who desire more of the abundant life Jesus came to give us.

Dive Deeper: Study Acts 8; Acts 10; Acts 19:1-7.

March 28

BAPTISMS

Acts 19:1-6

"While Apollos was at Corinth, Paul took the road through the interior and arrived at Ephesus. There he found some disciples ² and asked them, 'Did you receive the Holy Spirit when you believed?' They answered, 'No, we have not even heard that there is a Holy Spirit.' ³ So Paul asked, 'Then what baptism did you receive?' 'John's baptism,' they replied. ⁴ Paul said, 'John's baptism was a baptism of repentance. He told the people to believe in the one coming after him, that is, in Jesus.' ⁵ On hearing this, they were baptized in the name of the Lord Jesus. ⁶ When Paul placed his hands on them, the Holy Spirit came on them, and they spoke in tongues and prophesied."

When Paul encountered these believers, it appears he may have been given spiritual discernment to notice something different about them. Perhaps he sensed something, or Someone, was missing.

Apparently, he did not doubt whether they were believers based on how he asked this most important first question. Perhaps he was both shocked and excited that they "had not even heard there is a Holy Spirit."

Learning they had indeed repented of their sins, they were again baptized in water to demonstrate their decision to follow Jesus. Paul must have been filled with joy to be able to be used of God to then also empower these young believers with His Holy Spirit. Spiritual gifts were immediately manifested with this baptism of fire and power.

TODAY'S CHALLENGE:

There is always more to receive of His Presence for those who sincerely seek to know God better. Tell the Father you are longing for more of Him, and be ready to receive.

Dive Deeper: Study Acts 19; Luke 11:9-13; Acts 1:4-5, 8.

March 29

THE HOLY SPIRIT SPEAKS

Acts 13:2
"While they were worshiping the Lord and fasting, the Holy Spirit said, 'Set apart for me Barnabas and Saul for the work to which I have called them.'"

Isaiah 30:21
"Whether you turn to the right or to the left, your ears will hear a voice behind you, saying, 'This is the way; walk in it.'"

John 15:26
Jesus said, "When the Advocate comes, whom I will send to you from the Father—the Spirit of truth who goes out from the Father—he will testify about me..."

I have never heard the audible voice of God the Father, or God the Son. But, I very definitely daily hear the voice of God, the Holy Spirit! Yes, as the verses above prove, the Holy Spirit speaks to us. Are you listening?

This "still, small voice" of the Spirit comes to me in my thoughts from deep inside my heart or human spirit. There He, the Spirit of the Father and the Son, dwells in me, always ready and willing to lead me, instruct me, and point me to Jesus.

It is the noise and distractions of "the world" that compete for our attention. Sin, self and Satan do their best to drown out the precious voice of the Spirit. He is a "gentleman", and as such, does not impose Himself upon our free will. That is why it is so very important that we constantly choose to seek His voice and receive His instructions obediently.

TODAY'S CHALLENGE:

Be still. Be very quiet within. Listen. Listen. Listen. He will sow His seeds of love and instruction in your heart. You must constantly prepare the ground. Soak in His Presence.

Dive Deeper: Study John 14; John 16:12-15; 1 Kings 19:11-13.

March 30

DO NOT GRIEVE THE SPIRIT

Ephesians 4:29-31

"Do not let any unwholesome talk come out of your mouths, but only what is helpful for building others up according to their needs, that it may benefit those who listen. ^{30}*And do not grieve the Holy Spirit of God, with whom you were sealed for the day of redemption.* ^{31} *Get rid of all bitterness, rage and anger, brawling and slander, along with every form of malice."*

The Holy Spirit is a Person the same as God the Father, and God the Son. As such, it is possible to grieve Him by our words, actions and thoughts. Rather than disappointing Him, we should do our best to please Him.

In our daily lives, we must be constantly aware how we are interacting with people along our path, and dealing with challenges along the way. The enemy of our souls is always lurking about waiting for any opportunity we give him to tempt us to act out in ways similar to our "old man" prior to Christ. When we do, we grieve the Holy Spirit living in us.

Don't fall for the tricks, lures and devices of the enemy. The Spirit of Christ inside you knows the correct words and responses. Seek His guidance, and His peace, in the middle of the battle. Determine daily to do your best to please God in your thoughts, words and deeds.

TODAY'S CHALLENGE:

Tell the Father, aloud, that you desire to be led by the Spirit today, and not by the flesh, the world, or the devil. Rededicate and recommit yourself daily to pleasing the Father, Son and Spirit.

Dive Deeper: Study Ephesians 4; Galatians 1:10; Colossians 1:10; 1 Thessalonians 2:4; 1 Thessalonians 4:1; Hebrews 13:16.

March 31

THE SPIRIT DECIDES

1 Corinthians 12:11
"All these are the work of one and the same Spirit, and he distributes them to each one, just as he determines."

Acts 16:7
"When they came to the border of Mysia, they tried to enter Bithynia, but the Spirit of Jesus would not allow them to."

God, the Holy Spirit, makes decisions that help us, and guide us in His way for our lives. He chooses paths we may not be able to see, or are not wise enough to choose. It becomes increasingly important for us to wait, listen and come into agreement with His Will for our lives.

The Spirit has many gifts He will manifest in and through us at the right time, the right place, and with the right people. But, He decides when, where and how. As we learn to hear His still, small voice, we are able to partner with Him in His work.

In Acts 16:6-10, apparently Paul and his companions had a plan to minister the Gospel in Asia, but were prompted not to go by the Holy Spirit. Then, they came to the border of another region, and were not allowed to enter, again by the Spirit. Finally, the Spirit used a vision with Paul to direct him to go instead to Macedonia.

Are you seeking God's guidance daily? If so, are you quick to obey?

TODAY'S CHALLENGE:

Ask the Father to help you learn how to better hear the Spirit of Jesus, the Holy Spirit, as He makes decisions to benefit you. Tell your Heavenly Father that today you desire to make good choices guided by His Spirit who is with you, and within you!

Dive Deeper: Study Acts 16; 1 Corinthians 12:7-11; Hebrews 2:4.

April 1

FOOL'S DAY

1 Corinthians 1:18
"For the message of the cross is foolishness to those who are perishing, but to us who are being saved it is the power of God."

1 Corinthians 4:10
"We are fools for Christ..."

Before I was truly saved in prison, while I was climbing the corporate ladder, April 1st seemed to me to be a sign of positive change each year. Invariably, this time of year was when raises and promotions were announced. Something of significance always seemed to occur in the Spring. I thought April Fool's Day was "my lucky day".

At the time, I thought I had everything under control, and that I was doing a good job running my life. I didn't think I needed God.

What is the one-letter word in the middle of the word pride? "I". That's right, overcome with pride I was heading toward destruction. I thought I was wise, but I was a fool.

On my bunk in prison in the Spring of 2009, I began to face the truth. I wasn't doing such a great job of running my own life - I had to face the facts of where I ended up, and how I got there!

Today the Cross is no longer foolishness to me, and I am glad to say I am a fool for Christ!

TODAY'S CHALLENGE:

Talk to your Heavenly Father about where you stand with Him and His Son, Jesus, Who is the Truth. Ask the Holy Spirit to reveal wisdom through the Spirit of Christ.

Tell the Father, you are willing to be a fool for Christ for all of eternity. You will never regret it!

Dive Deeper: Study 1 Corinthians chapters 1 and 4.

April 2

DO NOT LIE TO GOD

Acts 5:3-4

"Then Peter said, 'Ananias, how is it that Satan has so filled your heart that you have lied to the Holy Spirit and have kept for yourself some of the money you received for the land? ⁴ Didn't it belong to you before it was sold? And after it was sold, wasn't the money at your disposal? What made you think of doing such a thing? You have not lied just to human beings but to God.'"

Lying to God the Holy Spirit has serious consequences. We do not deceive Him; we are only deceiving ourselves.

In this passage, Paul clearly confronts the lying spirit of the enemy who influenced Ananias to lie about the nature and amount of his gift. The enemy deceived Ananias, and he tried to deceive leaders anointed by the Spirit to shepherd the Church. Plainly, Paul points out that the Holy Spirit is God.

Why do we feel like we can get away with disobedience? Do we really believe God does not see what we are doing? Do we close our eyes and do it anyway hoping God has closed His eyes? Usually the consequences of our self-deception and lying to God are not as severe as it was for Ananias in physical death, but what are we doing to our spirit man?

TODAY'S CHALLENGE:

Ask the Father to help you face the areas of your life where you are not being honest with yourself and with God. Jesus gave you the Spirit as your Helper. Be honest with Him. Be honest with yourself.

Do not lie to God.

Dive Deeper: Study Acts 5; Isaiah 63:10; Matthew 12:30-32; Mark 3:28-30.

April 3

THE GLORY OF THE LORD

2 Corinthians 3:18
"And we all, who with unveiled faces contemplate the Lord's glory, are being transformed into his image with ever-increasing glory, which comes from the Lord, who is the Spirit."

In this passage, Paul declares the glory of the Lord is the Spirit. The very essence of our Lord is His Holy Spirit, His Glory. By His Glory, Who is the Spirit, He is transforming us daily into the image of Christ.

This is confirmed as God's purpose for us in Romans 8:29, where Paul says that God has predestined us to be conformed to the image of His Son. The Glory of God dwells in us, and it is His job to progressively change us into the very likeness of Jesus. This is the process known as sanctification.

The Spirit desires to remove everything in us that is not like Christ, so that His likeness is ever increasing in us, thereby allowing His Glory to be a Light in the darkness. He removes the impurities from us over time so we are an increasingly pure reflection of the Glory of God.

To the extent we see Jesus more clearly through His Holy Spirit, we are attracted by His Beauty and Glory. This attraction, like a strong magnet to metal, draws us increasingly to Him.

TODAY'S CHALLENGE:

Tell your Heavenly Father that you desire to be filled today with His Glory, His Holy Spirit, so that you can be increasingly transformed into the image of Jesus. Ask the Holy Spirit to reveal areas where you need to "deny self", and follow Jesus.

Receive His Glory.

Dive Deeper: Study 2 Corinthians 3; Romans 8:29; Ephesians 4:22-24.

April 4

GOD REVEALS BY HIS SPIRIT

1 Corinthians 2:9-10
"What no eye has seen, what no ear has heard, and what no human mind has conceived — the things God has prepared for those who love him — [10] these are the things God has revealed to us by his Spirit. The Spirit searches all things, even the deep things of God."

This passage is often used in sermons to foreshadow the mysteries of Heaven to be revealed when we leave our temporary earthly assignment. Certainly, there are many tremendous surprises awaiting us.

However, Paul is also informing us that the Spirit of God the Father knows all things, and desires to begin to reveal them to us now, in this life. By reviewing the entire passage of 1 Corinthians 2:6-16, we see Paul is speaking about the Wisdom of God revealed by His Spirit enabling us to have the mind of Christ.

Paul tells us in verse 11 and 12, *"no-one knows the thoughts of God except the Spirit of God. We have not received the spirit of the world, but the Spirit Who is from God, that we may understand what God has freely given us."*

Brothers and Sisters, this is exciting Truth. The Spirit of God in you desires to reveal the deep things of God to you, so you are better able to live the abundant life Jesus came to give you (John 10:10)!

TODAY'S CHALLENGE:

Ask your Heavenly Father to give you the mind of Christ. Tell Him you desire to understand the deep things of God that can help you today.

Allow God to reveal them by His Spirit.

Dive Deeper: Study 1 Corinthians 2.

April 5

GOD'S SPIRIT LIVES IN YOU

1 Corinthians 3:16
"Don't you know that you yourselves are God's temple and that God's Spirit dwells in your midst?"

In the Garden, God walked personally with Adam and Eve until sin prevented them from being in His Presence. In the wilderness, God's Presence dwelled inside the tabernacle in the Holy of Holies, and then similarly in the Temple, but He was not among the people; and, Ezekiel later sees the vision of the Glory of God departing even from the Temple in Ezekiel chapter 10.

The Father has always desired to dwell among His people. But He cannot live in sin. Jesus came to restore us to relationship with the Father forever. Jesus became the very sin the Father could not even bear to even look upon so that we could be made the righteousness of God in Christ (see 2 Corinthians 5:21).

The veil of separation of God's Presence in the Temple has been forever opened to us through the torn Body of His Son, Jesus.

God Himself has prepared a dwelling place again forever. His Presence, His Holy Spirit, dwells in you! The Spirit of the Father, and the Spirit of the Son, lives in us who have truly repented and believed the Gospel!

Have you really stopped to meditate on this amazing Truth? You are God's Temple!

TODAY'S CHALLENGE:

Be still and know that He is God. Thank the Father for making your body a place for His Holy Spirit to live. Meditate on the amazing miracle of God's Presence with you today.

God's Spirit lives in you!

Dive Deeper: Study 1 Corinthians 3; John 20:21-22; 1 Corinthians 6:19-20; Ephesians 2:22; Ezekiel 10:18; 2 Corinthians 5:21.

April 6

THE SPIRIT OF TRUTH

John 15:26
"But when the Helper comes, whom I shall send to you from the Father, the Spirit of truth who proceeds from the Father, He will testify of Me."

The Father and Jesus, the Son, determined in their Wisdom that we would need a Helper. How magnificent that our Helper, Teacher, Counselor and Guide comes to us as the Spirit of the Father and the Spirit of the Son!

Jesus perfectly represented the Father and always pointed people to the Father. Similarly, the Holy Spirit will always point people to Jesus. The Spirit of Truth represents perfectly the One Who is the Truth.

Therefore, the Holy Spirit will always counsel us, and help us, in perfect harmony with Jesus, Who is the Living Word. We can be certain that the voice of the Spirit will never contradict the Word of God.

Since Jesus told us repeatedly that He only does what the Father does, and says what the Father says, we can be confident that the Holy Spirit perfectly represents the Father too. Yet, the Father and the Son think so highly of the Spirit that they agreed to send Him to help us.

All three Persons of the Trinity are in harmony, and desire to help us in our restored relationship with God by always proclaiming Truth, and guiding us to the One Who is Truth.

TODAY'S CHALLENGE:

Spend some quiet time with the Father thanking Him and Jesus for sending you the Spirit of Truth. Ask the Father to give you a renewed hunger and thirst for His Word so that you will better recognize and obey the voice of the Holy Spirit.

Dive Deeper: Study John 15.

April 7

THE ETERNAL SPIRIT

Hebrews 9:14
"How much more, then, will the blood of Christ, who through the eternal Spirit offered himself unblemished to God, cleanse our consciences from acts that lead to death, so that we may serve the living God!"

God has always been, and will always be. He is eternally "I AM".

Therefore, all three persons of God are eternal. The Father, Son and Holy Spirit were not created and they will never cease to be. They are the uncaused First Cause of everything. They are Endless and Everlasting.

A.W. Tozer wrote, "God dwells in eternity, but time dwells in God. He has already lived all our tomorrows as He has lived all our yesterdays... Out of eternity our Lord came into time to rescue His human brethren whose moral folly had made them not only fools of the passing world but slaves of sin and death as well."[1]

Jesus willingly and obediently offered Himself to God as the final, unblemished sacrifice for all of our sins, for all time. The Word tells us He accomplished this through the Eternal Holy Spirit so that we may serve the living God.

The Holy Spirit Who lives in you is the One Who is able to perfectly serve the Father. Our challenge is to more perfectly surrender to Him daily as He accomplishes this in and through us.

TODAY'S CHALLENGE:

Ask the Father to help you learn how to more fully surrender to His Eternal Spirit so that you may better serve Him. Thank Him that the Blood of Jesus cleanses your conscience, and has set you free forever from time, sin and death.

Dive Deeper: Study Hebrews 9.

[1] A.W. Tozer, The Knowledge of the Holy, Harper and Row Publishers, copyright 1961.

April 8

THE SPIRIT IS ALL-POWERFUL

Luke 1:35
"The angel answered, "The Holy Spirit will come on you, and the power of the Most High will overshadow you. So the holy one to be born will be called the Son of God."

Have you ever stopped to consider the phrase "the power of the Most High"?

Traditionally the emphasis of this verse focuses on the fact that the Holy Spirit "overshadowed" Mary, which of course speaks to the Virgin Birth. But today, let's consider God's Power.

Theologically, God's power is referred to as "omnipotent" which means, "having all power". The word derives from Latin, is often translated as "almighty" in our Bible, and is never used with anyone but God. God alone is Almighty.

A.W. Tozer wrote, "Sovereignty and omnipotence must go together. One cannot exist without the other. To reign, God must have power, and to reign sovereignly, He must have all power... Since God is also infinite, whatever He has must be without limit; therefore God has limitless power, He is omnipotent."[1]

Stop and consider this amazing fact: the One with unlimited power dwells in you! That fact alone should make it easier for us to want to surrender to His leadership daily. Realizing how weak we are in our own selves should encourage us to let His power take control.

TODAY'S CHALLENGE:

Thank the Father for His unlimited power that resides in you in the form of His Holy Spirit. Ask Him to help you be a clear channel through which His power may flow to positively influence and minister to those around you.

Dive Deeper: Study Luke 1.

---

[1] A.W. Tozer, <u>The Knowledge of the Holy</u>, Harper and Row Publishers, copyright 1961.

April 9

THE SPIRIT IS EVERYWHERE PRESENT

Psalm 139:7-10
"Where can I go from your Spirit? Where can I flee from your presence? [8] If I go up to the heavens, you are there; if I make my bed in the depths, you are there. [9] If I rise on the wings of the dawn, if I settle on the far side of the sea, [10] even there your hand will guide me, your right hand will hold me fast."

There is nowhere we could ever be where the Presence of God the Holy Spirit is not.

God is omnipresent. A. W. Tozer explains, "God is everywhere here, close to everything, next to everyone... there is no place in heaven or earth or hell where men may hide from His presence. The scriptures teach that God is at once far off and near, and that in Him men move and live and have their being."[1]

It comforts me to consider how God was with me even in the midst of all my sin. He waited patiently for me to finally come to the end of myself in prison and cry out to Him in surrender. Likewise, His presence kept me safe, taught me, and set me free even while I was still incarcerated.

God is with you too right now, right where you are! Believe that.

TODAY'S CHALLENGE:

Be still and know that He is God. He is with you. He will never leave you. Tell Him you want to recognize His Presence with you all day.

Dive Deeper: Study Psalm 139; Psalm 46:10.

---

[1] A.W. Tozer, The Knowledge of the Holy, Harper and Row Publishers, copyright 1961.

April 10

THE SPIRIT LOVES

Romans 15:30
"I urge you, brothers and sisters, by our Lord Jesus Christ and by the love of the Spirit, to join me in my struggle by praying to God for me."

The Holy Spirit loves. John tells us that God is love. Love is an attribute of God. We know love is not all He is because He is also Grace, Truth, Mercy, Justice and many other attributes as well.

Love is not God, but God is love. God is perfect love. His love is aptly and beautifully described by Paul in 1 Corinthians 13:4-10. Stop and prayerfully meditate on that passage. Don't rush through it.

A.W. Tozer writes, "From God's other known attributes we may learn much about His love. We can know, for instance, that because God is self-existent, His love had no beginning; because He is eternal, His love can have no end; because He is infinite, it has no limit; because He is holy, it is the quintessence of all spotless purity; because He is immense, His love is an incomprehensibly vast, bottomless, shoreless sea before which we kneel in joyful silence and from which the loftiest eloquence retreats confused and abashed." [1]

Jesus told us in John 13:34-35, that we are to love others the way He loves us. In my own strength that seems impossible, but the Holy Spirit is able to perfectly love others through me if I allow Him.

TODAY'S CHALLENGE:

Thank the Father for His perfect love in His Son by His Holy Spirit. He loves you!

Dive Deeper: Study Romans 15; 1 John 4:7-21; 1 Corinthians 13:4-10.

[1] A.W. Tozer, The Knowledge of the Holy, Harper and Row Publishers, copyright 1961.

April 11

THE SPIRIT SPEAKS

Acts 8:29
"Then the Spirit said to Philip, "Go near and overtake this chariot."

Acts 13:2
"While they were worshiping the Lord and fasting, the Holy Spirit said, 'Set apart for me Barnabas and Saul for the work to which I have called them.'"

Learning to hear the Holy Spirit when He speaks is crucial to building an intimate personal relationship with God the Father. Jesus paid the highest price in the universe so that we could be restored to the Father. I believe this intimacy of relationship is only possible through the Spirit of God Who dwells in us.

Building a relationship with anyone requires some form of effective communication. For the most part, this primarily involves some form of verbal communication, ability to hear, and a response. While there are some people who have severe hearing and speaking disabilities, they learn to communicate in very specialized ways. Relationships require communication.

Most Christ-followers have never heard an audible voice, rather they sense distinct words or instructions in their mind that their heart understands as divine in origin. The Holy Spirit gives ideas and impressions that never conflict with the Word, and generally are not what your natural inclination, or fleshly desire, would normally be.

Scheduling time daily to be still, listen, and talk with God are important first steps.

TODAY'S CHALLENGE:

Ask the Father to help you to hear and respond to His Holy Spirit today. Ask Him something, then be still and listen. Give Him a response. He longs for conversation with you.

Dive Deeper: Study Acts 8.

April 12

THE DOVE

Matthew 3:16
"As soon as Jesus was baptized, he went up out of the water. At that moment heaven was opened, and he saw the Spirit of God descending like a dove and alighting on him."

It is impossible in this world to ever fully define God, but we can try to communicate His attributes by saying He is "like" something with which we are more familiar. John the Baptist expressed His recognition of the Holy Spirit coming to Jesus after His baptism "like" a dove. The dove is a symbol of the Holy Spirit.

"**Doves** have long been a symbol for **eternal peace**. God chose the **white dove** to portray the Holy Spirit. ... The **dove** is commonly seen in Christian art with Mary as a symbol or **care, devotion, purity** and **peace**."[1]

"If the **affable** and **meek** nature of the dove personality evokes some derision from more aggressive birds, it gets **respect** because of its association with peace, and as the symbol of coming together in **harmony**, doves are released on many occasions to symbolize **cooperation** and **non-aggression**."[2]

In the secular-based descriptions above, key words and phrases stand out: eternal peace, white dove, care, devotion, purity, peace, affable, meek, respect, harmony, and non-aggression. Did you know these are all characteristics of a dove?

Another fact I have observed is that doves are disrupted or disturbed easily. Carefully cultivate and host the Spirit's Presence.

TODAY'S CHALLENGE:

Tell the Father you want to learn more about the characteristics and attributes of His Holy Spirit. Ask Him to help you cultivate an appreciation of His purity, calmness, peace and sensitivity.

Dive Deeper: Study Matthew 3.

---

[1] Dove Symbolism – Pure Spirit, www.pure-spirit.com/more-animal-symbolism/602-dove-symbolism, 1/11/19.
[2] Doves – Browse the Animals, https://animalinyou.com/animals/dove/, 1/11/19.

April 13

WIND AND FIRE

Acts 2:1-4
"When the day of Pentecost came, they were all together in one place. ² Suddenly a sound like the blowing of a violent wind came from heaven and filled the whole house where they were sitting. ³ They saw what seemed to be tongues of fire that separated and came to rest on each of them. ⁴ All of them were filled with the Holy Spirit and began to speak in other tongues as the Spirit enabled them."

Often times in the Bible, wind and fire are symbols of the Holy Spirit of God. Today's passage has both of them in evidence in the same event. As you read other passages of Scripture, pause and consider the implications of those words appearing as to how the passage might describe something about the Spirit.

As I think about wind, I am reminded of both positive and negative effects. For example, a cool breeze on a hot day versus a cold blast in winter. I think of the wind supporting the majestic wings of an eagle in flight, as opposed to the death and destruction caused by a tornado. The wind carries away the useless chaff while winnowing wheat, versus carrying life-giving pollen and spores for plants.

When I consider fire, I think of its ability to refine impurities out of metal, harden steel, and destroy useless debris. Fire provides light and warmth. It commands respect.

TODAY'S CHALLENGE:

Ask the Father to help you see similar attributes of wind and fire in His Holy Spirit. Take some time to reflect on how the Holy Spirit works with you to refresh, support, distribute, refine, harden, illuminate and warm your life.

Dive Deeper: Study Acts 2; compare with 1 Kings 19:11-13.

April 14

LIVING WATER

John 7:38-39
"Jesus said, 'Whoever believes in me, as Scripture has said, rivers of living water will flow from within them.' [39] *By this he meant the Spirit, whom those who believed in him were later to receive..."*

1 Corinthians 12:13
"For we were all baptized by one Spirit so as to form one body—whether Jews or Gentiles, slave or free—and we were all given the one Spirit to drink."

Another symbol of the Holy Spirit is water, or living water. In Scripture, it is instructive to consider the word "water" to determine if, in context, the word might be symbolizing something about the Holy Spirit of God.

In John 7, Jesus refers to rivers of living water that will flow from a true believer. As we surrender to His Holy Spirit, Jesus is able to positively impact and minister to others around us. I believe this may also refer to the individual love language, or prayer language, the Spirit brings with Holy Spirit baptism. Praying "in the Spirit" can build up, or edify, and bring life to our own spirit man (see Jude 1:20-21).

In today's passage, Paul uses water and the Spirit together to refer to new life in baptism, and that we all have access to the One and same Spirit to drink of his life-giving flow of power, purity and unity.

In John 4, Jesus told the woman at the well to ask Him for life-giving water that forever quenches spiritual thirst, and becomes a spring of eternal life. Are you thirsty?

TODAY'S CHALLENGE:

Tell the Father you desire to drink of His Living Water in the form of His Holy Spirit today. Let Him satisfy your deepest longings.

Dive Deeper: Study John chapters 4 and 7.

April 15

DO NOT BLASPHEME THE SPIRIT

Matthew 12:31
"And so I tell you, every kind of sin and slander can be forgiven, but blasphemy against the Spirit will not be forgiven."

In this verse, Jesus says that it is a very serious sin to blaspheme the Holy Spirit; so serious that it will not be forgiven. The Greek work from which "blasphemy" is translated here means malicious talk, slander, insult or curse. By inference, it may also mean to abuse, refuse or deny.

Because of the context surrounding this verse, some theologians feel blasphemy "involves attributing the ministry and miraculous power of the Holy Spirit (such as the authority to drive out demons and power to heal the sick) to Satan rather than God. It involves a deliberate rejection of the Holy Spirit's witness to Christ and the gospel."[1]

I have often heard it said that if you are concerned about so seriously blaspheming the Spirit that you aren't forgiven, then it is a good sign that, in fact, you haven't blasphemed Him. Someone in that condition would never care about whether they had or not.

If you are concerned, then to be sure of your secure position in Christ, repent to the Father of any way you might have done this in the past, and get it covered under the Blood. There is no sin that the Blood of Jesus cannot cleanse. Those who remain unforgiven have never repented.

TODAY'S CHALLENGE:

Talk to the Father about your desire to always honor and revere Him and His Holy Spirit. Repent to Him if you feel any conviction from the past regarding blasphemous words or actions you might have had. Thank Him for the security of your salvation in Christ Jesus.

Dive Deeper: Study Matthew 12; consider today's verse in light of Isaiah 63:10; Mark 3:28-30; Acts 5:3-5; Ephesians 4:30; 1 Thessalonians 5:19; 1 Timothy 1:13.

[1] Explanatory note for Matthew 12:31, <u>Life in The Spirit Study Bible,</u> by Zondervan Publishing, copyright 1992, 2003 by Life Publishers International.

April 16

DO NOT RESIST THE SPIRIT

Acts 7:51
"You stiff-necked people! Your hearts and ears are still uncircumcised. You are just like your ancestors: You always resist the Holy Spirit!"

In order to be led by the Holy Spirit (instead of the world, the flesh or the devil), we must be attentive, willing and obedient. Pride and stubbornness prevent us from following the Spirit's lead.

As Christians, the fleshly attitudes of our heart are cut away by the Holy Spirit in His progressive work of making us more like Christ Jesus. This process is "sanctification", and its purpose is to set us apart to serve God with all our hearts, and to make us more holy.

As long as we pride-fully think we can manage our own lives our own way, we will resist the still, small voice of the Spirit in His attempt to lead us on the narrow path. Success in the Christian walk comes as we turn our attentions away from the distractions of the world, listen carefully for the Spirit's voice, and choose to be obedient to His instructions.

Learning to do this becomes easier when we stop and consider where our own efforts to run our own lives left us – in prisons of our own making while "in the free world", and eventually behind steel bars, concrete walls and razor wire.

TODAY'S CHALLENGE:

Ask your Heavenly Father to help you learn to listen and obey His Holy Spirit. Tell Him you want to be more like Jesus today. Decide to work on listening constantly for the Spirit as you go about your routine today.

Do not resist the Holy Spirit.

Dive Deeper: Study Acts 7.

April 17

DO NOT INSULT THE HOLY SPIRIT

Hebrews 10:29
"How much more severely do you think someone deserves to be punished who has trampled the Son of God underfoot, who has treated as an unholy thing the blood of the covenant that sanctified them, and who has insulted the Spirit of grace?"

Webster's Dictionary defines "to insult" as treating with contempt, rudeness or disrespect. The Greek word translated in this passage as "insulted" also means to mistreat or damage. The context of the passage surrounding this verse refers to someone who continues to knowingly sin willfully after having received the Holy Spirit in salvation.

This kind of behavior does not treat God with respect and ignores the tremendously high price Jesus paid with His Blood to purchase our freedom from sin. It is the kind of attitude that enables the personal deception that grace will continue to cover intentional sin after salvation despite of what one does or how often one does it.

This disrespectful, rude and insulting approach to life displays no reverent fear for God, in front of Whom we will one day all stand in judgment. Carefully consider Hebrews 10:30-31.

Grace does not give us license to sin, it gives us the power not to sin! This power of God is His Holy Spirit. In this passage, He is referred to as the "Spirit of grace".

TODAY'S CHALLENGE:

Tell the Father you repent from all the ways you have ever insulted His Holy Spirit. Thank the Father for the sacrifice of Jesus. Ask Him to identify, and help you to turn away from, intentional sin in your life.

Do not insult the Holy Spirit.

Dive Deeper: Study Hebrews 10.

April 18

DO NOT GRIEVE THE HOLY SPIRIT

Ephesians 4:30
"And do not grieve the Holy Spirit of God, with whom you were sealed for the day of redemption."

Webster's Dictionary defines "to grieve" as causing emotional distress, sorrow or undue burden. The Greek word translated in this passage as "grieve" also means to cause sadness. The context of the passage surrounding this verse contains specific and practical instructions for Christian living.

In Ephesians 4:29-32, Paul is instructing us about behavior that is not to be part of our daily walk, and most of it involves our words, and actions which follow from unwholesome talk of any kind. For example, our words can portray anger, and lead us into fights, both physical and verbal. We may be harboring bitterness and resentment for something someone else did or said. We might be "talking trash" or desiring revenge towards them.

All this behavior and speech grieves the Holy Spirit of God. These things are directly opposed to the attributes and fruit of the Holy Spirit that He desires to bring forth in our lives. Paul tells us to be kind and compassionate to one another, and quick to forgive every offense against us in the same way Christ has forgiven us.

The words we speak should be carefully selected to build others up, not tear them down. Our thoughts, words and actions should be positive in every way, not negative in any respect.

TODAY'S CHALLENGE:

Ask the Father to help you be more sensitive today to the speech and actions that will please Him, and thereby positively represent Christ to all those around you.

Do not grieve the Holy Spirit.

Dive Deeper: Study Ephesians 4; Isaiah 63:10; 1 Thessalonians 5:19.

April 19

DO NOT QUENCH THE HOLY SPIRIT

1 Thessalonians 5:16-19
"Rejoice always, [17] pray continually, [18] give thanks in all circumstances; for this is God's will for you in Christ Jesus. [19] Do not quench the Spirit."

Webster's Dictionary defines "to quench" as to put out, extinguish or subdue. The Greek word translated in this passage as "quench" also means to snuff out. The context of the passage surrounding this verse contains Paul's instructions to the Christians in Thessalonica regarding their interaction with one another, the world and God.

One of the fruits of the Spirit, and a character attribute of Jesus, is joy. Expressing joy can become a more natural constant expression of a Christian the more one focuses on things that matter for eternity. Thinking about the consistent faithfulness of God towards us even when we fail in our faith towards Him causes us to be joyful in the midst of trials.

At first glance, "praying continually" seems impossible, or at the least, very impractical. However, prayer is conversation with God, and since His Holy Spirit is always in us and with us, an ongoing discussion with Him during our normal day can become a natural process. After all, He is our Friend, Helper and Counselor – someone we can converse with often.

An attitude of gratitude, or sincere ongoing thankfulness towards God, naturally results the more we focus on every good thing He has done and is doing in our lives.

If we are not joyful, prayerful and thankful, we quench the Holy Spirit of God.

TODAY'S CHALLENGE:

In an attitude of constant conversation with the Spirit today express joy and sincere thanks.

This is God's will for you today.

Dive Deeper: Study 1 Thessalonians 5.

April 20

HOPE AND A FUTURE

Jeremiah 29:11
*"For I know the plans I have for you," declares the L*ORD*, "plans to prosper you and not to harm you, plans to give you hope and a future."*

I declare April 20, 2009, as my "re-birth day" in prison, when I totally surrendered my life to serve my Lord and Savior, Jesus Christ. It happens also to be my actual date of birth 57 years earlier!

About a month earlier, after I had written my family to ask forgiveness for the many ways I had hurt and offended them, I received letters from both my brothers expressing their forgiveness towards me and extending their love and assistance.

Tears welled up in my eyes as I read their kind words of mercy and compassion. It had been a very long time since I was capable of relieving my heart though tears. Being alone, lying on my bunk, God began to encourage my heart through a verse my brother wrote in his letter.

I believe this was the first time I had ever read or heard about the verse written above, Jeremiah 29:11. I needed hope. I needed encouragement. I thought my life, for all practical purposes, was over because of a past full of poor choices and sin. I did not know God still had a plan for me - a plan to prosper me, and not to harm me.

That very day I chose to believe God forgave my past, and that I could trust Him to provide hope and a good future for me. What a tremendous birthday present!

TODAY'S CHALLENGE:

Believe God. He forgives your past, and has a good plan for your future. Receive hope.

Dive Deeper: Study Jeremiah 29:1-23; Romans 15:4, 13; Job 42:10, Isaiah 61:7; Zechariah 9:12; Hebrews 6:18-20, 7:18-19; 10:23; Psalm 16:8-9, 11; 31:24; 25: 3-5; 33:18-22; 42:5; 62:5-8; Proverbs 10:28; 11:7; 23:18; 24:14, 20; Titus 1:2, 2:13

April 21

GOD'S GIFT

Matthew 1:18, 20
"This is how the birth of Jesus the Messiah came about: His mother Mary was pledged to be married to Joseph, but before they came together, she was found to be pregnant through the Holy Spirit... ²⁰ But after he had considered this, an angel of the Lord appeared to him in a dream and said, "Joseph son of David, do not be afraid to take Mary home as your wife, because what is conceived in her is from the Holy Spirit."

On behalf of humanity, an innocent girl received the most magnificent gift – Jesus was conceived in Mary by God, the Holy Spirit.

This Divine Intervention into history must be the single most significant event for all of eternity. God injects Himself into fallen, restrictive, three-dimensional space to take upon Himself the penalty for all sin, for all time, so that we may have an opportunity to choose whether we will have an intimate personal relationship with our Heavenly Father God.

His Holy Spirit exercised ultimate Creative Power to bring this about. In similar fashion as with Creation in the beginning where the Spirit hovered over the deep waiting to carry out the Word, the Spirit's Presence came upon Mary to create the Living Word, Jesus. Later in the new testament, we learn the Holy Spirit was also intimately involved in the creation of His Body – the Church.

Like Mary, let us receive this Ultimate Gift from God, His Son, Jesus!

TODAY'S CHALLENGE:

Tell the Father you desire to obediently receive His Most Precious Gift. Ask Him to help you more fully appreciate all the ways He exercises His Creative Power to save you and all of humanity.

Dive Deeper: Study Matthew 1:18-25; Luke 1:26-38; Genesis 1:1-2; John 20:21-22; Acts 2:1-4.

April 22

THE SPIRIT UPON JESUS

Matthew 3:16
"As soon as Jesus was baptized, he went up out of the water. At that moment heaven was opened, and he saw the Spirit of God descending like a dove and alighting on him."

Yesterday we learned how the Holy Spirit came upon Mary for the benefit of all humanity. Today, we see the Spirit coming upon Jesus for Him; and, through Him, for us!

When Jesus was ready to officially begin His earthly ministry, He presented Himself in a public demonstration of submission to God the Father. Our Father expressed His complete pleasure with His Son and sent His Spirit to be upon Jesus. To John the Baptist, the Spirit appeared like a dove and remained upon Jesus.

The Father empowered the Son with everything He would need to complete His rescue mission. In the Old Testament, we see the anointing power of the Spirit coming upon someone for a particular task but withdrawing later. When He came upon Jesus the Spirit remained.

At Pentecost, under an open Heaven, the Holy Spirit came upon us as Believers so that we may be empowered to accomplish our mission. Jesus sent us out to disciple and baptize others, but He did not send us alone; He and the Father gave us His Holy Spirit. The Father is pleased with us when we allow Him to remain!

TODAY'S CHALLENGE:

Talk to the Father today about how you may more faithfully host His Presence in your life. Ask Him to show you how to allow the Spirit more freedom to lead you, and tell the Father you will obediently follow.

Dive Deeper: Study Matthew 3; Luke 3:21-22.

April 23

THE SPIRIT LED JESUS

Luke 4:1-2
"Jesus, full of the Holy Spirit, left the Jordan and was led by the Spirit into the wilderness, ²where for forty days he was tempted by the devil…"

Jesus was full of the Holy Spirit, and led by the Spirit. If Jesus needed the Holy Spirit so do we!

The beginnings of the first stage of the ministry of Jesus was not in the Temple, or among the throngs of people who would later surround Him; rather, He was in the wilderness with only the Holy Spirit of His Father. There in the desert the man Jesus learned to follow the Divine Spirit.

He was sustained during forty days of testing, and empowered to say "no" to the temptations of Satan. When the enemy presented an enticing argument, Jesus was led by the Spirit to use the Word to specifically counter Satan for success. He did not need anything but the Word and the Spirit to overcome every temptation.

Similarly, in our own wilderness experience, we must be led by the Spirit, and emboldened by the Word of God. We must be able to counter specific temptations with specific scriptures for victory. We must be willing to be led by the Spirit so that we learn and grow through every test and trial.

We must daily be filled with the Spirit. See Ephesians 5:15-20.

TODAY'S CHALLENGE:

Ask the Father to reveal more of Himself to you through His Holy Spirit today. Tell Him you want to be continuously filled, and led, by His Spirit. When you encounter temptations and trials today utilize the Word and the Spirit to overcome. He will sustain you!

Dive Deeper: Study Luke 4; Matthew 4:1-17; Ephesians 5:15-20.

April 24

THE SPIRIT ANOINTED JESUS

Luke 4:14, 18
"Jesus returned to Galilee in the power of the Spirit, and news about him spread through the whole countryside... (Jesus said,) [18]"The Spirit of the Lord is on me, because he has anointed me to proclaim good news to the poor. He has sent me to proclaim freedom for the prisoners and recovery of sight for the blind, to set the oppressed free..."

The anointing of Jesus by the Holy Spirit must have been so evident to everyone with whom He came into contact, that they immediately understood He was no ordinary rabbi or prophet. People were drawn to Him and to His uniqueness.

In his first public address in a synagogue, He proclaimed He was the anointed One Isaiah had written about 700 years earlier. He found the place in the scroll of Isaiah, read the prophecy, and proclaimed that it had been fulfilled in Him.

The same anointing available to Jesus is also available to us. Our challenge is to learn to submit, allow His Holy Spirit to lead us, and be willing to be quickly obedient. There are multitudes who need to hear the Good News so they can be set free from every form of bondage. As they see the anointing on us while we daily become more like Jesus, the Spirit will draw them to the Father.

TODAY'S CHALLENGE:

Thank the Father that by His grace the same Spirit that anointed Jesus lives in you. Ask Him to help you become more submissive and obedient so that His Spirit will impact others through you today.

You are anointed and appointed! Live like it.

Dive Deeper: Study Luke 4:14-44; Isaiah 61:1-4; Acts 2:22; Acts 10:37-38.

April 25

THE SPIRIT TESTIFIES OF JESUS

John 15:26
Jesus said, "When the Advocate comes, whom I will send to you from the Father—the Spirit of truth who goes out from the Father—he will testify about me."

The Holy Spirit will always testify of Jesus. The Spirit points us to Christ, leads us in the ways of Christ, and desires to conform us ever increasingly into the very image of Christ Jesus. If you sense a "leading" that does not match up to Christ Jesus and His Ways, you are not following the Holy Spirit's voice.

Jesus sent us a Helper, Advocate, Friend and Guide. The Holy Spirit is the Supreme Gift available to us from the Person of Ultimate Sacrifice Who proclaimed Himself to be the Truth.

The Source of all Truth is the Spirit of the Father from Whom we were given the most Preeminent Gift, Jesus. The Father's heart is Jesus. The Father's Spirit is Truth. How could He testify to us of Anyone but Jesus?

Our supreme desire ought to be the daily pursuit of deeper, intimate relationship with God the Father, God the Son, and God the Holy Spirit. Today's scripture reveals more about each Person in the Godhead.

Knowing the individual Persons of God helps us have a deeper, more meaningful relationship with God. Study the Persons. Learn to relate to each Person's uniqueness.

TODAY'S CHALLENGE:

Thank the Father for the Spirit of Truth, the Holy Spirit, Who will always teach you about Jesus. Ask the Father to show you how to develop a more intimate relationship with each of the Three Persons of God.

This is about relationship, not religion.

Dive Deeper: Study John 15; John 14:6; John 8:32; John 1:14, 17.

April 26

THE SPIRIT RAISED JESUS

Romans 8:11
"And if the Spirit of him who raised Jesus from the dead is living in you, he who raised Christ from the dead will also give life to your mortal bodies because of his Spirit who lives in you."

Romans 1:4
"...and who through the Spirit of holiness was appointed the Son of God in power by his resurrection from the dead: Jesus Christ our Lord."

If you will really stop to consider the significance and reality of these two scriptures, it will almost blow your mind, and overwhelm your heart. Read them again. Ask your Teacher, the Holy Spirit to explain their meaning.

The abundant life Jesus came to give us (see John 10:10) is instantly available to us now as we continue our earthly journey. How? By the very Spirit Who was instrumental in bringing Life back to our Savior and Lord.

It was the Resurrection of Jesus that dealt the death-blow to our enemy. The Word tells us that the Power of God to accomplish this was administered through the Spirit of Holiness, His Holy Spirit, Who by this act solidified Jesus as the Son of God, and crowned Him King of kings.

Saint of God, this is the very same Spirit Who dwells in you! Meditate on 1 Corinthians 3:16.

TODAY'S CHALLENGE:

Thank the Father for His Spirit of Holiness Who raised Jesus from the dead. In light of this truth, make it a goal to learn how to totally surrender to the Spirit's leadership of your life moment by moment. Thank the Father that everything you need for the abundant life already dwells in you.

Dive Deeper: Study Romans 8; 2 Corinthians 4:13-14; 1 Peter 3:18; John 10:10; 1 Corinthians 3:16.

April 27

YOU ARE NOT YOUR OWN

1 Corinthians 6:19-20
"Do you not know that your bodies are temples of the Holy Spirit, who is in you, whom you have received from God? You are not your own; ²⁰ you were bought at a price. Therefore, honor God with your bodies."

God does not dwell any longer in temples made by man; rather, He lives in the re-born believer's body, a temple God made. The price He paid for this was the Blood of His Son, Jesus.

When we are born from above God sends His Holy Spirit to live in us. He wants to dwell in a clean body. The Spirit's job of progressive sanctification makes us ever more holy, and sets us apart for more of God's service.

Our job is to participate with the Holy Spirit in this clean-up job by seeking intimate relationship with Him daily so that we will more willingly, and completely, surrender every part of our lives to Him. Submitting to His still small voice to lead us along the narrow path is crucial.

We must realize that we do not belong to ourselves any longer; we belong to God. It is His choice and responsibility to make us into the image of Jesus. We must be good stewards of our temple.

TODAY'S CHALLENGE:

Tell the Father how much you treasure His Presence. Ask Him to make you more aware that His Holy Spirit accompanies you everywhere you go. Ask Him to help you remember that He is right there with you in whatever you are doing.

Think about where you go and what you do. God is with you.

Dive Deeper: Study 1 Corinthians 6; 1 Corinthians 3:16; Ephesians 2:22; John 20:21-22.

April 28

SPIRITUAL MANIFESTATION GIFTS

1 Corinthians 12:7-11
"Now to each one the manifestation of the Spirit is given for the common good. [8] To one there is given through the Spirit a message of wisdom, to another a message of knowledge by means of the same Spirit, [9] to another faith…, to another gifts of healing …, [10] … miraculous powers, … prophecy, … distinguishing between spirits, … speaking in different kinds of tongues, and … the interpretation of tongues. [11] All these are the work of one and the same Spirit, and he distributes them to each one, just as he determines."

The Holy Spirit manifests His Power in believers for the benefit of others through various visible and/or audible gifts. He chooses the timing, and person, through whom to manifest these depending on the particular circumstances, and the willingness of a humble believer to allow Him to display His gift through them.

If we, of our own will, attempt to exercise these, we are not operating in His anointing. However, we must be sensitive to respond to His prompting when He is making the choice of what to do and when to do it. Then He will work in and through us to accomplish what He determines.

This submission and obedience on our part requires child-like faith. Only as a child will we enter the Kingdom work God is doing on the earth.

TODAY'S CHALLENGE:

Thank the Father for the many gifts He manifests by His Holy Spirit in and through us for the benefit of others. Ask Him to show you how to better participate in His Kingdom work.

Be willing. Be available. Be obedient.

Dive Deeper: Study 1 Corinthians 12.

April 29

GOD RESTORES

Zechariah 9:12
"Return to your fortress, you prisoners of hope; even now I announce that I will restore twice as much to you."

I abandoned my son, Andy, when he was only two years old. Pride, selfishness and self-deception took me on a path to total destruction.

Until he was twelve, I stayed in touch and spent time with him somewhat regularly during the years, but I was in large part absent from his life. From age twelve to age twenty-four, I saw him only once. I was too involved in a life of sin and self to care, and too "stuck on stupid" to change.

After I was saved in prison, I began writing him every month but never heard from him. I continued to write anyway. I prayed for restoration of our relationship regularly.

One year after my release from prison, God arranged for me to be able to go for a ministry-related meeting to the city where Andy lived. I had reached out to Andy by text since he never answered my calls. He responded to a text! We had a marvelous reunion, and he told me he had saved every one of my letters.

Today, God is still continuing to restore our relationship, and I am patient to wait in faith. In the eight years since my release, I have been with him about five times. He doesn't yet contact me, but he sometimes responds as I continue to reach out to him. Today is his birthday.

Don't give up on family relationships. God can and will restore in His time. Be patient and faithful.

TODAY'S CHALLENGE:

Thank the Father that He will deliver on His promise to restore your family. Keep your eyes on Him. Let Him work on their hearts as he transforms you.

Dive Deeper: Study Zechariah 9; Malachi 4:6.

April 30

SPIRITUAL FRUIT

Galatians 5:22-23
"But the fruit of the Spirit is love, joy, peace, forbearance, kindness, goodness, faithfulness, [23] gentleness and self-control. Against such things there is no law."

I have heard it taught that there is one Spiritual fruit, love, and that the other eight attributes flow from that one gift. Others teach that the word "fruit" here is actually plural in the Greek, and that all nine attributes are individual fruits the Spirit brings forth.

Either way, these attributes ought to be realized in us as character qualities of Christ. The Spirit desires to produce them in ever-increasing measure in the lives of fully surrendered believers. God's will is that we be made into the image of His Son. See Romans 8:29.

As branches, we are to abide, or remain, in the Vine, Jesus. The life force, sap, flowing through the branches from the vine has been likened to the Holy Spirit. The believer does not strive to produce fruit by his own efforts. Rather, the Holy Spirit produces fruit naturally as we stay connected to Jesus.

The Word tells us as Jesus is, so are we in this world (1 John 4:17). When He is revealed, we shall be like Him (1 John 3:2). There is no natural law that would prevent the Holy Spirit from bringing forth in us all the character qualities of Christ.

TODAY'S CHALLENGE:

Thank the Father for the fruit He produces by His Holy Spirit in and through you to make you more like Jesus. Ask Him to help you intentionally abide in the Vine so that the Spirit flows.

Don't get in His way. Allow Him to work.

Dive Deeper: Study Galatians 5; Colossians 3:12-17; John 15:1-17; Romans 8:29; 1 John 4:17; 1 John 3:2.

May 1

THE LOVE OF THE SPIRIT

Romans 15:30
"Now I beg you, brethren, through the Lord Jesus Christ, and through the love of the Spirit, that you strive together with me in prayers to God for me..."

We have previously seen that the Holy Spirit is the Spirit of Truth (see April 6), and we know He is also the Spirit of the Father (see April 5). Since God is Love, the love of His Spirit will be a major factor in our lives as Christians.

The Body of Christ must come together in love. Love abides forever, and it never fails. The Holy Spirit, in love, gently convicts believers of sin, rather than condemning them in shame. The foremost fruit of the Spirit is love (see April 30), and the evidence that we follow Jesus will be our walk of love (see John 13:34-35).

Paul urges Christians to unite in prayer for specific purposes. The power of agreement in prayer cannot be overstated. Notice that Paul requests them to "strive" in prayer. Prevailing prayer requires diligence, faith and patience. It is a key component in our spiritual armor.

Through the Lord Jesus Christ, Who is full of Grace and Truth, Paul knows that believers who strive together in prayer, and walk in love, will see victory.

Do you see areas in your life where there is a need for unity, prayer and love?

TODAY'S CHALLENGE:

Tell the Father you are grateful for the love of the Holy Spirit in your life. Ask Him to identify areas where you need more unity with the body of Christ, and to give you wisdom as to how to prevail in prayer and walk in love today.

Dive Deeper: Study Romans 15; John 13:34-35, 1 Corinthians 13.

May 2

THE PERFECT TEACHER

John 14:26
"But the Advocate, the Holy Spirit, whom the Father will send in my name, will teach you all things and will remind you of everything I have said to you."

Psalm 32:8
"I will instruct you and teach you in the way you should go; I will counsel you with my loving eye on you."

Even our favorite teachers made mistakes. The Holy Spirit never does. Those same teachers specialized in one or two subjects. The Holy Spirit perfectly knows everything!

Jesus wanted His disciples to know with certainty they would not be left alone to carry out the Great Commission. He assured them that He and the Father knew they needed a Helper, Teacher and Counselor to teach them daily how to apply the truths Jesus had given them, and to remind them of everything He had taught them. He wanted them to have continuous counsel for clear direction, and the Power of God for Kingdom success.

It was so important for them, they were instructed not to go anywhere or do anything until they had received power from on high and the gift the Father had promised – The Holy Spirit.

Likewise, we need direction, instruction and counsel to achieve the plans the Father and Son have for us. As we continue to read and absorb the Word, we need our Helper to remind us of key verses at critical times when the enemy tempts us. Aren't you glad you have the Perfect Teacher?

TODAY'S CHALLENGE:

Tell the Father how much you need His direction today. Thank Him for sending you His Holy Spirit, and tell Him you want to listen and obey your Teacher.

Dive Deeper: Study John 14; Psalm 32.

May 3

THE ONE TRUE GUIDE

John 16:13
"But when he, the Spirit of truth, comes, he will guide you into all the truth. He will not speak on his own; he will speak only what he hears, and he will tell you what is yet to come."

Although the Godhead is comprised of three distinct Persons of the Father, Son and Holy Spirit, they are always in perfect agreement instantly. They never have to have a strategy meeting, or a vote on what to do.

Consequently, Jesus told His disciples that anytime the Spirit spoke to them or otherwise guided them, they could be sure He was speaking for the Father and the Son. Furthermore, they could know with certainty that He would always proclaim or reveal absolute truth because He is the Spirit of Truth.

Since the Spirit is also the Spirit of Prophecy in that He always has the testimony of Jesus (see Revelation 19:10), we can be certain He knows future events, and can guide us with that in mind. We can trust Him to tell us things to come through a word of prophecy or wisdom.

We should always seek the guidance of the Holy Spirit even for the simplest of daily decisions. This is a picture of true surrender, submission and humility. The best thing for us to know is that "of our own selves, we can do nothing", but "with Him all things are possible".

TODAY'S CHALLENGE:

Thank the Father that He has given you the Spirit of Truth to overcome all the lies of the enemy. Tell Him you trust Him to guide you one day at a time into your future.

Dive Deeper: Study John 16; Isaiah 30:19-21; John 14:26; Revelation 19:10.

May 4

CONVICTION

John 16:8, AMP
"And He, when He comes, will convict the world about [the guilt of] sin [and the need for a Savior], and about righteousness, and about judgment..."

Those of us who have been prisoners, all had a specific time when we learned we had been convicted of the charges levelled against us. Another person, or group of persons, condemned us and declared punishment. When this happened, we were first labeled as "convicts".

For a Christian, the word "convict" in today's verse does not imply condemnation and punishment. For those of us who are in Christ Jesus, and are led by the Spirit, there is no condemnation. See Romans 8:1-2.

Rather, the Holy Spirit gently exposes, refutes and convinces us of areas of our life where we are falling short of the righteousness of Christ so that we will not return to the guilt of ongoing sin. Our Savior has delivered us from the power of sin, and we are free to make right choices by the leadership of the Holy Spirit.

The Spirit makes us aware of God's standard of righteousness in Christ Jesus, shows us what sin is, and gives us the power to overcome the world.[1] When we miss the mark, He calls us to repentance. We must always have a heart that desires to be obedient and we must be quick to repent when we are not. See 1 John 1:9.

TODAY'S CHALLENGE:

Ask the Father to empower you today to walk in the righteousness of Christ. Listen for the Holy Spirit's direction along the right path, and His gentle conviction if you start to wander.

Dive Deeper: Study John 16; Romans 8:1-2; 1 John 1:9.

---

[1] Life in the Spirit Study Bible published by Zondervan.

May 5

A TRUE FRIEND

Proverbs 18:24, AMP
"The man of too many friends [chosen indiscriminately] will be broken in pieces and come to ruin, But there is a [true, loving] friend who [is reliable and] sticks closer than a brother."

True friends are hard to find. For example, how many of our "friends" visit us while we are incarcerated, or put money on our account so we can make phone calls or buy hygiene items? Very few, if any, right?

Yet, if we are really blessed, we finally find someone who sticks with us through hardship, encourages us when we are down, gives us direction when we are uncertain, provides wise advice when we seek it, and does not abandon us when we are difficult to get along with. They model for us how to be a true friend too. Such a friend is rare and invaluable.

Having once been so selfish and manipulative of people, it is amazing to me now how God has given me several truly unselfish and unconditionally loving friends. I never dreamed people could be so genuine and caring as those whom God has brought into my life. Once we put Him first in everything, He transforms us so we can be a true friend to others and He places the right people in our lives.

The Holy Spirit is our very best friend. He never abandons us, and loves us unconditionally even when we are sometimes acting un-loveable. He encourages us and gives us hope.

TODAY'S CHALLENGE:

Thank the Father for His unconditional love and friendship through His Holy Spirit.

Cherish your true friends, and the One Who is True.

Dive Deeper: John 15:9-17; 1 Corinthians 13; 1 John 4:7-12.

May 6

THE SPIRIT INTERCEDES FOR US

Romans 8:26, AMP
"In the same way the Spirit [comes to us and] helps us in our weakness. We do not know what prayer to offer or how to offer it as we should, but the Spirit Himself [knows our need and at the right time] intercedes on our behalf with sighs and groanings too deep for words."

As a believer, we are never left on our own because we always have the Holy Spirit. This is also true when it comes to prayer.

In Heaven, we have Jesus interceding for us (see Hebrews 7:25; 1 John 2:1), and on earth, we have the Holy Spirit to help us when we do not know how to pray. Sometimes it is hard to express ourselves completely from the deepest part of our being. We run out of words before we feel a release deep inside of the yearning and striving associated with the request.

The Holy Spirit is able to express our deepest feelings for us in intercession when we "pray in the Spirit" with groans, syllables and phrases in which our mind does not engage. Paul refers to praying with his spirit and singing with his spirit in 1 Corinthians 14:15.

Jude 1:20 says to "build yourselves up in your most holy faith and pray in the Holy Spirit." The Holy Spirit's intercession on our behalf makes us stronger!

TODAY'S CHALLENGE:

Ask the Father to help you express your prayer requests more completely by His Holy Spirit's intercession. Tell Him you want to learn to pray powerfully and effectively in any way He provides. Surrender to the expression by the Holy Spirit of your deepest needs and concerns.

Dive Deeper: Study Romans 8:26-28; Hebrews 7:23-25; 1 John 2:1-2; 1 Corinthians 14:14-15; Jude 1:20.

May 7

THE SPIRIT PRAYS GOD'S WILL

Romans 8:27, AMP
"And He who searches the hearts knows what the mind of the Spirit is, because the Spirit intercedes [before God] on behalf of God's people in accordance with God's will."

Notice that today's verse starts with the word "And", so it is associated with the previous verse and is a continuing thought. Consequently, I suggest you re-read Romans 8:26 and yesterday's devotional.

Our Father searches our hearts. He knows us completely, and so does His Holy Spirit Who lives inside every believer. Because He is the Spirit of the Father, and the Spirit of the Son, our intercessor, the Holy Spirit, knows the perfect will of God for us and prays on our behalf accordingly.

Our spiritual desires and yearnings find their source in the Holy Spirit Who dwells within us. The Holy Spirit joins with us to help and empower us to be victors instead of victims in our circumstances. But He also acts in addition to or apart from us to intercede and intervene for us by appealing to the Father on our behalf of our needs in accordance with God's will. When we are helpless, the Holy Spirit is truly our Helper.[1]

What a tremendous benefit it is to us for us to pray in the spirit and allow the Holy Spirit to pray God's perfect will and plan for our lives. The Spirit knows the Plan!

TODAY'S CHALLENGE:

Thank our Heavenly Father for His Holy Spirit in you. Tell Him you trust His perfect will and plan for your life. Ask the Holy Spirit to help you pray for complete manifestation daily of His will and plan.

Dive Deeper: Study Romans 8:26-28; 1 Corinthians 14:14-15; Jude 1:20.

---

[1] Life in the Spirit Study Bible published by Zondervan.

May 8

WORKING TOGETHER FOR GOOD

Romans 8:28, AMP

"And we know [with great confidence] that God [who is deeply concerned about us] causes all things to work together [as a plan] for good for those who love God, to those who are called according to His plan and purpose."

Similar to yesterday, notice that today's verse starts with the word "And", so this verse continues the thought begun in Romans 8:26. Therefore, it would be helpful to review the previous two day's devotionals for purposes of continuity.

When we allow the Holy Spirit to intercede with sighs, groans and syllables uttered by and through us, we know He is praying the perfect will of God over our lives. Because He is God, and knows the mind of the Father, the Spirit knows exactly what to pray at just the right time in every circumstance and how to perfectly express it.

Therefore, as a true believer in love with, and dependent on, our Father, we can be certain that He will take even the worst of circumstances and use it for our good when we allow the Holy Spirit to intercede on our behalf.

In faith, we must always choose to trust God with the outcome of every situation when we have thoroughly prayed through with our mind, and with our spirit.

TODAY'S CHALLENGE:

Tell the Father you trust Him to implement His perfect plan for your life. Surrender completely to the intercession on your behalf by His Spirit. Recommit your total love for and to the Father, and depend on Him to work everything out for good in your life today.

Dive Deeper: Study Romans 8:26-28; 1 Corinthians 14:14-15; Jude 1:20.

May 9

HOLY SPIRIT DIRECTION

Acts 13:2
"While they were worshiping the Lord and fasting, the Holy Spirit said, 'Set apart for me Barnabas and Saul for the work to which I have called them.'"

In order for us to be led daily by the Spirit instead of the flesh, we must be obedient to follow His direction. When He speaks, we listen and do what He says.

The disciples were seeking the Lord and His Presence by worshiping and fasting. In response to their pressing in for more of Him, the Holy Spirit gave them direction. Saul, who was later called Paul, and Barnabas, responded to this direction. For this, we should all be very thankful because Paul ended up writing more than half of the New Testament we study today; and, they helped take the Gospel to the nations.

Many people say they have never heard the Spirit speak to them. Personally, I have never heard an audible voice, but on a daily basis, I feel His impressions in my mind and heart, and I try to respond with instant obedience.

An intimate personal relationship with the Father is only possible because of Jesus; and, it is developed through the Spirit's ongoing communication with us, and our obedient response to Him.

The more time we spend alone with God in prayer, Bible study, worship and/or fasting, the better we will hear the direction of the Spirit for our lives.

TODAY'S CHALLENGE:

Ask the Father to help you learn to listen and obey His direction for your life through His Holy Spirit. Be still, and listen to the small voice within the deepest part of your being.

Follow His direction.

Dive Deeper: Study Acts 13; Isaiah 30:19-21; John 15:26-27; John 16:12-15.

May 10

THE LIVING WORD

John 1: 1, 14
"In the beginning was the Word, and the Word was with God, and the Word was God... ¹⁴ The Word became flesh and made his dwelling among us. We have seen his glory, the glory of the one and only Son, who came from the Father, full of grace and truth."

Jesus, the Name above all names, became the Living Word of the Father when He took on flesh and came to dwell among us. The Holy Spirit initiated the physical process of this miraculous incarnation of Jesus with His visitation to Mary.

Jesus manifested the Glory of the Father; and, the Father's grace and truth for humanity was on display through the life of Jesus. The power of the Holy Spirit achieved God's mighty works through Jesus who intentionally and willingly humbled Himself to be a man led by the Spirit of God.

Jesus personified everything the Father intended for us, and He was the manifestation of the living and active Word of God. His Truth pierced the hearts of those to whom He ministered, and He was able to discern the thoughts and intents of the hearts of all who encountered Him. He was anointed by, and led by, the Holy Spirit in every way, every day.

What a magnificent example we have in Christ Jesus! We too will see the Living Word bring forth fruit in our lives when we are led by the Spirit daily.

TODAY'S CHALLENGE:

Ask the Father to give you more revelation about His Son through His Word today. Listen for the Holy Spirit to expound upon Truth.

Cherish the Living Word.

Dive Deeper: Study John 1:1-14; Isaiah 55:10-11; Revelation 19:13; Hebrews 1:1-3; Colossians 1:15-18; Colossians 2:9; Psalm 33:6; Psalm 107:20; Psalm 147:18; Acts 10:37-38.

May 11

THE ACTIVE AGENT IN CREATION

Genesis 1:2
"Now the earth was formless and empty, darkness was over the surface of the deep, and the Spirit of God was hovering over the waters."

Yesterday we were reminded that Jesus, the Word, was in the beginning with God at the moment of Creation. Today, we see that the Holy Spirit was present as well, and waiting for the Father to speak the Word.

Our verse states that the Spirit of God was hovering over the waters. With air and water is the potential for life, and all the potential in the Universe was brought forth from the mouth of the Father when He spoke the Living Word for the Holy Spirit to implement. The breath of God, the Holy Spirit, carried forth the Word to create. The Holy Spirit is the active creative power of the Father.

The Spirit was not only active at Creation. He was also active in the Incarnation of Jesus, the last Adam (see Matthew 1:18-23). The Spirit was actively involved in the indwelling of the first believers (see John 20:21) and every believer since then. The creation of "the Church" with power was initiated by the Holy Spirit at Pentecost (see Acts 1:4-8 and 2:1-4).

In the Resurrection, the Holy Spirit was the active force the Father used in creating "the Second Man" by raising Jesus from the dead (see Romans 8:11, 29; Hebrews 9:14; and Colossians 1:18). Finally, the Holy Spirit was involved in creating the "new you" (see John 3:5 and 2 Corinthians 5:17)!

TODAY'S CHALLENGE:

Thank the Father for His Word, Jesus, and the active power of Creation, His Holy Spirit.

Allow His active, creative power to lead you today.

Dive Deeper: Study Matthew 1:18-23; John 20:21-22; Acts 1:4-8; Acts 2:1-4; Romans 8:11, 29; Hebrews 9:14; Colossians 1:18; John 3:5-8; 2 Corinthians 5:17.

May 12

THE SPIRIT AND THE WORD

2 Peter 1:20-21
"Above all, you must understand that no prophecy of Scripture came about by the prophet's own interpretation of things. [21] For prophecy never had its origin in the human will, but prophets, though human, spoke from God as they we carried along by the Holy Spirit."

2 Timothy 3:16
"All Scripture is God-breathed..."

Yesterday we learned that the breath of God, the Holy Spirit, carried forth the Word from the Father. The Hebrew word translated as Spirit in Genesis 1:2 means breath, or wind. Similarly, the Greek words translated as Spirit, and God-breathed, in today's scriptures carry essentially the same meaning. That is, scripture comes from Divine inspiration, not the inspiration of men.

We know man can make mistakes; man is fallible. God is infallible, and His words are without error. So, we can trust Scripture to be true and infallible because it was God-breathed, or Divinely given through the Holy Spirit.

The prophets and disciples who contributed to canonized scripture were powerfully anointed, led by the Holy Spirit, and totally committed to their calling. In fact, they were so submitted and set apart for God that they faced severe ridicule and persecution for speaking out. I am certain there were many times that they wished they could be silent but felt compelled to speak or write anyway.

A high price has been paid by many over the centuries to write, publish and share the Word of God. Surely, the Spirit of God continues to watch over His Word!

TODAY'S CHALLENGE:

Tell the Father how much you appreciate having access through your Bible to what He has chosen to reveal of Himself through the Spirit-inspired Scriptures.

Dive Deeper: Study 2 Peter 1; Romans 15:4; Hebrews 4:12; 1 Thessalonians 2:13; John 10:34-36; Psalm 12:6.

May 13

SPIRIT GIVES BIRTH TO SPIRIT

John 3:6

"Flesh gives birth to flesh, but the Spirit gives birth to spirit."

John 1:12-13
"Yet to all who did receive him, to those who believed in his name, he gave the right to become children of God—[13] children born not of natural descent, nor of human decision or a husband's will, but born of God."

When the Bible refers to us being "born of God", "born from above", and "born again" it is communicating the true nature of our new spirit man. The Holy Spirit draws us to salvation, and creates us anew, spiritually speaking. See 2 Corinthians 5:17.

As the active agent in Creation (see May 11), the Holy Spirit's role in making us a new creation is crucial and primary. We cannot re-create ourselves, but when we finally submit to God, His Holy Spirit begins to do His work.

After being "born of God", the Holy Spirit then begins in us the process of sanctification to set us apart for God and make us progressively more holy.

Those "born of God" cannot make sin a habitual practice in their lives. As a believer, one's desires are changed so as to love God sincerely and endeavor from the heart to please God and avoid evil. This is accomplished only through the grace given to believers in Christ, through a sustained relationship with Christ and through dependence on the Holy Spirit.[1] Are you experiencing a new life in Christ?

TODAY'S CHALLENGE:

Think about how your life has changed since you have been "born of God". Tell the Father you will surrender more and more to His Holy Spirit's sanctification process.

Dive Deeper: Study John 3; 2 Corinthians 5:17-21; John 1:10-13.

---

[1] Life in the Spirit Study Bible, published by Zondervan, article on "Regeneration".

May 14

INCARNATION AND THE SPIRIT

Matthew 1:18, 20
"This is how the birth of Jesus the Messiah came about: His mother Mary was pledged to be married to Joseph, but before they came together, she was found to be pregnant through the Holy Spirit... [20] But after he had considered this, an angel of the Lord appeared to him in a dream and said, 'Joseph son of David, do not be afraid to take Mary home as your wife, because what is conceived in her is from the Holy Spirit.'"

The Holy Spirit has been involved with Jesus from the beginning. They were together at the Creation (see May 11), and the Holy Spirit was the active power of God to come upon Mary to conceive her precious child, Jesus.

Why is the virgin birth important to the Christian faith? Jesus Christ, God's Son, had to be free from the sinful nature passed on to all other human beings by Adam. Because Jesus was born of a woman, he was a human being; but as the Son of God, Jesus was born without any trace of human sin. Jesus is both fully human, and fully divine.[1]

The only way for Jesus to be born sinless was for Him to be conceived by the Holy Spirit. There were no iniquities passed down to Him in the bloodline of a natural father. Knowing this, we will want to cooperate with the Holy Spirit's process of sanctifying us to make us more holy.

TODAY'S CHALLENGE:

Thank your Heavenly Father for the supernatural conception and birth of Jesus. Ask Him to help you more fully understand and appreciate the significance of Jesus being both human and Divine.

Dive Deeper: Study Matthew 1:18-25; Luke 1:26-38.

---

[1] Life Application Study Bible, published by Zondervan.

May 15

FULL, LED AND EMPOWERED

Luke 4:1, 14
"Jesus, full of the Holy Spirit, left the Jordan and was led by the Spirit into the wilderness…¹⁴ Jesus returned to Galilee in the power of the Spirit, and news about him spread through the whole countryside."

Oh, what an awesome God we serve. Like Jesus, we are able to be full of the Spirit, led by the Spirit and empowered by the Spirit! We are the living temple where we are able to host the very presence of God, filled to over-flowing with His anointing, and emboldened to spread the Good News to all.

If Jesus needed to be full, led and empowered, don't we? How could we ever really expect to do the things He did without all of His Spirit? See John 14:12.

For those of us who are, or have been, incarcerated, there is a day when we will leave our own "Jordan" and return to the wilderness of the world. Surely, we must seek all of the Holy Spirit's power and anointing to success-fully transition back into freedom.

When our "cellies", families, former friends and co-workers see the trans-formation God did in us, news of Him will spread out all around us! Our testimony of a truly changed life by the power of the Holy Spirit will bring God the Father glory, and please our Lord and Savior, Jesus!

TODAY'S CHALLENGE:

Talk to the Father about your need and desire to be full, led and empowered by His Holy Spirit just like Jesus. Seek to learn all you can about hosting His Presence so that your life will be totally and forever transformed.

Dive Deeper: Study Luke 4; John 14:12-14; Acts 10:37-38.

May 16

CLEANSING OUR CONSCIENCE

Hebrews 9:14
"How much more, then, will the blood of Christ, who through the eternal Spirit offered himself unblemished to God, cleanse our consciences from acts that lead to death, so that we may serve the living God!"

Because of the sacrificial death, resurrected life, and Blood of Jesus, we are cleansed of our past, and have been given the Holy Spirit so that we may serve our Father with a clear conscience.

That is almost an unbelievable truth for me because I remember how very depraved, perverted and sinful my life was before Jesus found me, and saved me, in prison in 2009. Yet, I testify that He has cleansed my conscience; and, when the devil reminds me of my past, I remind him of his future.

The Holy Spirit progressively sanctifies us after we truly repent and surrender to God. He teaches us the truth of the cleansing of our conscience by the Blood, and the power available to us to serve God with all our being. Through sanctification, we are set apart and made progressively more holy.

The Spirit reveals the righteousness of God in Christ Jesus offered to us because of His unblemished sacrifice. In Him alone are we counted as righteous, so we may approach the Father with confidence! See Hebrews 4:16.

TODAY'S CHALLENGE:

Tell the Father how grateful you are for the cleansing Blood of Jesus to enable you to live with a clear conscience. Promise Him you will repent quickly whenever you are convicted by His Spirit anytime you begin to stray from His narrow path. Thank Him for the new life you have been given in Christ!

Dive Deeper: Study Hebrews 9; Hebrews 4:16; Hebrews 6:10-12; 1 Peter 1:1-2; 2 Peter 1:3-4.

May 17

INCOMPARABLE GREAT POWER

Ephesians 1:18-20
"I pray...that you may know...[19]his incomparably great power for us who believe. That power is the same as the mighty strength [20] he exerted when he raised Christ from the dead..."

For so many years I felt powerless. Long before I was incarcerated behind razor wire and steel bars, I was imprisoned by addictions, hopelessness, depression, shame, pride, greed and a myriad of other bondages. I did not think anything would ever change because I did not have the power to change them. Have you ever felt this way?

After I fully surrendered to God while in prison, I began to learn about the Power of God the Father available to me through His Holy Spirit Who lived in me. I now have the Power! This power is the same Power that resurrected Jesus from the dead and seated Him forever in Heavenly places. God is Almighty, that is, He possesses all power.

The fact that this same Power in the Person of the Holy Spirit will lead me, teach me, comfort me, and help me is almost beyond comprehension, but it is true! I see Him manifest more of this daily in my life as I learn to more fully surrender and submit in obedience to Him.

Are you experiencing this more every day? Seek. Surrender. Submit. Obey.

TODAY'S CHALLENGE:

Ask our Heavenly Father how you may know more of His incomparable resurrection power for living the abundant life Jesus came to give you. Seek Him today with all your heart. He will be found by you and reveal His Power in the form of His Holy Spirit.

Dive Deeper: Study Ephesians 1:3 – 2:10.

May 18

LAY DOWN YOUR LIFE

John 10:17-18
"The reason my Father loves me is that I lay down my life—only to take it up again. ¹⁸ No one takes it from me, but I lay it down of my own accord. I have authority to lay it down and authority to take it up again. This command I received from my Father."

Jesus was not murdered. He voluntarily laid down His life as a sacrifice. He took up His glorified body at the Resurrection.

God the Father gave Him the authority to do this. At the Cross He died as "the last Adam", but at the Resurrection He arose as "the Second Man", "the firstborn among many brothers". See 1 Corinthians 15:45, 47; and Romans 8:29.

God will not crucify our "old man". He asks us to do that voluntarily. His intent is not to make our old man better, rather it is to make us a totally "new creation" after we deny self, and willingly submit to our death on the cross with Jesus. See 2 Corinthians 5:17.

He has given us authority in Christ Jesus to lay down our old life and take it up again in the form of a new person. What a magnificently powerful truth this is!

Have you denied self? We must do this daily so we will have our new life

TODAY'S CHALLENGE:

Tell the Father you are glad you are a new creation in Christ Jesus by His Holy Spirit living in you. Ask Him to help you learn to deny self daily.

Rededicate your life to Him today. Deny self.

Dive Deeper: Study John 10; Romans 8:29; 1 Corinthians 15:45, 47; 2 Corinthians 5:17-21.

May 19

THE SPIRIT OF HOLINESS

Romans 1:4
"...who through the Spirit of holiness was appointed the Son of God in power by his resurrection from the dead: Jesus Christ our Lord."

1 Peter 1:15
"But just as he who called you is holy, so be holy in all you do..."

It was very intimidating when I first read what Peter wrote to "be holy". Why? Because I knew how unholy I used to be, and that I will never be perfected until I see Jesus.

Holiness is the primary goal of sanctification, which is an ongoing process. It begins when we first surrender to the Lordship of Jesus and the Leadership of the Holy Spirit. To be "sanctified" is to be "set apart", to be "made holy".

Of our own selves, this is an impossible task. But, we have the Spirit of Holiness abiding in us. This is one of His primary tasks. In Christ, the Spirit is progressively making us more holy.

I have heard people say we are all children of God, but that is not true. We are all "God's creations", but Romans 8:14 says, *"...those who are led by the Spirit of God are the children of God."*

Are you willing to be led by the Spirit? Are you letting Him do his work in you to make you holy? He will not force you. You must desire it.

TODAY'S CHALLENGE:

Tell the Father you want to allow His Spirit of Holiness, His Holy Spirit, to do His work of sanctification in you today. Ask the Father to help you willingly submit to His Hand as the Potter.

Be moldable clay today. Stay on the potter's wheel.

Dive Deeper: Study 1 Peter 1:13 – 2:12; Romans 12:1-2; Colossians 3:1-17; Romans 8:5-17.

May 20

THE SPIRIT GLORIFIES JESUS

John 16:13-14
"But when he, the Spirit of truth, comes, he will guide you into all the truth. He will not speak on his own; he will speak only what he hears, and he will tell you what is yet to come. ¹⁴ He will glorify me because it is from me that he will receive what he will make known to you."

Jesus, Who is "the Truth" (John 14:6), knew we would need a Helper and Guide after He ascended. He and the Father sent "the gift the Father promised" (Acts 1:4), the "Spirit of truth" to fulfill this role in our lives.

Jesus finished His work perfectly and completely, and the Father recognized this truth by resurrecting Him from the grave, and seating Him above all things forever in Heaven. Jesus reconciled mankind back to the Father through Himself by the Cross and Resurrection. In this life, we must choose where we will spend eternity, and Jesus enabled us to choose Heaven by grace alone, through faith alone, in Him alone!

However, until Heaven, the Spirit of Christ, and the Spirit of the Father, the Holy Spirit, has been given to us to represent and glorify Jesus. When we receive guidance and instruction from the Spirit, we can be certain it is coming directly from Jesus. When we obey, we are glorifying God!

TODAY'S CHALLENGE:

Thank the Father for His incredible Gift, His Holy Spirit. Tell Him you will listen for guidance and truth from Jesus through His Holy Spirit. Make a decision to be led by the Spirit today, and firmly resolve that you will be obedient to His promptings.

Dive Deeper: Study John 16; John 14:6; Acts 1:4.

May 21

FOR YOUR GOOD

John 16:7
"But very truly I tell you, it is for your good that I am going away. Unless I go away, the Advocate will not come to you; but if I go, I will send him to you."

Imagine for a few minutes you were one of the original twelve disciples of Jesus. After having spent every day in the very near presence of Jesus for more than three years, you are with Him on Passover eve.

It finally sinks in that Jesus is "going away" after having been told several times before this very evening. Anxiety, worry, concern, fear, and confusion must have attacked them all in various degrees.

Why is He going, and where? Is He really coming back for them, and when? How will they get by until He returns? Will they be able to continue their fellowship, and live the new way Jesus had been demonstrating daily? Jesus had been telling them they would be hated, persecuted, and kicked out of the synagogue. What would happen to them without Jesus?

Then Jesus says it is better for them if He goes away. WHAT?!?!? How could this be possible?

Jesus could only be in one place at one time while He was restricted to His earthly body. But, He explained, He would send another Helper just like Him Who could be with them in every place, at all times, regardless of how far apart they physically might be from one another.

It took about fifty-three days, until Pentecost, for this truth to finally manifest. It really was better for them (and us) that Jesus go!

TODAY'S CHALLENGE:

Think deeply about this today.

Dive Deeper: Study John 16.

May 22

YOU ARE WITNESSES

Acts 1:4-5, 8
"On one occasion, while he was eating with them, he gave them this command: 'Do not leave Jerusalem, but wait for the gift my Father promised, which you have heard me speak about. ⁵ For John baptized with water, but in a few days you will be baptized with the Holy Spirit.'... ⁸ But you will receive power when the Holy Spirit comes on you; and you will be my witnesses in Jerusalem, and in all Judea and Samaria, and to the ends of the earth."

When you are baptized with the Holy Spirit, you receive power. In fact, the Bible indicates that the Holy Spirit is the very power of God Almighty present on this Earth. Everything the Father does is in, and through, the power of His Spirit.

We need this power to live the abundant life Jesus came to give us. Our lives should be so gloriously transformed that our actions, character, love and compassion speak more loudly to others than even the very words that come from our mouths. People should see such a difference in our lives that they would know we "had been with Jesus." See Acts 4:13.

This is part of what it means to be a "witness". A witness is one who testifies, and who gives evidence. A witness is someone who was present at a particular event or transaction, who will testify that it has taken place.

Will you testify today?

TODAY'S CHALLENGE:

Thank the Father for His Holy Spirit and ask Him to give you the power to be a witness of all the glorious work He is doing in your life.

Dive Deeper: Study Acts 1:4 – 2:41; Acts 4:13.

May 23

MARY NEEDED THE SPIRIT

Acts 1:14
"They all joined together constantly in prayer, along with the women and Mary the mother of Jesus, and with his brothers."

In the Upper Room on the day of Pentecost, there were 120 men and women obediently waiting to "receive power from on high" which had been promised by Jesus (see Luke 24:49). Mary, the mother of Jesus, and her other sons, were there that day in the assembly of faith-filled disciples.

During the earthly ministry of Jesus, His mother must have been proud of Him, marveled at His miracles, and was amazed at His wisdom and teachings. But, we can imagine, she was also worried about the threats of the religious leaders against someone so brash as to call God His Father, and to equate Himself with God!

At the foot of the Cross, her pain and grief must have overwhelmed her to the point that she must not have been able to stand or walk without assistance from John, the beloved disciple and friend of Jesus.

The Good News of the Resurrection on the third day must have been unbelievable until she witnessed Him herself. Can you imagine what she said to her other children, and how they might have responded?

We know one thing for sure though. Mary and her other sons were compelled by their hope and joy to wait in the Upper Room to receive the One with Power Jesus sent!

TODAY'S CHALLENGE:

Ask the Father to fill you more full of His power, joy and hope through His Holy Spirit living in you.

Mary needed the Spirit. So do we.

Dive Deeper: Study Acts 1; Luke 24:49.

May 24

SPIRIT-ENABLED TONGUES

Acts 2:1-4
"When the day of Pentecost came, they were all together in one place. ² Suddenly a sound like the blowing of a violent wind came from heaven and filled the whole house where they were sitting. ³ They saw what seemed to be tongues of fire that separated and came to rest on each of them. ⁴ All of them were filled with the Holy Spirit and began to speak in other tongues as the Spirit enabled them."

There has been quite a bit of discourse and writings about this first appearance of Spirit-enabled tongues in the New Testament, as well as a lot of controversy and confusion.

I don't know all the answers or ramifications concerning this gift that came with Power, but I know a few over-riding truths that lead me to want to know more. I am willing to keep an open mind because I want absolutely everything the Holy Spirit wants to empower and bless me with. Do you?

This in fact was prophesied about 700 years earlier in Isaiah 28:11 – but also see Isaiah 28:1-15 for context with the entire chapter. Verse 12 indicates there is rest and refreshment for us!

Isaiah 28:13 implies knowledge from His Word accompanies it, and I imagine this includes the "Rhema", God-spoken Word referred to in Romans 10:17, where we are told that "faith comes by hearing…". Isaiah 28:15 talks of protection. Jude 1:20-21 talks of being built up, or edification.

Rest, refreshment, knowledge, protection and edification - do you think these may all be part of the many benefits of tongues?

TODAY'S CHALLENGE:

Tell the Father you want Him to progressively reveal why He and Jesus sent the Holy Spirit with the gift of tongues.

God has all the answers. Ask Him.

Dive Deeper: Study Acts 2:1-22; Isaiah 28:1-15; Jude 1:20-21; Romans 10:17.

May 25

GOD DOES NOT CHANGE

Hebrews 6:17
"Because God wanted to make the unchanging nature of his purpose very clear to
the heirs of what was promised, he confirmed it with an oath."

Malachi 3:6
"I the LORD do not change. So you, the descendants of Jacob, are not destroyed."

There is no doubt we will be learning more about God for all of eternity. For now, however, God has revealed Himself through His Word, and His Spirit. Jesus said if we have seen Him, the Living Word, we have seen the Father. He has given us enough Truth in the here and now so we can choose to enter into an eternal relationship with Him.

God does not change. His very nature is unchanging. He has confirmed this. We can count on God to consistently apply love, mercy, grace, justice and judgment.

What we learn of God's faithfulness, principles, justice and judgment in the Old Testament prepares us to discover His unconditional love, mercy and grace demonstrated in and through Jesus as related to us in the New Testament. He always preserves a remnant of those who will seek Him with all their heart, surrender to the Lordship of Jesus, and follow the leadership of the Holy Spirit!

The unchanging nature of His purpose is to offer the intimacy of eternal relationship with the Father to the heirs of salvation through Jesus Christ by His Holy Spirit.

TODAY'S CHALLENGE:

Worship the Father in appreciation of His unchanging and unconditional love, grace and mercy to you. Tell Him you desire above all else to accept His offer of intimate relationship with Him.

Dive Deeper: Study Malachi 3; Hebrews 13:8; James 1:17; Psalm 102:25-27; Psalm 90:2.

May 26

HE IS ALWAYS WITH US

Matthew 28:20
"...And surely I am with you always, to the very end of the age."

In John 14:15-20, Jesus had explained that He and the Father were going to send the Spirit of Truth to help them, and be with them forever.

Jesus knew His work in His earthly body was about to be finished, but He wanted His disciples, and those who believed in Him through them, to know they would always have a Helper, Advocate, Counselor and Friend. The Spirit of the Father, and the Spirit of Christ, that is, the Holy Spirit, would fulfill all these promised roles, and He would never leave them.

Jesus, as a man, could only be in one place at a time. In John 14:12, Jesus said those who follow Him would do greater works than He did. Pretty unbelievable, right? Yet, when you multiply all the efforts of all the disciples in different places manifesting miracles through the same power of the Holy Spirit that anointed Jesus, one might imagine these as "the greater works".

Jesus Himself said all this was possible "because I am going to the Father". He knew that the Holy Spirit Who had been with them as the anointing of Jesus will now be in them (John 14:17).

Could this be one reason He told them to wait until they received power from on high before they went out to fulfill the Great Commission (Matthew 28:18-19)?

TODAY'S CHALLENGE:

Thank the Father that you are never alone. Tell Him you want to be fully empowered to do the works of Jesus by the power and anointing of the Holy Spirit.

Dive Deeper: Study Matthew 28:18-20; John 14:15-20; John 14:12; Exodus 33:15-16; Joshua 1:5-9; Zephaniah 3:17; Deuteronomy 31:8.

May 27

JESUS IS ALWAYS THE SAME

Hebrews 13:8
"Jesus Christ is the same yesterday and today and forever."

In this world of constant change, consternation and confusion seem the order of the day. Yet, great comfort is gained when we consider the profound truth that Jesus will never change.

As I consider this, I am thankful Jesus will always love sinners but will never condone sin. He was not afraid to be with sinful, disobedient and rebellious people, but a true encounter with Him left them changed and willing to obey Him when He said, "Go, and sin no more."

Since He is the Truth, I find confidence knowing that truth does not change. It does not evolve. It is not relative to what is happening in society. It is fixed and constant because He is.

Knowing His work is forever finished, complete and perfect allows me to place all my Faith in Him. No-one has ever done what He did, nor will they ever. Nothing needs to be added, and it cannot be changed. It is forever sufficient for my salvation.

My faith, loyalty and allegiance to Jesus will never be misplaced because He is forever in His Place, high above all else with everything under His feet. Realizing I am seated with Him in Heavenly places (Ephesians 2:6), I am thankful I am forever the undeserving recipient of His mercy, love, kindness and grace.

TODAY'S CHALLENGE:

Ask the Father to help you fully realize and appreciate the eternal, unchanging nature of Jesus. Tell the Holy Spirit you would like more complete revelation of this truth.

Think deeply about what this means to you.

Dive Deeper: Study Hebrews 13; Malachi 3:6; James 1:17; Hebrews 6:17; Psalm 90:2; Psalm 102:25-27.

May 28

LET THE SPIRIT WORK

Philippians 2:13
"...for it is God who works in you both to will and to do for His good pleasure."

Zechariah 4:6
"Not by might nor by power, but by My Spirit, says the Lord Almighty."

It amazes me that God has decided to accomplish His work on earth through imperfect people who are fully surrendered to Him. Jesus told His disciples not to go anywhere or do anything until they received power from God in the form of His Holy Spirit.

In the same way, when we are surrendered, listening and obedient, the Holy Spirit in us will lead us where He wants us to go so He can do what He wants to do through us for others. It is not our might or power, but His Spirit.

God Himself is working in us to accomplish His will in and through our lives. As we learn to fully submit to His Leadership and Lordship He is able to bring forth the fruit in our lives through which He desires to benefit and bless others – love, joy, peace, patience, kindness, goodness, gentleness, faithfulness, and self-control. This fruit certainly enriches us, but these character qualities of Christ are primarily beneficial to those with whom we are in daily contact.

We must stay attached to the Vine (John 15:1-5), so He can bring forth fruit. Without Him we can do nothing. He brings forth fruit that remains (John 15:16).

TODAY'S CHALLENGE:

Ask the Father to do what He wills in your life that will bring Him pleasure. Tell Him you want His Spirit to do the work.

Don't get in His way.

Dive Deeper: Study Philippians 2; John 15:1-5, 16; Zechariah 4:1-7.

May 29

YOU ARE SEALED BY THE SPIRIT

Ephesians 4:30
"And do not grieve the Holy Spirit of God, with whom you were sealed for the day of redemption."

In what ways does the Spirit seal us for the day of redemption?

The Greek word translated in this passage means "to seal, to put a mark on an object to show possession, authority, identity, or security."

After we come to Christ in true repentance, surrender to His Lordship over our lives, and submit to the Spirit's leadership, we can know we are eternally secure. He has marked us as His forever. We must voluntarily let Him "possess" us. Before Christ, I was possessed by evil spirits, now I only want to be possessed by the Holy Spirit!

Once sealed, we must allow Him to have total authority over us. We must also recognize and receive the authority Christ Jesus has given us (see Matthew 28:18). Consequently, the enemy has no authority over us except the authority we give him when we open the door through sin.

The Holy Spirit seals us also as a sign of identity. We must know who we are in Christ. We cannot believe the accusations of the enemy against us; rather, we must confess and believe what God says about who we are in Christ. Meditating upon, and memorizing, scriptures related to our new identity on a daily basis is important to combatting the constant accusations and lies of the enemy.

TODAY'S CHALLENGE:

Thank our Father that you are sealed for the day of redemption by the Holy Spirit. Ask Him to help you understand the authority and new identity you have now in Christ.

Dive Deeper: Study Ephesians 4.

May 30

THE HOLY SPIRIT TESTIFIES

Hebrews 10:15-17
"The Holy Spirit also testifies to us about this. First he says: ¹⁶ 'This is the covenant I will make with them after that time, says the Lord. I will put my laws in their hearts, and I will write them on their minds.' ¹⁷ Then he adds: 'Their sins and lawless acts I will remember no more.'"

With the Holy Spirit, we have an internal witness who testifies to us about the Way and the narrow path associated with our Christian walk; and, reminds us of God's unconditional love and forgiveness when we stray.

After we are saved, we have the great blessing of the daily guidance by the Holy Spirit, and He testifies to, and for, us! The Greek word translated in verse 15 as "testifies" means to testify, give testimony, commend, speak well of, and vouch for.

We have learned that the Holy Spirit will always testify of Jesus, so we have His help to know how to live the Christian life the way Jesus instructed. While we have His Word in our Bibles, we also have the inner witness to speak well of, and commend to us, the law of the Spirit of life in Christ Jesus.

We also have the Spirit to vouch for the fact that our sins are forgiven, and God is not holding our past against us so we are no longer bound by the law of sin and death (see Romans 8:1-2).

What a great witness He is for us!

TODAY'S CHALLENGE:

Ask the Father to help you appreciate and listen to the inner witness of His Holy Spirit today.

Dive Deeper: Study Hebrews 10; John 16:7-15; Romans 8:1-2.

May 31

THE SPIRIT GIVES REAL LIFE

Romans 8:11
"And if the Spirit of him who raised Jesus from the dead is living in you, he who raised Christ from the dead will also give life to your mortal bodies because of his Spirit who lives in you."

Not only does the Holy Spirit indwell a Christian, He gives life to our mortal bodies in ways we could not previously imagine before salvation.

Prior to my salvation in prison, I can see now that I had not really lived life to the fullest. Even when I had a great job, family and material possessions, I was empty inside, and had no peace and contentment.

Then, when I suddenly and foolishly walked away from my family and my job, and lost all those possessions, I was overcome with depression, hopelessness, and despair. I was also still empty, and without peace. Inside, I was filled with turmoil, indecision, self-accusation, and self-loathing.

Now I understand progressively more every day what it really means to have the abundant life Jesus came to give us (see John 10:10). The same powerful Spirit the Father used to resurrect Jesus (see April 26 devotional) lives in me, and powerfully provides everything I was missing before Christ!

As I learn to more fully surrender to Him, I am blessed with more of His fruit – love, joy, peace, patience, kindness, gentleness, faithfulness and self-control. These are the character qualities of Christ, and in Him alone is real life!

TODAY'S CHALLENGE:

Thank the Father for real life in Christ through His Holy Spirit living in you. Write down some of the differences between your life prior to salvation, and now. Rejoice and be glad!

Dive Deeper: Study Romans 8; John 10:1-10; John 5:24, 39-40.

June 1

STRENGTH AND ENCOURAGEMENT

Acts 9:31
"Then the church throughout Judea, Galilee and Samaria enjoyed a time of peace and was strengthened. Living in the fear of the Lord and encouraged by the Holy Spirit, it increased in numbers."

When we are in bondage of any kind, there are plenty of days we especially need strength and encouragement. Great peace indwells us in the form of the Holy Spirit; and, He provides these needed qualities if we let Him.

As we have already learned, the Holy Spirit administers all of God's power on this earth, and since He lives in us, this power is available to us. He is our Helper, Strengthener, Teacher, Encourager, Counselor, Friend and Guide. What is the secret for us to be able to allow Him to work freely in our lives?

I believe this verse tells us that the fear of the Lord is key. "The fear of the Lord is the beginning of wisdom, and knowledge of the Holy One is understanding." See Proverbs 9:10. The fear of the Lord is reverence, respect, and awe.

We host the very presence of God! As we develop an intimacy of relationship with the Father, because of the Son, through the Holy Spirit, we will know Him better. In this knowing, we will want to honor, love, revere, and respect the awesomeness of Him. As a result, we will want to do our best to obey Him.

The more in tune we are with the Holy Spirit, the more peace, strength and encouragement He provides.

TODAY'S CHALLENGE:

Take time to dwell on the many magnificent attributes of God, and ask the Father to teach you the fear of the Lord by His Spirit. Wisdom, knowledge and understanding will increase, and you will be strengthened and encouraged in Christ by His Spirit!

Dive Deeper: Study Acts 9; Proverbs 9:10.

June 2

FRUIT OF LIFE

Galatians 5:22-23
"But the fruit of the Spirit is love, joy, peace, forbearance, kindness, goodness, faithfulness, ²³ gentleness and self-control. Against such things there is no law."

For far too long, most of us bore bad "fruit of the flesh" always leading to death described in Galatians 5:19-21, which immediately precedes today's passage.

The Holy Spirit in us brings about the good "fruit of the Spirit" that always leads to life (see also April 30 about staying connected to the Vine). Jesus desires that we all bear fruit and that the fruit would last (see John 15:16).

How can we participate in the Holy Spirit's work of bringing forth all this great fruit in our lives?

These character qualities of Christ enumerated in today's passage come forth in us in greater abundance as we learn to more fully surrender to the Lordship of Christ Jesus, and completely submit to the Leadership of the Holy Spirit.

My experience is that the more I seek and love God with all my heart, soul, mind and strength; the more I desire to be obedient to Him. Blessings follow obedience. To me, the peace, joy, love and other fruit of the Spirit being manifested in my life are such good blessings that I want more!

There is absolutely no comparison between the previous fruit of darkness and the flesh we used to have; and the light and spiritual blessings we have now in the fruit of life in the Spirit.

TODAY'S CHALLENGE:

Ask the Father to show you how to allow Him to bring forth more spiritual fruit in your life. Which character qualities listed above are already evident? Which ones need to grow?

Dive Deeper: Study Galatians 5; Colossians 3:12-17; John 15:16.

June 3

GLORIFYING JESUS

John 16:14
"He will glorify me because it is from me that he will receive what he will make known to you."

Since we have the Spirit of Christ living in us, we can be certain that the Holy Spirit will always lead us in paths that glorify God, but we must always be willing to follow along the Path.

Jesus said that He is the Way, so that means He is the Path. We know we enter in through the narrow gate by grace alone, through faith alone, in Christ alone. But we are led along the narrow path by our Guide, Friend, Teacher and Counselor – the Holy Spirit.

Problems arise more frequently for us when we re-assert our own lordship over our lives and want to do things our own way. We take ourselves off the narrow path through our failure to listen and follow the prompting of the Holy Spirit. He always wants to lead us in the way of Jesus, but He is a gentleman and will not force us to obey.

Because of the finished work of Jesus on the Cross, everything the Father has is available to true believers by the Holy Spirit. The Spirit receives everything we need daily to stay on the path of abundant life now, and throughout all eternity, but we must choose to ask for His leadership and obediently follow Him.

Our lives bring glory to God when we do.

TODAY'S CHALLENGE:

Thank the Father for Jesus and the Holy Spirit. Tell Him you want to better hear and follow the Holy Spirit in everything you do today.

Bring glory to God today as you walk the narrow path.

Dive Deeper: Study John 16; Matthew 7:13-14.

June 4

THIRSTING FOR MORE

1 Corinthians 12:13
"For we were all baptized by one Spirit so as to form one body—whether Jews or Gentiles, slave or free—and we were all given the one Spirit to drink."

Acts 1:5
Jesus said, "For John baptized with water, but in a few days you will be baptized with the Holy Spirit."

The Baptism of the Holy Spirit operates first at the level of making us all part of the Body of Christ. None of us can come to Christ unless the Father draws them (John 6:44), and this occurs when the Spirit convicts us of sin, righteousness and judgment (John 16:18). Upon genuine repentance and confession of faith, we become part of the Body of Believers.

However, before Jesus ascended, He reminded His disciples of His promise that He and the Father would send them a Helper Who would give them the power they needed to fulfill the Great Commission (Acts 1:8; 2:33; Mark 16:15-20).

A few days earlier they had received the Holy Spirit from the resurrected Christ upon Whom they now believed (John 20:22), so they then became part of the Body of Christ by the Spirit. So, just before His ascension, Jesus was describing another act of the Spirit – His baptism for power.

We are all given the same as the disciples, but do we want it? Are we thirsty for more of the Holy Spirit so we can fulfill our particular commission, plan and purpose?

TODAY'S CHALLENGE:

Tell the Father that you thirst for more of the Holy Spirit. Ask Him to fill you afresh daily. Drink deeply of His Spirit today.

Dive Deeper: Study 1 Corinthians 12; John 6:44; 16:8, 20:22; Acts 1:8, 2:33; Mark 16:15-20.

June 5

CLOTHED WITH POWER

Luke 24:49
Jesus said, "I am going to send you what my Father has promised; but stay in the city until you have been clothed with power from on high."

Acts 1:8
Jesus said, "But you will receive power when the Holy Spirit comes on you..."

What does this power actually do that we receive from the Baptism of the Holy Spirit as discussed yesterday? Why is it important to us? What difference can we expect it to make in our lives as Christians?

From the day of Pentecost, the disciples were given boldness, strength, courage and perseverance from the Baptism of the Holy Spirit. Three thousand came into faith that day, and they devoted themselves to the apostles' teaching and to their fellowship with one another. They were filled with awe, and many wonders and miraculous signs were done (see Acts 2:41-43).

Perhaps Paul was referring to being "clothed with power" when he instructed the Colossians to clothe themselves with compassion, kindness, humility, gentleness and patience; and to walk in forgiveness, love, peace and thankfulness (see Colossians 3:12-17).

Brothers and sisters, in the two paragraphs above, we have seen that being clothed with power by the Baptism of the Holy Spirit resulted in boldness, strength, courage, perseverance, devotion, fellowship, awe, wonders, signs, compassion, humility, gentleness, patience, forgiveness, love, peace and thankfulness!

By my own personal experience, I can testify all these are being manifested in increasing amounts and frequency in my life. They are all available to you too.

TODAY'S CHALLENGE:

Ask the Father to clothe you with power. Ask Him to Baptize you in His Holy Spirit, and to fill you to overflowing with Himself.

Dive Deeper: Study Luke 24; Acts 2:41-43; Colossians 3:12-17.

June 6

SOMETHING WAS MISSING

Acts 8:14-17
"When the apostles in Jerusalem heard that Samaria had accepted the word of God, they sent Peter and John to Samaria. [15] When they arrived, they prayed for the new believers there that they might receive the Holy Spirit, [16] because the Holy Spirit had not yet come on any of them; they had simply been baptized in the name of the Lord Jesus. [17] Then Peter and John placed their hands on them, and they received the Holy Spirit."

Isn't this passage interesting? New believers came into faith in Samaria. The Samaritans were not ethnically fully Jewish, and so were looked down upon, and treated as second-class citizens. Those of us in prison or any other form of bondage can easily identify with their treatment.

When Peter and John arrived, they must have readily seen something lacking in these new believers. Their faith, outwardly portrayed by water baptism, brought them into the Body of Christ, but something more remained for them to receive.

Perhaps what was lacking was the process of sanctification. One of the jobs of the Holy Spirit in a Believer is to set them apart for God's service, and begin the process of making them more holy.

Left to our own devices, we are powerless to transform ourselves. It comes only by the power of the Holy Spirit working in and through us progressively over time as we obediently submit to His leadership.

Is something missing in your life as a Believer?

TODAY'S CHALLENGE:

Tell the Father you want to submit to everything the Holy Spirit wants to do in you. Ask Him to give you whatever He sees missing in your life.

Dive Deeper: Study Acts 8.

June 7

SCALES FELL, EYES OPENED

Acts 9:17-18
"Then Ananias went to the house and entered it. Placing his hands on Saul, he said, "Brother Saul, the Lord—Jesus, who appeared to you on the road as you were coming here—has sent me so that you may see again and be filled with the Holy Spirit." [18] Immediately, something like scales fell from Saul's eyes, and he could see again. He got up and was baptized..."

I suggest you also read this account of Saul's conversion in Acts 22:1-16.

After his Damascus Road encounter with the Living Lord Jesus, Saul must have immediately become a Believer, for he did not argue with Jesus, and got up to do what he was told. Another indication of conversion was, in Damascus, he chose to begin a complete fast of food and water, in spite of how helpless he must have felt due to his blindness.

What is happening in this temporary physical realm is often a reflection of what is happening in the eternal spiritual realm. Saul's blindness must have brought him to a point of weakness and humility like perhaps nothing ever had in his life.

He was seeking spiritual enlightenment by fasting (verse 9), which led to much prayer (verse 11). Jesus, in answer to Saul's prayers, sent Ananias to lay hands on Saul to receive the Holy Spirit knowing he would need this power to proclaim the name of Christ to the Gentiles (verse 15).

Something like scales fell from his eyes and he could see. He began to preach that Jesus is the Son of God (verse 20)!

TODAY'S CHALLENGE:

Ask the Father to open your eyes to the power of the Holy Spirit.

Dive Deeper: Study Acts 9:1-31; Acts 22:1-16.

June 8

THE SPIRIT IS FOR EVERYONE

Acts 10:44-47
"While Peter was still speaking these words, the Holy Spirit came on all who heard the message. ⁴⁵ The circumcised believers who had come with Peter were astonished that the gift of the Holy Spirit had been poured out even on Gentiles. ⁴⁶ For they heard them speaking in tongues and praising God. Then Peter said, ⁴⁷ 'Surely no one can stand in the way of their being baptized with water. They have received the Holy Spirit just as we have.'"

What happened at Pentecost was not just for the 120 followers assembled in the Upper Room. Nor was it only for the Jewish Believers in Jesus. The gift was available to all, even those the Jews considered outsiders, that is, the Gentiles.

A lot of us who have been in any form of bondage have at one time or another felt like outsiders too. But God is no respecter of persons, what He did for one He will do for all.

This particular case is somewhat noteworthy because the power and anointing of the Holy Spirit came upon those who heard Peter's message even before he was finished. He didn't even have an "altar call". The Word went forth and the Spirit moved!

Those with Peter were convinced because they heard them speaking in tongues and praising God. The Baptism of the Holy Spirit so thrills and empowers your spirit that you cannot help but praise God, and when you run out of words, the Spirit will pray through you supernaturally!

TODAY'S CHALLENGE:

Think about the power of the Holy Spirit, and spend some time just praising God from your spirit. You will be uplifted, encouraged, renewed and refreshed.

Dive Deeper: Study Acts 10; Romans 8:26-28.

June 9

DID YOU RECEIVE?

Acts 19:1-2
"While Apollos was at Corinth, Paul took the road through the interior and arrived at Ephesus. There he found some disciples ² and asked them, "Did you receive the Holy Spirit when you believed?" They answered, "No, we have not even heard that there is a Holy Spirit."

It grieves me to know so many good brothers and sisters in Christ who have not even heard that there is a Holy Spirit.

I can't help but think of when Paul was describing for Timothy what mankind would be like in the last days, he listed a long list of troubling characteristics, and ended it by referring to those who "have a form of godliness, but deny its power." See 2 Timothy 3:1-5.

Could Paul have been referring to a large segment of true believers who are saved for eternity, but not experiencing much of the abundant life available to them right now (see John 10:10) because they do not acknowledge the very power they need?

When we get saved, we are not expected to just hold on for the rest of this life on earth waiting for Heaven to fulfill us. No, eternal life began the day we gave our heart to Jesus, and we can receive the gift of empowerment by the Holy Spirit in order for us to be overcomers here and now, and continuing throughout all of eternity.

Did you receive the Holy Spirit when you believed?

TODAY'S CHALLENGE:

Tell the Father you want to understand more about His Gift to you in the form of His Holy Spirit. Ask Him to empower you to be an overcomer today.

Dive Deeper: Study Acts 19; 2 Timothy 3:1-5; John 10:10.

June 10

JESUS BAPTIZES

Mark 1:8
"I baptize you with water, but he will baptize you with the Holy Spirit."

In this passage, John the Baptist was speaking of Jesus Who would come after him. Similar passages are in Matthew 3:11, and Luke 3:16. He was distinguishing his baptism of repentance from the Baptism of the Holy Spirit Jesus would bring.

In John 4:2, we learn that Jesus did not baptize believers in water, rather His disciples did this. I have often wondered if Jesus did this intentionally so that His Baptism with the Holy Spirit and fire (see March 14) would be set apart from baptism into the faith?

At age 12, I was baptized in water but I don't think I got anything except wet. Can you relate?

In prison, I wanted to announce my inward profession of faith by the outward act of baptism as an indication to myself and others that I was willing to be held accountable for my decision to commit my life to Christ.

I had truly repented of my sin and was ready to turn away from sinful habits. Baptism in water that time resulted in an inward knowing that I was really saved. Yet, I still struggled with sin in some areas.

It wasn't until I asked Jesus to baptize me with His Holy Spirit that I began to feel empowered to actually turn from sin, and resist the many temptations the devil brought my way.

Have you received this power?

TODAY'S CHALLENGE:

Tell the Father you want Jesus to baptize you so that you are empowered to resist temptation, and can be purified with the Refiner's fire.

Dive Deeper: Study Mark 1; Matthew 3:11; Luke 3:16; John 4:2.

June 11

FAN INTO FLAME

2 Timothy 1:6-7
"For this reason I remind you to fan into flame the gift of God, which is in you through the laying on of my hands. [7] For the Spirit God gave us does not make us timid, but gives us power, love and self-discipline."

Paul's last letter to his son in the faith, Timothy, is more significant to me when I consider the fact that Paul knew he would soon give his life for the gospel of Jesus. His letter was written from prison, apparently after he already knew the fate that awaited him. I assume he believed this might be his last chance to write.

In that light, he reminds Timothy of the sincere faith of his mother and grandmother that Paul confidently stated resided in Timothy. Therefore, as a sincere believer, Paul encourages Timothy to "fan into flame the gift of God".

In previous devotions we have learned about the "gift of God" to which Paul is referring, the power and anointing of the Baptism of the Holy Spirit. In some translations it says to "stir up the gift of God that lies within you".

Paul wants to strengthen Timothy, but he reminds Timothy he already has all the power he needs to be able to walk in love with soundness of mind for discipline and self-control. This is all available through the Spirit.

Are you too a sincere believer? Fan into flame - stir up the gift - that is in you by the Holy Spirit of God!

TODAY'S CHALLENGE:

Tell the Father you want to walk in courage, love and self-discipline today through the sound mind of Christ given you by the Holy Spirit.

Dive Deeper: Study 2 Timothy 1; 1 Corinthians 12:4-13.

June 12

LAST DAYS' OUTPOURING

Joel 2:28-29
"And afterward, I will pour out my Spirit on all people. Your sons and daughters will prophesy, your old men will dream dreams, your young men will see visions. ²⁹ Even on my servants, both men and women, I will pour out my Spirit in those days."

In the context of the entire second chapter of Joel, it is clear the Lord Himself is prophesying of "the day of the Lord" (Joel 2:1-2), after His people, Israel, are regathered in the land. I encourage you to stop and read the entire chapter.

Peter, on the day of Pentecost, referred to this passage in explaining what had happened, so he believed they were then "in those days" because of the outpouring of the Holy Spirit.

So many prophetic scriptures have already been fulfilled concerning the last days. In fact, Dr. David Jeremiah says that all the prophecies that must be fulfilled before the second coming of Christ have, in fact, already been fulfilled. He could come any day.

In view of this, the power and anointing of the Holy Spirit that the Father wants to pour out on His sons and daughters becomes ever more important with each passing day. Romans 8:14 says, *"For those who are led by the Spirit of God are the children of God."*

Brothers and sisters in Christ, in these last days, we must have all of the Holy Spirit, and make a decision daily to be led by the Spirit.

TODAY'S CHALLENGE:

Ask the Father to pour out more of Himself through His Holy Spirit so that you are overflowing for the benefit of others today wherever you go and whatever you do.

Dive Deeper: Study Joel 2; Acts 2:1-22; Romans 8:14.

June 13

TEST THE SPIRITS

1 Thessalonians 5:19-22
"Do not quench the Spirit. [20] Do not treat prophecies with contempt[21] but test them all; hold on to what is good, [22] reject every kind of evil."

1 John 4:1
"Dear friends, do not believe every spirit, but test the spirits to see whether they are from God, because many false prophets have gone out into the world."

One of the manifestation gifts of the Holy Spirit is the "distinguishing of spirits" (1 Corinthians 12:10), and this gift is available to all true believers. The Spirit makes this available to us, but we have to let Him manifest it in us as, and when, He determines we need it (1 Corinthians 12:11).

This is another reason why we must not quench the Spirit, because we are instructed by both Paul and John to test prophecies, and test the spirits, to see whether or not they are from God. False teachings and false prophets abound.

Jesus warned repeatedly in Matthew 24, Mark 13, and Luke 21, that we must be careful not to be deceived in the last days leading up to His return. He said, *"For false messiahs and false prophets will appear and perform great signs and wonders to deceive, if possible, even the elect."*

So, I want to be sure I am among "the elect", don't you? I am convinced we all need the manifestation gift of distinguishing or discernment of spirits.

TODAY'S CHALLENGE:

Tell the Father you want to be able to better discern the spirits of false teaching or false prophecies by the Spirit's manifestation gift. Ask Him to help you learn to listen and obey His Holy Spirit.

Dive Deeper: Study 1 Thessalonians 5; Matthew 24:4-5, 11, 24; Mark 13:5-6, 22; Luke 21:8; 1 Corinthians 12:10-11.

June 14

INSPECT THE FRUIT

Matthew 7:15-17, 20
Jesus said, "Watch out for false prophets. They come to you in sheep's clothing, but inwardly they are ferocious wolves. [16] By their fruit you will recognize them. Do people pick grapes from thorn bushes, or figs from thistles? [17] Likewise, every good tree bears good fruit, but a bad tree bears bad fruit... [20] Thus, by their fruit you will recognize them."

Yesterday we learned about testing the spirits so we are not deceived. Today, we are further warned about false prophets, which I believe includes false teachers and false shepherds.

We must not be taken in by someone's outward appearance, by flattering speech, or by the image they project. On the outside they seem fine, even sincere, but on the inside they might be something else entirely.

Good trees bring forth good fruit, but bad trees bear bad fruit. Jesus wants us to be fruit inspectors. What kind of spiritual fruit is being produced? The fruit of the Spirit is love, joy, peace, patience, kindness, goodness, gentleness, faithfulness and self-control.

We must examine the spiritual fruit being brought forth from those prophets, teachers and shepherds who influence us as Christians. By the power and discernment of the Holy Spirit in us, we will be able to distinguish good and bad fruit.

Anything that does not line up with the Word is false. Jesus told the Father, "Thy word is truth."

TODAY'S CHALLENGE:

Ask the Father for more of His Spiritual discernment so you can judge good fruit from bad fruit. Tell the Holy Spirit you will listen for His prompting today as you cautiously inspect the fruit of those influencing your Christian walk.

Dive Deeper: Study Matthew 7; Galatians 5:22-25; Colossians 3:12-17.

June 15

FALLING IN THE SPIRIT

Revelation 1:17
John wrote of his encounter with Jesus, "When I saw him, I fell at his feet as though dead..."

John 18:6
"When Jesus said, 'I am he,' they drew back and fell to the ground."

Ezekiel 44:4
"...I looked and saw the glory of the LORD filling the temple of the LORD, and I fell facedown."

It does not surprise me that when somebody encounters the presence of the Lord they often fall down. Some may be overwhelmed by His Glory, others may fall to their face in an act of reverence and respect. Still others are overcome by His anointed power.

Here are other instances: Matthew 17:6; Acts 9:4-8; Ezekiel 1:28; 3:23, and 43:3; Daniel 8:17-18; and Daniel 10:8-9. Some fall forward, some fall back. Others may go to their knees.

Sometimes when people go forward for ministry at the end of a service, the anointing of the Presence is so strong they may fall as if fainting. This is sometimes called being "slain in the Spirit" but I don't think that is an actual Biblical term. "Falling under the anointing" seems more accurate to me.

I never believed in this until it happened to me, and it has happened several times, without anyone touching me. My advice is, if you ever fall, stay lying down and let the Spirit minister to you His love, peace and healing.

For some, the personal ministry of the Holy Spirit is received without falling. It is not about falling, but about receiving what the Spirit wants to give you.

TODAY'S CHALLENGE:

Look up all the scriptures referenced above and ask the Holy Spirit to explain their significance.

Dive Deeper: Study Matthew 17:6; Acts 9:4-8; Ezekiel 1:28; 3:23, 43:3; Daniel 8:17-18; 10:8-9.

June 16

DRUNK IN THE SPIRIT

Acts 2:15
"These people are not drunk, as you suppose. It's only nine in the morning!"

Ephesians 5:18-19
"Do not get drunk on wine, which leads to debauchery. Instead, be filled with the Spirit, [19] speaking to one another with psalms, hymns, and songs from the Spirit. Sing and make music from your heart to the Lord..."

At Pentecost, the 120 dedicated, obedient followers of Jesus were so overcome with the power of the Holy Spirit that they acted and sounded like people who were drunk! Most of us have been to parties in our old way of life where there was an overabundance of alcohol. We can all attest that a person definitely behaves and talks differently when they are "under the influence".

Peter assured them these were not drunk in the usual sense of the word, but referred to the last days' prophecy of Joel 2:28-29 (see June 12) indicating that the power of God's Spirit was being poured out. Part of the manifestation was in their speech, but I am certain there were other indications of unusual early morning behavior as well, such as thanking God, praising Him, and singing from the depths of their spirit songs never heard or learned before.

Paul exhorts the Ephesians not to be drunk in the usual sense of the word; rather, instead of being full of alcohol, they should be full of the anointed, powerful Spirit of God. When we are, Paul says, what we are full of will overflow!

TODAY'S CHALLENGE:

Ask the Father to fill you with His anointing that it will overflow to give glory to Him.

Be filled with, and under the influence of, the Spirit today!

Dive Deeper: Study Acts 2:1-22, 32-33; Joel 2:28-29; Isaiah 29:9-10.

June 17

LAUGHTER AND JOY

Romans 14:17
"For the kingdom of God is not a matter of eating and drinking, but of righteousness, peace and joy in the Holy Spirit..."

Psalm 126:2-3
*"Our mouths were filled with laughter, our tongues with songs of joy. Then it was said among the nations, "The Lord has done great things for them."
³ The Lord has done great things for us, and we are filled with joy."*

One of the fruits of the Holy Spirit is joy. True joy spills over into genuine, wholesome laughter. For example, the child of promise, Isaac, means in the Hebrew "he laughs". Sarah was overcome with joy and laughter and declared others would laugh with her (see Genesis 21:3, 6).

One of the Psalms of Hebrew worship, shown above, declared they were filled with laughter and joy when they considered the great works God had done in and for them.

In Romans 14:17, Paul defines the Kingdom of God not having to do with physical activities, but consisting of spiritual qualities resulting from the Holy Spirit – righteousness, peace and joy.

I had heard of "holy laughter" that would sometimes manifest when the anointed power of the Holy Spirit was present, and I didn't quite know what to think. But then I experienced it for real! I could not stop the joyous laughter that was spilling uncontrollably from me. I left that service more refreshed than I had been in many years. Sometimes, laughter really is the best medicine!

TODAY'S CHALLENGE:

Spend time alone in the presence of the Father considering all the great things He has done. You will feel true joy rising up. You might even laugh out-loud!

Dive Deeper: Study Romans 14; 1 Thessalonians 5:16-18; Philippians 4:4; John 16:24; Psalm 118:24; Proverbs 17:22; Isaiah 55:12; Isaiah 61:3; Psalm 33:21; Proverbs 10:28.

June 18

TREMBLING AND TERROR

Daniel 8:17
"As he came near the place where I was standing, I was terrified and fell prostrate."

Matthew 17:6
"When the disciples heard this, they fell facedown to the ground, terrified."

Matthew 28:4
"The guards were so afraid of him that they shook and became like dead men."

Being in the very close proximity to the Holiness and Power of God can fill us with terror.

In Matthew 17:6 above, the Greek word translated as "terrified" has different meanings depending on the context. For example, it can mean to fear, to be afraid, or alarmed; which are contexts that are an impediment, or hindrance, to faith and love. In other contexts, it means to reverence, respect or worship; which indicates a proper fear of God. I recommend you read Daniel 10:7-11 where you will see the effects of the Presence of the Angel of the Lord on some men with Daniel, and on Daniel himself.

Depending upon where one perceives they stand with God, they may be fearful, afraid or alarmed; and even run and hide. These, I think, would be natural reactions of unbelievers. True believers, however, may shake, tremble and fall to their knees, but I suspect it would be more out of reverence, respect and worship; perhaps even physical weakness in the face of great power.

In services where the power of God fell among the people, I have personally seen both sets of reactions. I fell to my knees, bowed myself as low as I could, and worshiped.

TODAY'S CHALLENGE:

Consider how you will react when confronted with His Anointed Presence.

Dive Deeper: Study Matthew 28.

June 19

SPEECHLESS

Luke 1:22
"When he came out, he could not speak to them. They realized he had seen a vision in the temple, for he kept making signs to them but remained unable to speak."

Ezekiel 3:26
"I will make your tongue stick to the roof of your mouth so that you will be silent and unable to rebuke them, for they are a rebellious people."

Daniel 10:15-17
"While he was saying this to me, I bowed with my face toward the ground and was speechless. [16] Then one who looked like a man touched my lips, and I opened my mouth and began to speak. I said to the one standing before me, 'I am overcome with anguish because of the vision, my lord, and I feel very weak. [17] How can I, your servant, talk with you, my lord? My strength is gone and I can hardly breathe.'"

There are times in our lives when something happens and we are left speechless. Certainly, in the Presence of God we are likely to be speechless for a time as I am sure we will be overcome with the Majesty and Beauty of our Loving King.

I can be pretty talkative, especially about God. Yet, there are times when I am overcome with thankfulness and adoration for Him saving someone like the very ungodly person I once was, and I don't know how to express my feelings in normal speech. In times like these, I utilize my prayer language in prayer and praise. The Spirit knows how to pray and praise for me. See Romans 8:26-28.

TODAY'S CHALLENGE:

If you don't have a heaven-sent love and prayer language, ask our Father. See Luke 11:11-13.

Dive Deeper: Study Daniel 8; Luke 11:11-13; Romans 8:26-28; Jude 1:20-21.

June 20

WEEPING

Hebrews 5:7
"During the days of Jesus' life on earth, he offered up prayers and petitions with fervent cries and tears to the one who could save him from death, and he was heard because of his reverent submission."

Matthew 26:75
"Then Peter remembered the word Jesus had spoken: 'Before the rooster crows, you will disown me three times.' And he went outside and wept bitterly."

Revelation 5:4
"I wept and wept because no one was found who was worthy to open the scroll or look inside."

As boys, we most likely heard someone say, "Real men don't cry". We were taught to hold in our emotions, especially sadness, anger or pain; and, we might have been subject to great embarrassment or ridicule if we broke down. Even if we were alone, we subjected ourselves to self-condemnation.

There is no calculating how much damage has been done in our families, or society in general, by the fact that men will not express their most tender of emotions in weeping.

There is something about the anointing and presence of God after salvation that brings tears of joy and thankfulness as we focus on His Goodness towards us. Sometimes there may be tears of regret when we consider how we used to be before being saved and transformed.

I am not ashamed of my tears. When I consider the passages today, three men I deeply admire and respect were overcome with weeping. These were the strongest of men.

TODAY'S CHALLENGE:

Express your emotions to your Father. Don't be ashamed to cry. You are in good company.

Dive Deeper: Study Matthew 26; Mark 14:72; John 11:35; John 20:11.

June 21

TRAVELING BY THE SPIRIT

Acts 8:39-40
"When they came up out of the water, the Spirit of the Lord suddenly took Philip away, and the eunuch did not see him again, but went on his way rejoicing. ⁴⁰ Philip, however, appeared at Azotus and traveled about, preaching the gospel..."

2 Corinthians 12:2-4
"I know a man in Christ who... was caught up to the third heaven. Whether it was in the body or out of the body I do not know—God knows. ³ And I know that this man... ⁴ was caught up to paradise and heard inexpressible things, things that no one is permitted to tell."

Revelation 4:1-2
"After this I looked, and there before me was a door standing open in heaven. And the voice I had first heard speaking to me like a trumpet said, "Come up here, and I will show you what must take place after this." ² At once I was in the Spirit, and there before me was a throne in heaven with someone sitting on it."

Apparently the Power of God the Holy Spirit sometimes supernaturally transports people for His purposes. Luke describes in the Acts passage something which appears to involve what we would now describe as "tele-transportation" of his entire body.

Paul wasn't sure whether he was transported, or caught up, to Heaven physically in his body, or just spiritually. John, in Revelation describes what may have only happened in the Spirit. Would recent terms for this include an "out-of-body experience"?

Isn't it interesting that recent cultic, "new age" beliefs (which I believe are demonic) are only now describing what some Christians experienced 2,000 years ago?

TODAY'S CHALLENGE:

Study today's passages in context. Ask the Holy Spirit for His insight.

Dive Deeper: Study Ezekiel 3:14; 8:3; 11:24; 2 Corinthians 12:1-6.

June 22

FIRE AND THE SPIRIT

Hebrews 12:29
"for our 'God is a consuming fire.'"

Acts 2:3
"They saw what seemed to be tongues of fire that separated and came to rest on each of them."

Luke 3:16
"...He will baptize you with the Holy Spirit and fire."

The Bible has many other references tying together fire with the Spirit of God, or the Angel of the Lord. For example, you could also check out: Exodus 3:2; 24:17, 40:38; Leviticus 9:24.

See also what Paul writes in 1 Thessalonians 5:12-22 where it implies, in verse 19, that we can diminish the fire of the Holy Spirit in our lives by failing in Christian actions and speech.

The word "Fire" brings to mind many different things including power, purity, holiness, destruction, warmth, security, heat, illumination, flame, protection, renewal, enthusiasm, and zeal. Certainly the Holy Spirit of God can be related to many of these same words, and can personalize several of them for us in our Christian lives.

Have you experienced the Holy Spirit's purity, power, security, illumination, protection, renewal, enthusiasm and zeal? Has He refined your life by burning away some of your old trash in His ongoing work of sanctification in you? Have you personally felt the fire of the Holy Ghost Baptism?

TODAY'S CHALLENGE:

Tell your Father you want to better understand the symbols of fire associated with His Glory and His Holy Spirit.

Dive Deeper: Study Exodus 3:1-6, 24:17, 40:38; Leviticus 9:24; 1 Thessalonians 5:12-22.

June 23

DEATH AND LIFE

Romans 6:23
"For the wages of sin is death, but the gift of God is eternal life in Christ Jesus our Lord."

For most of my life, I worked hard for the devil for wages that I now know lead only to death. Can you relate?

Have you too been deceived by the enemy into seeking fulfillment in everything he could throw your way, finally realizing that none of it really mattered?

Think about this. Serving the world, the flesh and the devil is really hard work. The "rewards" are always temporary, and never fully satisfying. One is always left feeling a little cheated, a little more lost, and still alone. A person feels like the next raise, the next hit, the next sexual encounter, or the next illicit thrill, will be "the one", but invariably, it isn't.

Hopelessness, depression and despair are always lurking in our minds, and only self-medication can keep us from thinking about how poor we really are, and how little we hang on to, from our wages from sin. But the effects of self-medication are fleeting too.

Finally, in a prison bed, I came to the end of myself and cried out to God to rescue me. I had been a walking dead man far too long. If there was true life in Him, I wanted it. I no longer worked or strived, I simply received the Gift in faith.

TODAY'S CHALLENGE:

Tell the Father you will receive His Gift of salvation and eternal life through His Son, Jesus. Ask the Holy Spirit to fill the former emptiness inside with the unconditional love, and complete acceptance, found only in the Father.

Have you received His Gift?

Dive Deeper: Study Romans 6.

June 24

CHRIST LIVES IN ME

Galatians 2:20
"I have been crucified with Christ and I no longer live, but Christ lives in me. The life I now live in the body, I live by faith in the Son of God, who loved me and gave himself for me."

Read this verse again slowly, and really think about what it says. At first it seems contradictory and nonsensical. Yet, there is marvelous truth that can be experienced increasingly daily if we will begin to think this way.

Paul tells us elsewhere that we should consider our "old man" to be dead (Romans 6:11), and that we are "new creations" in Christ Jesus. We are to remember that old things have passed away, and all things have become new (2 Corinthians 5:17).

We are to consider ourselves as having been crucified with Christ, and that we too were raised from the dead with Him in a new life. The Spirit of Christ now lives in us, the Holy Spirit. He wants to live His Life through us. The One Who loved us so much He gave Himself for us wants to express His new life in and through us!

If we live in daily surrender and submission to His Spirit in us, and we are dedicated to obedience to His promptings, we are really living and walking by faith.

This scripture is a marvelous truth worth memorizing and confessing daily!

TODAY'S CHALLENGE:

Ask the Father to help you more fully realize the truths expressed in our verse of scripture today. Write down this verse, and carry it with you today to meditate upon. Work on memorizing it.

Dive Deeper: Study Galatians 2; Romans 6:11; 2 Corinthians 5:17-21.

June 25

A NEW CREATION

2 Corinthians 5:17, AMP
"Therefore if any person is [ingrafted] in Christ (the Messiah) he is a new creation (a new creature altogether); the old [previous moral and spiritual condition] has passed away. Behold, the fresh and new has come!"

Have you been grafted into the Tree of Life in Christ Jesus?

As I considered this in my own life, I envisioned that I had previously been a wild branch on the tree of death, or the tree of knowledge of good and evil. I had been trained up to do good, but the more I learned and practiced evil, the more it destroyed me. I was dying and useless.

Was this you too?

But I learned from Paul, in Romans 11:17-24, how we were grafted in to Christ through faith. When we are grafted into Christ, everything associated with our past is gone, and we are provided new life totally from the Source of Life itself, that is, Christ. See also John 15:1-8.

God's answer to the condition of a sinful man is not to try to improve him slowly over time. Rather, God kills the old man, and resurrects a totally new creation, one that never existed before.

In God's eyes, we are instantly made new in Christ Jesus. In Christ we have access to a totally new way of living in freedom, and we do not have to continue to be in bondage to our past. However, we experience this freedom daily only as we allow ourselves to be led by the Spirit.

TODAY'S CHALLENGE:

Tell the Father how much you appreciate having the opportunity for a totally new life in Christ. Ask the Holy Spirit to teach you how to make this verse ever more true in your daily experience.

Are you a new creation?

Dive Deeper: Study 2 Corinthians 5; Romans 11:17-24; John 15:1-8.

June 26

BE SET FREE

John 8:34-36

"Jesus replied, 'Very truly I tell you, everyone who sins is a slave to sin. [35] Now a slave has no permanent place in the family, but a son belongs to it forever. [36] So if the Son sets you free, you will be free indeed.'"

Before I truly gave my heart and life to Christ, it seemed I could not do anything but sin. Occasionally, I made a meager attempt to do a kind and loving unselfish act, but afterwards I realized I had a sinful motive or attitude in doing it.

No matter how often I tried, or how much I wished I could be different, I felt hopeless, helpless, and trapped. I was a slave to sin, and I thought nothing would ever change.

This led to the very dark bondage of suicidal depression. I was homeless and unemployed. I didn't feel as if I mattered. I was a loner, and belonged to nothing and no-one except sin and the devil.

Others around me could not help me; they were slaves too. Our master, the devil, was not interested in setting anyone free.

But when I came to know the Son, I learned He defeated my old master. He had the power to set me free. He had the will for me to be free as He proved in His sacrificial death. In His victorious resurrection, He conquered sin and led long-held captives free forever.

I was one of them. Have you been set free by the Son?

TODAY'S CHALLENGE:

Thank the Father for making a way through Jesus for you to be part of God's family forever. Ask the Holy Spirit to help you walk in freedom today from all past bondages.

Dive Deeper: Study John 8.

June 27

COME TO YOUR SENSES

Luke 15:17-20
"When he came to his senses, he said, 'How many of my father's hired servants have food to spare, and here I am starving to death! [18] *I will set out and go back to my father and say to him: Father, I have sinned against heaven and against you.* [19] *I am no longer worthy to be called your son; make me like one of your hired servants.'* [20] *So he got up and went to his father..."*

One of my favorite Bible chapters is Luke 15. I can really identify with the lost sheep, and the lost coin. I especially see myself in the wayward prodigal son. I recommend you re-read the entire chapter. With which part do you most identify?

Like most of us, the prodigal son thought he knew best how to run his own life. He left his family and, I suppose, went off to "find himself". For a while, he was living it up with his new friends, but when his money ran out, his "friends" were nowhere to be found. Is this beginning to sound personally familiar?

As a Jew, he was never to be around pigs, but the only job he could find was slopping the hogs, so now he had also abandoned his faith. It was here that he finally came to his senses.

He knew he still had a home, so in true repentance he made a decision to turn back, humbled himself, and asked forgiveness. His father lovingly received him, no questions asked.

TODAY'S CHALLENGE:

Tell the Father you realize you have made many mistakes, but you are ready to repent and come home. He loves you. He's been patiently waiting to welcome you.

Dive Deeper: Study Luke 15; Psalm 34:18, 51:17.

June 28

CALL UPON THE LORD

Psalm 118:5, AMP
"Out of my distress I called upon the Lord; the Lord answered me and set me free and in a large place.'"

As I read this verse, it occurs to me that we cannot be set free unless we call upon the Lord. Unfortunately, most people do not call upon the Lord until they are in a place of severe distress, and have exhausted everything else they can think of to try to set themselves free. That would be me. You too?

A place of distress is often one of captivity or bondage. It is usually very restrictive in the sense that there seems to be no escape. This could be a physical prison, or some other emotional bondage like addiction or depression.

I went to prison one time, late in life, but I had been in emotional bondage for years. I had been in great distress for quite some time due to bi-polar illness, homelessness, unemployment, suicidal depression, depravity, perversion, pride, greed, and drug addictions. But until I went to prison I was too proud to call upon the Lord.

On my bunk, ten months into my sentence, I finally got real with myself, and with God. I told Him, "I realize I'm not doing such a hot job of running my own life, look where I ended up! God, please help me. If you can do anything with my life now, I will serve you with all of my heart for all of my days." The Lord answered me and set me free!

TODAY'S CHALLENGE:

From your own personal place of distress today, call upon the Lord. Tell Him you want to be free.

Dive Deeper: Study Psalm 118; Jeremiah 33:3; Psalm 40:1-5; Psalm 34:4.

June 29

NO WATER, ONLY MUD

Jeremiah 38:6
"So they took Jeremiah and put him into the cistern... They lowered Jeremiah by ropes into the cistern; it had no water in it, only mud, and Jeremiah sank down into the mud."

Even a committed, true believer is not exempt from trouble. Sometimes life circumstances put us in a place from which we can see no relief or escape. It is times like these that really test our faith.

Perhaps others brought us to this place merely by us being in the wrong place at the wrong time. Their poor choices and/or sin impacted us as well as them. Or maybe our own lapse of judgment took us down the wrong path that ended in a very difficult place.

Other times, through no apparent fault of our own, we find ourselves in what we view as a hopeless situation, and we feel helpless to do anything about it. Regardless of how we got there, we need to be rescued.

Jeremiah was a dedicated servant of the Lord and one of God's most reliable prophets to His people, Israel. He had been proclaiming the Word of the Lord as he had been instructed, but it was not a popular message. Sometimes, people don't really like hearing the truth.

Jeremiah did not give up, and did not turn away from God. God knew his situation and used a former enemy to pull him out of the pit not long before he would have died.

Wherever the difficult place is you are now, don't give up. Stay true to God, He will pull you out.

TODAY'S CHALLENGE:

Tell God your only hope lies in Him. Call out to him today in faith.

Dive Deeper: Study Jeremiah 38; James 1:2-5, 12; John 16:33; Romans 5:3-5; Romans 8:35-39; 1 Peter 1:6-9; 1 Peter 4:12-14; 2 Corinthians 1:3-7; 11:23-27.

June 30

SOWING AND REAPING

Galatians 6:7-8
"Do not be deceived: God cannot be mocked. A man reaps what he sows. ⁸ Whoever sows to please their flesh, from the flesh will reap destruction; whoever sows to please the Spirit, from the Spirit will reap eternal life."

God does not change. The word we use for this attribute of God is "immutable". Similarly, God has laws He set in place that do not change. One of these is the law of sowing and reaping.

In this scripture today, Paul says there are reliably natural consequences to our actions, and we cannot fool God into changing them no matter how smart or clever we think we are.

For example, if a farmer sows corn into the ground, he can never expect to harvest potatoes instead of corn. Similarly, apple seeds sown yield apple trees, and eventually apples will be reaped, not oranges.

In the past, many of us have sown fleshly acts to please our own lusts and desires, and we have reaped plenty of heartache and destruction back not only upon ourselves, but upon our loved ones as well. Bad decisions always have bad consequences; maybe not at first, but it is eventually inevitable.

The good news is that this law works the same way if we are sowing good decisions guided by the Spirit of God into our lives and the lives of others. We will always get good spiritual results.

What have you been sowing recently?

TODAY'S CHALLENGE:

Tell the Father you want to sow good seed into good ground. Ask the Holy Spirit to help you evaluate the seed you've been planting.

Dive Deeper: Study Galatians 6; Matthew 13:1-23.

July 1

CHASING AFTER THE WIND

Ecclesiastes 2:10-11
"I denied myself nothing my eyes desired; I refused my heart no pleasure. My heart took delight in all my labor, and this was the reward for all my toil. ¹¹ Yet when I surveyed all that my hands had done and what I had toiled to achieve, everything was meaningless, a chasing after the wind; nothing was gained under the sun."

Today's passage was written late in life by Solomon, reported to be one of the wisest men in the world during his day. He was also one of the richest men of his time, perhaps even for all time.

Although he started out with a heart dedicated to the One True God, Jehovah, over time he was influenced by his many wives and concubines to honor the gods of their pagan ancestors and former countries. Material riches, and his own importance in the eyes of others, became more important to Solomon than the God of Israel.

Having once been, in the world's eyes, at the top of the ladder of success, these verses really struck me as so very true in my own personal experience. Although I was raised in a Christian home by both parents, I turned my back on God as pride, money and self-importance took His place.

By the time I reached prison, and I took an honest review of my life, I too came to the conclusion that a life without God as the priority resulted in "everything was meaningless, a chasing after the wind, nothing was gained…"

"But God…" Life now has meaning. I have a Kingdom purpose. God is solidly on the throne of my life forever. The wind of the Holy Spirit has caught me!

TODAY'S CHALLENGE:

Tell God you will make Him your priority today. Take an honest look at your life.

Dive Deeper: Study Ecclesiastes 2:1-26, 12:13-14.

July 2

FUTILE THINKING

Romans 1:21-22
"For although they knew God, they neither glorified him as God nor gave thanks to him, but their thinking became futile and their foolish hearts were darkened. ²² Although they claimed to be wise, they became fools..."

I am pretty sure you personally know well at least one person who grew up knowing God and trying to structure their lives on His principles. Then, somewhere in their journey towards God and Heaven, they made a U-turn and went their own way. Maybe that person is you? Certainly it was me. See Isaiah 53:6.

So many people fall in the category Paul was describing in today's passage. When I went to college, I turned away from God and set out on my own figuring I could run my own life. I stopped recognizing the many blessings and talents I had as having come from Him, and began taking credit for everything myself.

As we pursue our own ways, we journey further into sin and our own hearts are darkened. The Light of God we once knew grows dimmer and dimmer, reduced to only a flicker of what it once was. Pride and worldly knowledge take the place of Biblical wisdom we once knew and applied to our lives; and, although we considered ourselves wise in the ways of the world, we became fools.

Often it takes a series of failures, leading to a very dark place, for us to finally wake up to the everlasting Goodness and unconditional Love of our Father in Heaven. For me, the Light finally penetrated the darkness of my heart on a prison bunk.

TODAY'S CHALLENGE:

Ask the Father to send the Light of Jesus into your heart by His Holy Spirit.

Dive Deeper: Study Romans 1; Isaiah 53:6.

July 3

EXCHANGING TRUTH FOR A LIE

Romans 1:24-25
"Therefore God gave them over in the sinful desires of their hearts to sexual impurity for the degrading of their bodies with one another.[25] *They exchanged the truth about God for a lie, and worshiped and served created things rather than the Creator—who is forever praised. Amen."*

Each of us has been given free will to make our own decisions. God does not force Himself upon His created ones.

But a seed of rebellion was planted in each of us from our ancestors in the Garden, so pretty much all of us try to do life our own way instead of God's way. So often, we succumb to the ever increasing temptations of the world, the flesh and the devil; and, a little is never enough. Can you relate?

The truth is God wants what is best for us, and He patiently waits for us to return to Him. But, similar to the serpent's implication to Eve that God was withholding something good from her, we fall into the trap of believing the lie of the enemy that what the world offers us in material things and sexual enticement is better.

Having once traveled very far down that same road, I can now attest to the truth that God is Supremely Good, and He has much better things awaiting us when we repent and return to Him with all of our heart.

TODAY'S CHALLENGE:

Talk to the Father about your desire to have the best He has for you through your faith in Jesus. Ask the Holy Spirit to lead you today in the path of God's perfect will for your life.

Follow Him.

Dive Deeper: Study Romans 1; John 14:6; Luke 15:11-24; Isaiah 53:6.

July 4

STAND FIRM FOR FREEDOM

Galatians 5:1
"It is for freedom that Christ has set us free. Stand firm, then, and do not let yourselves be burdened again by a yoke of slavery."

One of the biggest lies of the enemy is that there is total freedom in serving the devil because "anything goes". In fact, "Do as thou wilt" is the Luciferian motto of secular humanists worldwide.

The truth takes a while to dawn on us, if it ever does, but "doing our own thing" results in bondages of every kind. We become enslaved to the very things we thought would help us live free. Eventually, we are imprisoned by lust, materialism, pride, selfishness, addictions, greed and many other things, as we pursue "freedom" to be who we want to be. Does this sound familiar to you?

I too was enslaved to sin, and experienced many different forms of bondage. What Good News it was when I learned that Jesus paid a price to purchase my freedom from sin so that, if I made the choice to be free from the power of sin, I could turn and follow Him. Instead of being an unwilling slave to sin, I could choose to be a voluntary servant of righteousness.

I am learning to re-submit and re-commit daily to the Lordship of Jesus, and the Leadership of the Holy Spirit, so that I will not "let myself be burdened again by a yoke of slavery." Are you determined to stay free?

TODAY'S CHALLENGE:

Tell the Father how much you appreciate freedom in Christ Jesus. Ask the Holy Spirit to point out any remaining bondages, and choose to turn from them and live free today.

Stand firm for freedom.

Dive Deeper: Study Galatians 5; 2 Corinthians 3:17; 1 Peter 2:16; Isaiah 61:1; Romans 6:1-2, 7, 11, 18; Romans 8:1-4; John 8:31-32, 36.

July 5

GOD GAVE THEM OVER

Romans 1:24, 26, 28
"Therefore God gave them over in the sinful desires of their hearts to sexual impurity... [26] Because of this, God gave them over to shameful lusts... [28] Furthermore, just as they did not think it worthwhile to retain the knowledge of God, so God gave them over to a depraved mind..."

Have you ever noticed Paul's emphasis that "God gave them over"? Three times in five verses Paul stressed that God gives men the free will to decide the course of their lives, but there are always increasingly worse consequences.

I suggest you read the entire passage of Romans 1:18-32. If your Bible had pictures, mine would be there in that very passage as the poster child of that lifestyle.

My own steady, downward spiral into reprobation, perversion and depravity started when, similar to verse 21, I refused any longer to acknowledge God. He let me have my way. He gave me over to the sinful desires of my heart to every kind of sexual impurity as stated in verse 24; the shameful lusts described in verse 27; and, depraved, perverted thoughts of every kind leading to the lifestyle enumerated in verse 29-31. As verse 32 states, I even took pleasure in seeing others do the same things. I am not exaggerating.

"But God..."! Oh, how very thankful I am that regardless of how far I fell, or how long I stayed there, God was ready to receive me home when I came to Jesus for forgiveness in true repentance.

TODAY'S CHALLENGE:

Thank the Father that what He does for one He will do for all. If you haven't yet done so, today would be a great day to turn around.

Repent. Receive His unconditional love and forgiveness.

Dive Deeper: Study Romans 1:18-32; Luke 15:11-24.

July 6

WITHOUT HOPE AND WITHOUT GOD

Ephesians 2:12
"...remember that at that time you were separate from Christ, excluded from citizenship in Israel and foreigners to the covenants of the promise, without hope and without God in the world."

Although there are many very unpleasant and disgusting memories, sometimes I intentionally think about my life before Christ while I was still separate from Him.

I remember the absolute hopelessness, and the abject despair of my circumstances, and the fact I was completely convinced nothing would ever get better. In fact, I was in constant fear everything would get worse, and it did.

I cringe when I think about my formerly filthy and blasphemous language. I start to feel shame again for my sexually immoral lifestyle. My heart starts to grieve again for the despicable ways I treated people, especially my family and friends.

Surely I was a picture of what it meant to be "without hope and without God." Can you see yourself here too? Oh, brothers and sisters in Christ, how glorious it is to be totally forgiven, forever accepted, and unconditionally loved. How very wonderful it is to be filled with joy, peace, and especially hope!

Paul wrote, *"May the God of hope fill you with all joy and peace as you trust in him, so that you may overflow with hope by the power of the Holy Spirit."* Romans 15:13

Are you still without hope and without God? Come to Christ.

TODAY'S CHALLENGE:

Ask the God of Hope to fill you once again with joy and peace so that you may overflow with hope by the power of the Holy Spirit. Tell Him you want to be His child forever. Trust in Him.

Dive Deeper: Study Ephesians 2; Romans 5:6-10.

July 7

STILL A SON

Luke 15:20-24

"So he got up and went to his father. But while he was still a long way off, his father saw him and was filled with compassion for him; he ran to his son, threw his arms around him and kissed him. ²¹ The son said to him, 'Father, I have sinned against heaven and against you. I am no longer worthy to be called your son.' ²² But the father said to his servants, 'Quick! Bring the best robe and put it on him. Put a ring on his finger and sandals on his feet. ²³ Bring the fattened calf and kill it. Let's have a feast and celebrate. ²⁴ For this son of mine was dead and is alive again; he was lost and is found.'"

After the prodigal son finally came to his senses, he turned around and started home. I love how Jesus said, "his father saw him while he was still a long way off and was filled with compassion for him."

The son was welcomed home, not as a servant who would have to work for acceptance; but still as the son he was, and never stopped being, fully restored to the father by grace in love.

The robe represents righteousness. The ring represents authority. Shoes represent son-ship, not servanthood. Immediate acceptance and restoration. What a marvelous act of grace, mercy and love on the father's part.

Our Heavenly Father is the same way. And I am so very thankful He saw me while I was still a long way off. Is He still looking for you?

TODAY'S CHALLENGE:

Thank the Father for accepting you as a son or daughter. Think about His mercy and love towards you.

Welcome home. Don't wander off.

Dive Deeper: Study Luke 15.

July 8

OUT OF THE SLIMY PIT

Psalm 40:1-3
*"I waited patiently for the L*ORD*; he turned to me and heard my cry. ² He lifted me out of the slimy pit, out of the mud and mire; he set my feet on a rock and gave me a firm place to stand. ³ He put a new song in my mouth, a hymn of praise to our God. Many will see and fear the L*ORD *and put their trust in him."*

When we finally admit to ourselves that we are at our lowest point, and we are trapped with no way out, it is there and then that our genuine cry for help from God will be heard.

Until a person realizes they are drowning they don't cry out for help. A person has to know they are lost before they desire to be found.

It doesn't matter how far you have fallen, or how hopelessly mired down you are in sin and circumstances, God is able to reach down and lift you out.

He doesn't just pull you out and abandon you, He cleans you up by His Holy Spirit. He sets your feet firmly on the Rock, Who is Christ, where you are able to stand firmly on the Word! You are restored to His original plan for your life.

In your gratitude, you will give Him praise through your testimony to others, so that many will see Him, reverently admire His awesomeness, and put their trust in Him!

Join me in proclaiming, "God is Good!"

TODAY'S CHALLENGE:

Tell the Father how grateful you are for Him pulling you up out of your own deep, muddy, miry pit. Ask the Holy Spirit to help you share your testimony today.

Dive Deeper: Study Psalm 40.

July 9

DELIGHT IN WEAKNESSES

2 Corinthians 12:9-10
"But he said to me, 'My grace is sufficient for you, for my power is made perfect in weakness.' Therefore, I will boast all the more gladly about my weaknesses, so that Christ's power may rest on me. ¹⁰ That is why, for Christ's sake, I delight in weaknesses, in insults, in hardships, in persecutions, in difficulties. For when I am weak, then I am strong."

In this world, and especially in prison, there are predators looking for signs of weakness in potential prey. So, in the natural, we try to hide our weaknesses, often even to ourselves. Therefore, at first glance, today's verses seem nonsensical.

Whether in the free world or confined, Christians still learn to protect themselves from predatory behavior, and sometimes we need to come together and stand up for one another.

However, in the spiritual realm as we advance in the Kingdom, admitting our weaknesses is crucial. Pride works against us, but we must realize apart from Christ we can do nothing (John 15:5). In humility, recognizing an area of life where we struggle is the first step for inviting the strength of the God to take over by His Holy Spirit.

Realizing "by myself I can do nothing" (John 5:30) is the best place I can be as moldable clay in the Potter's Hands; or as a surrendered, submitted vessel for God's use for special purposes (2 Timothy 2:20-21). The more I step back, the more He steps up. I need Him!

TODAY'S CHALLENGE:

Tell the Father you realize He wants to work in and through you. Ask the Holy Spirit to show you any areas where you have not recognized a need for His strength in your weakness.

Be strong. Acknowledge weakness.

Dive Deeper: Study 2 Corinthians 12; John 15:5; John 5:30; 2 Timothy 2:20-21.

July 10

EARNESTLY SEEK HIM

Hebrews 11:6
"And without faith it is impossible to please God, because anyone who comes to him must believe that he exists and that he rewards those who earnestly seek him."

I was raised up going to church, but when I went to college I turned my back to God and pretty much went my own way for most of the next 40 years. The only real faith I had was in myself, and I was not trying to please God, only people. Have you done this too?

Although I achieved quite a measure of worldly success, and was fortunate to have a wonderful wife and infant son, I never gave God any credit for how He had blessed me. Although I confessed that I knew God, I lived as if He didn't exist.

Out of pride, I foolishly abandoned everybody from my previous life to begin a new career in Nashville's music industry. I failed miserably, and lost everything. Faith in myself was no longer possible. Pleasing people in Nashville was beyond impossible.

It took a few years, but when I finally reached bottom, and put aside my pride, I cried out to God. I always believed He existed, but out of desperation at the end of my rope, I came to Him. He did not turn me away.

I began to seek Him with all my heart, and my desire to know Him better has only increased over time. It is very true in my life that He rewards those who earnestly and diligently seek Him.

TODAY'S CHALLENGE:

Tell the Father you are placing all your faith in Him. Ask the Holy Spirit to teach you how to follow hard after God, and earnestly seek Him today.

Dive Deeper: Study Hebrews 11; Lamentations 3:19-26; Jeremiah 29:11-14; Acts 17:26-28; Deuteronomy 4:29-31; Psalm 9:9-10; Proverbs 8:17; Proverbs 2:1-5.

July 11

KNOWLEDGE OF THE HOLY

Proverbs 9:10
"The fear of the Lord is the beginning of wisdom, and knowledge of the Holy One is understanding."

In prison, not too long after I gave my life to Christ, on the table in the day room where everyone knows books left there are "up for grabs", I found a very tattered, thin, pocket-size paperback that has become my favorite book. It is <u>Knowledge of the Holy</u>, by A.W. Tozer.

Reverend Tozer writes short but very compelling chapters covering each of twenty major attributes of God. The primary verse for his book is today's scripture.

The fear of the Lord is often misunderstood. The more we seek Him with all our heart, the more we begin to learn and appreciate some of His most marvelous attributes. In so doing, our awe, reverence, love and respect for our Almighty God begins to increase dramatically. This fear of the Lord is the prerequisite to beginning to learn the wisdom of God.

Man's wisdom is no comparison to the wisdom of God. It is child's play. Foolishness. Yet, God in His grace has revealed some of His wisdom in His Word; and, Jesus became for us wisdom from God (1 Corinthians 1:30).

If we desire with all our heart to know God, He reveals more of His nature to us. He is Holy. We are not. We must start with that. As we begin to know the Holy One, we start to acquire true understanding.

I pray regularly for the fear of the Lord, wisdom, knowledge and understanding.

TODAY'S CHALLENGE:

Ask the Father to help you seek wisdom though a proper fear of the Lord; and lead you to more knowledge and understanding of His Holiness.

Dive Deeper: Study Proverbs 9; 1 Corinthians 1:30; Ephesians 3:10-11; Colossians 2:2-3.

July 12

MEDITATE ON THE WORD

Psalm 1:1-3
"Blessed is the one who does not walk in step with the wicked or stand in the way that sinners take or sit in the company of mockers, ² but whose delight is in the law of the LORD, and who meditates on his law day and night. ³ That person is like a tree planted by streams of water, which yields its fruit in season and whose leaf does not wither — whatever they do prospers."

I believe today's scripture reveals two of the secrets to consistently living the abundant quality of life Jesus came to give us (John 10:10). The first is, delight daily in God's Word and meditate on it continuously. The second is, surround yourself only with people who do the same.

When I consider the promises in verse 3, for those who meet the preceding requirements, I picture a large, healthy tree whose roots are sunk down deep into fertile ground extending out underneath the riverbed itself. The water from the stream would be constantly feeding the roots, keeping it in good health, enabling it to produce the fruit God designed for it, and supporting leaves that never even wilt.

This is like the provision, fruit, plan and endurance God has for those who are fully committed and dedicated to seeking Him and His Word daily. In so doing, they wisely choose their friends, and they prosper in everything they do. The favor of God surrounds them as a shield (Psalm 5:12).

TODAY'S CHALLENGE:

Tell the Father you desire to delight in His Word; and, you want it to soak deep within your spirit and soul. Ask the Holy Spirit to help you wisely choose companions.

Meditate on today's verses.

Dive Deeper: Study Psalm 1; John 10:10; Psalm 5:12.

July 13

THE DESTINATION

John 14:6
"Jesus answered, 'I am the way and the truth and the life. No one comes to the Father except through me.'"

As I consider this scripture, I am convinced Jesus is the one and only way to a particular destination; and, the destination is the Father. Truth and Life reside in Him. Jesus, the Son, perfectly represents and reveals the Father.

Jesus was responding to a question from Thomas about the way to where He was going. Thomas wanted to know the destination. Jesus did not say the destination was Heaven; rather, He emphasized that the primary destination was not a location, but a Person, the Father!

In the Old Testament, God had been revealed as Provider, Protector, Judge, Healer, Avenger, and Shepherd, as well as other roles; but, He was not revealed as "Father". His people, Israel, did not know Him in this way.

When Jesus came as the Son, He could introduce God as "Father". Jesus many times said things like, "I and the Father are One", "If you've seen me you've seen the Father', "I only do what I see the Father do, and I only say what I hear the Father say."

Jesus came to restore us to relationship to the Father – the same intimate relationship Adam and Eve had. Jesus is Truth. He is Life. And He is the only Way to Father God!

If you died today, are you certain of your destination?

TODAY'S CHALLENGE:

Thank the Father for His Son, Jesus. Ask the Holy Spirit to help you better comprehend the love and character of the Father. The Spirit will point you to Jesus. He reveals the Father.

He is a Good, Good Father.

Dive Deeper: Study John 14.

July 14

FRUIT OF THE FLESH

Galatians 5:16, 19-21
"So I say, walk by the Spirit, and you will not gratify the desires of the flesh... [19] The acts of the flesh are obvious: sexual immorality, impurity and debauchery; [20] idolatry and witchcraft; hatred, discord, jealousy, fits of rage, selfish ambition, dissensions, factions [21] and envy; drunkenness, orgies, and the like. I warn you, as I did before, that those who live like this will not inherit the kingdom of God."

We often teach and share about the fruit of the Spirit; for example, see April 30 and June 2.

However, before revealing the fruit of the Spirit, Paul first describes the "acts of the flesh", or we could say the "fruit of the flesh" (in contrast with Galatians 5:22-23).

Having been led by "the flesh" for the greatest part of my life, I already had a great deal of familiarity with most everything Paul lists here. In fact, Paul says they are obvious. If I didn't have Paul's list, I imagine I could have named many of these from personal experience. Couldn't you?

We have spent plenty of years serving the world, the flesh, and the devil. The ways of the world and the desires of the flesh just come naturally when we serve the devil instead of God.

After we choose to serve God, the Holy Spirit brings forth the right kind of fruit to benefit us and the Kingdom. Anyone who has truly repented will no longer regularly produce this "fruit of the flesh" because they do not continue to practice sin (1 John 5:18).

TODAY'S CHALLENGE:

Tell the Father you repent from the previous acts of the flesh. Ask the Spirit for His fruit.

Dive Deeper: Study Galatians 5; 1 John 5:18; 2 Timothy 3:1-5; Galatians 6:7-10.

July 15

PRESS ON

Philippians 3:13-14
"Brothers and sisters, I do not consider myself yet to have taken hold of it. But one thing I do: Forgetting what is behind and straining toward what is ahead, ¹⁴ I press on toward the goal to win the prize for which God has called me heavenward in Christ Jesus."

I previously shared my thoughts about the importance of "forgetting what is behind". See January 24. We can't move forward if we are stuck in our past. Yet, Paul says moving forward is the point!

In part, this is a picture of Paul running a race, perhaps it is a long distance. He says he is "straining" toward what is ahead. Could it be a crown or other reward?

In this context, the Miriam-Webster Dictionary says to "strain" means "to exert to the utmost", or "strive violently". Paul is intensely focused and striving for something. He is dedicated and determined; and I can imagine that he won't give up, give in or give out!

Paul says he will "press on". The dictionary definition in this context means "to follow through", "to force one's way", or, "to require haste or speed in action". He is hastily and forcefully moving forward, with intense focus, to follow through to his goal!

Paul has previously revealed in Romans 8:29 that the ultimate purpose of the Father for each of His children is to be conformed to the image of Christ so that Jesus is the "firstborn among many". This must be his prize!

Are you focused intensely on, and striving toward, this goal and prize?

TODAY'S CHALLENGE:

Tell the Father you will re-double your determination to allow the Holy Spirit to sanctify you and conform you to the image of Jesus.

Dive Deeper: Study Philippians 3; Romans 8:29.

July 16

SEVENTY TIMES SEVEN

Matthew 18:21-22
"Then Peter came to Jesus and asked, "Lord, how many times shall I forgive my brother or sister who sins against me? Up to seven times?"
²² Jesus answered, "I tell you, not seven times, but seventy times seven."

God's forgiveness is unconditional and unlimited. Ours should be too.

One of the biggest traps the enemy uses to ensnare Believers is "offense"; that is, being offended and holding un-forgiveness. One of the most important books John Bevere has written to date is The Bait of Satan. I heartily recommend this book to you.

This is so important, I suggest you re-read the material covered in three earlier devotionals – January 29-31. Go ahead, I will wait right here. :-)

The finished work of Jesus, through the Cross and Resurrection, enables God the Father to justifiably extend to us, by His grace, unlimited and unconditional forgiveness and mercy. He doesn't stop at seven times, or even 490 times, as long as we truly repent (see January 9), "He is faithful and just to forgive us our sins and cleanse us of all unrighteousness." See 1 John 1:9.

Even if the person does not come to you, admit their fault, and ask for your forgiveness (and they most often don't), you still must choose to forgive them. Holding un-forgiveness against anybody for anything is sinful, and thereby hinders your prayers, and hampers your relationship with God. See Mark 11:25. You don't necessarily have to continue a close relationship with someone who continues to hurt you, but you must continue to forgive.

TODAY'S CHALLENGE:

Ask the Holy Spirit to remind you of people who have hurt you. Forgive them, and ask the Father to forgive you for holding un-forgiveness towards them.

Dive Deeper: Study Matthew 18; Mark 11:25; Matthew 6:14-15.

July 17

SET FREE FROM SIN

Romans 6:6-7
"For we know that our old self was crucified with him so that the body ruled by sin might be done away with, that we should no longer be slaves to sin— 7 because anyone who has died has been set free from sin."

Let's look at three key phrases Paul uses in this passage: "ruled by sin", "slaves to sin", and, "set free from sin".

Prior to receiving salvation, everyone is "ruled by sin", albeit to varying degrees. I was pretty much a sinner to the nth degree, how about you? We could not help but sin because that was our very nature. Our spirit man was dead, at least in a coma, so our soul man always followed our "flesh".

We can only serve one master, and prior to Christ, we were "slaves to sin." We were helpless to resist the temptations of the world, the flesh and the devil. As hard as we might have sometimes tried, we generally gave in. We really did not have control over our lives; the enemy did.

Jesus paid the ultimate price - His Life, His Blood – to redeem us out of the slave market of sin. No longer would we be involuntarily mastered by sin; we could choose to be led by His Holy Spirit rather than our "flesh". We now have the very real option not to continue to sin!

Paul teaches us to always remind ourselves that our "old man" died, so we are no longer helpless to resist old temptations. We are free.

TODAY'S CHALLENGE:

Thank the Father for sending Jesus to purchase you back from the enemy. Ask the Holy Spirit to help you remember your old man is dead!

Anyone who has died has been "set free from sin."

Dive Deeper: Study Romans 6.

July 18

THE NEW IS HERE

2 Corinthians 5:17
"Therefore, if anyone is in Christ, the new creation has come: The old has gone, the new is here!"

Great news! We have been grafted into Christ, and our old man is dead! May I suggest you review the devotionals for June 25 and July 17?

This is absolutely one of my favorite verses. If you haven't yet done so, I urge you to memorize it and rehearse it to yourself daily. This is Truth, and applying it will set you free in Christ!

One of the most remarkable things about coming to Christ was that I really could start over. I did not have to keep bemoaning all the many mistakes I had made. I no longer had to buried in shame, guilt, remorse and embarrassment about my past. I could begin again because I was born again!

"The old has gone, the new is here!"

When I am led by the Spirit, I am "in Christ". When I give in to old man, fleshly temptations I am not then operating in Christ. I do not have to give into them since my old man is dead, but I need to consciously declare this aloud when temptation comes. I want to hear myself proclaim this because faith comes by hearing; and, when I do, I am submitting to God, and resisting the devil! See January 20.

All the promises of God are available to me in Christ. My new man lives daily in Him.

TODAY'S CHALLENGE:

Tell the Father you are thankful to have the opportunity to start over in Christ Jesus. Ask the Holy Spirit to help you memorize today's verse, and live it out today.

Dive Deeper: Study 2 Corinthians 5; 1 Samuel 10:6; Isaiah 43:18; Ezekiel 36:26; John 8:36; Romans 6:4; Galatians 5:1; Philippians 3:13.

July 19

POWERFUL DIVINE WEAPONS

2 Corinthians 10:3-4
"For though we live in the world, we do not wage war as the world does.⁴ The weapons we fight with are not the weapons of the world. On the contrary, they have divine power to demolish strongholds."

As Christians, we become aware of a spiritual war raging constantly around us in a dimension we cannot normally discern with our five senses. For example, see 2 Kings 6:15-18.

The weapons we use are not the worldly weapons we naturally think about when it comes to war; rather, they are powerful divine weapons. In Ephesians 6:10-18, Paul tells us about our enemy, the armor we use to protect us from his attacks, and our arsenal of weapons.

Notice that the armor is defensive, but there are two offensive weapons: wielding the sword of the Spirit which is the Word of God; and, praying in the Spirit.

In the 2 Kings scripture, Elisha prayed to open the eyes of his servant, and he prayed to blind the eyes of his enemies. The most powerful prayers are those that use the Word of God; and, when we don't know how to pray, we can let the Spirit pray though us because He prays the perfect will of God the Father! See Romans 8:26-28.

Strongholds are fortified places, or fortresses, and in some cases, the Greek word is translated as "prisons". We cannot let the enemy imprison us and establish fortresses in our souls. You are able to demolish strongholds!

TODAY'S CHALLENGE:

Thank the Father for ultimate victory in the war over the enemy by Jesus. Ask the Holy Spirit to help you remember today that you are not fighting "for" victory, but "from" victory.

Use your weapons.

Dive Deeper: Study 2 Corinthians 10; 2 Kings 6:15-18; Ephesians 6:10-18; Romans 8:26-28.

July 20

FAITH COMES

Romans 10:16-17
"But not all the Israelites accepted the good news. For Isaiah says, 'Lord, who has believed our message?' [17] *Consequently, faith comes from hearing the message, and the message is heard through the word about Christ."*

Have you "accepted the Good News"? Have you "believed our message"?

We have all been given a measure of faith (Romans 12:3), which I believe is at least enough to believe and accept the Good News of Jesus Christ! But most of us would like to have more faith. Is that you? Have you ever said to yourself, "If I just had more faith..."? Be encouraged: faith comes. Faith can be increased!

We are not left with only the beginning measure of faith we were given in order that we could come to Christ. No, faith comes. It grows.

How? By the Word. Jesus is the Living Word, and He continues to speak to us through His written Word; and, by the Holy Spirit Who brings to our remembrance everything Jesus has told us. God's Word does not return without effect, and it is able to accomplish all God intends (Isaiah 55:11).

Memorizing and meditating upon scripture puts the Word inside us. Then, the Holy Spirit is able to bring it to our remembrance when we need to use it as a weapon (see July 19)! Speak the Word out loud to your mountain.

When we hear ourselves proclaim the Word of God over our situation and circumstances, we see the Word work. When we see the results, our faith increases!

TODAY'S CHALLENGE:

Tell the Father you want more faith. Thank Him for the faith to believe. Ask the Holy Spirit to help you memorize, and meditate upon, the Word He inspired. Rehearse it aloud often.

Dive Deeper: Study Romans 10; Joshua 1:8-9; Psalm 1:1-3; Isaiah 55:10-11.

July 21

LIAR OR LORD?

John 14:6
"Jesus answered, "I am the way and the truth and the life. No one comes to the Father except through me."

Some non-Christians have kind things to say about Jesus, but they will not say He is God. Many concede He was a "good teacher". Some say He was one of God's "prophets". Others say He was an "enlightened being", or "an ascended master". Most point to Him as a "good man"; possibly even the "best man" who ever lived, and a "good example" for us to follow.

But, these same people get very nervous, even angry, when someone states their belief that Jesus was, and is, God. And, they really get mad when someone asserts that Jesus is the only way to God.

Jesus very clearly equated Himself with God the Father many times in the Gospels. In fact, this was the primary reason (or excuse) the Pharisees gave for wanting to crucify Him (John 5:18). Jesus said, "If you have seen me you have seen the Father" (John 14:9). In John 10:30, Jesus said, "I and the Father are one."

If Jesus is not exactly who He said, He is a liar, or a lunatic, or both. In that case, He is not "good teacher", a "good man", or a "good example"; and He certainly is not worth following.

There is no doubt about Who Jesus claimed to be – God. He said He is <u>the</u> Way to the Father, not one of a number of options, or a choice among acceptable alternatives.

TODAY'S CHALLENGE:

Ask the Father to help you be prepared to respond correctly when someone doubts Jesus as God. Familiarize yourself with the writings of Lee Strobel or Josh McDowell.

Speak the truth in love.

Dive Deeper: Study John 14; John 5:18; John 14:9; John 10:30; Philippians 2:9-11.

July 22

NO OTHER NAME

Acts 4:12
"Salvation is found in no one else, for there is no other name under heaven given to mankind by which we must be saved."

In front of the Disciples, Peter proclaimed the revelation he had been given from God when he answered Jesus, "You are the Christ, the Son of the Living God." Yet, in his own strength, he was unable to cling to this truth, and he denied he even knew Jesus.

After being baptized with the Holy Spirit at Pentecost, Peter boldly preached the Truth to those in Jerusalem, and 3,000 souls were saved! He and John courageously refused to be silenced by the Sanhedrin, and were thrown in jail.

The next day, when they were brought out to appear before the rulers, elders and teachers of the law, they were asked "in what name did you do this?" Peter boldly proclaims, "It is by the name of Jesus Christ of Nazareth..." Courageously, he proceeds to declare Acts 4:12 shown above.

Peter, the first great evangelist, boldly proclaimed Jesus under the anointing of the Holy Spirit of God. He is a good Biblical example for us!

Today is the birthday of another great evangelist, Don Castleberry, founder of Freedom in Jesus Prison Ministries. He tells everyone he sees about Jesus. Many thousands of prisoners have given their lives to Jesus in and through Don's evangelistic ministry since he himself was saved in the Lubbock County Jail in the late 1970's.

I am proud to say Don is my best friend and mentor. He loves prisoners more than anyone I know, and he really loves Jesus!

TODAY'S CHALLENGE:

Pray for Don and Freedom in Jesus Prison Ministries. Maybe you could send Don a card. Send it to P.O. Box 939, Levelland, TX 79336

Dive Deeper: Study Acts 4; Matthew 16:16; John 14:6; Isaiah 43:11, 44:6-8, 45:22, 46:8-10.

July 23

NO OTHER SAVIOR

Isaiah 43:11
"I, even I, am the LORD, and apart from me there is no savior."

Isaiah 45:22
"Turn to me and be saved, all you ends of the earth; for I am God, and there is no other."

Jehovah God is speaking to us very clearly. This is hard to misunderstand. Many refuse to believe it; some reject it outright; and, others want to argue about it.

But, one day, everyone will have to face the One Who said it: Jehovah; the God of Abraham, Isaac and Jacob; the Maker of Heaven and Earth; the King of kings; the Lord of lords; the Father of our Lord Jesus Christ; the Great I AM; and, the King of Glory!

Everyone will face Him alone. Neither your mother, grandmother, dad - not even your "cellie" – will be by your side. We will all have to individually account for what we did about this truth when it was presented to us. Paul says no one will have an excuse. See Romans 1:18-20.

Christianity is "all inclusive" – anyone in "all the ends of the earth" may call on the Name of the Lord and be saved (Joel 2:32). However, it is "exclusive" in the sense that it is only for those who truly repent and "turn" solely to Jesus (John 14:6). We come to God only on His terms.

There is no middle ground, no gray area. Choose this day Whom you will serve.

TODAY'S CHALLENGE:

Pray to the Father, in Jesus' Name, that every unbeliever you know will come to surrender to God, by the drawing of their hearts by the Holy Spirit. Be specific. Pray for them regularly.

Watch God work.

Dive Deeper: Study Isaiah 43; Romans 1:18-20; Joel 2:32; John 14:6; Acts 4:12.

July 24

LIFT UP YOUR HEAD

Luke 21:28
"When these things begin to take place, stand up and lift up your heads, because your redemption is drawing near."

As "the Day of the Lord" quickly approaches, we should remember the signs Jesus so clearly enumerated shortly before He willingly gave up His Life for us on the Cross. We need to be awake and watching.

We should live with our hearts and heads lifted up in anticipation of His soon return! "Look up, your redemption is drawing near." What an exciting time to be alive!

In Matthew 24, Mark 13, and Luke 21, Jesus told us to look for certain events and signs, and He repeatedly warned of deception. He said to be aware of wars and rumors of wars; and, famines and earthquakes in diverse places. There will be great persecution; many will turn away from the faith; and, many will betray and hate one another.

False prophets will deceive many; wickedness will increase; and, the love of most will grow cold. The Gospel will be preached in the whole world, and there will be unequaled great distress. There will be great signs in the stars, sun and moon; with fearful events and great signs from Heaven.

There will pestilences in various places, and the world will hate Christians. Nations will be in anguish and perplexity at the roaring and tossing of the sea. Heavenly bodies will be shaken, and men will faint from terror.

All these are happening now. Don't run. Don't hide. Don't be afraid. Don't be preoccupied with temporary worldly distractions. Look up!

TODAY'S CHALLENGE:

Ask the Father to give you discernment by His Holy Spirit so you will not be deceived, and boldness to tell others about Jesus!

Dive Deeper: Study Matthew 24; Mark 13; Luke 21.

July 25

A THIEF IN THE NIGHT

1 Thessalonians 5:1-3
"Now, brothers and sisters, about times and dates we do not need to write to you, ² for you know very well that the day of the Lord will come like a thief in the night. ³ While people are saying, "Peace and safety," destruction will come on them suddenly, as labor pains on a pregnant woman, and they will not escape."

Many of us who have been imprisoned know one or more folks who were professional thieves. I suppose most everyone is a thief in some regard if they have ever stolen anything, large or small. But I am thinking of someone who has a lot of experience and didn't get caught.

Usually, a thief wants to get in quickly when no one is watching, perhaps while everyone is asleep. They arrive suddenly when no one is expecting them. If someone had been up, alert, waiting and watching, they would not be surprised or caught off guard.

The day of the Lord will come when no-one is expecting. In a spiritual sense, most of the world will be asleep. They will most definitely be surprised. This day is fast approaching. See July 24 devotional.

Jesus said no one knows the date or hour, only the Father; so Paul says, in verse 1, he does not need to address this specifically. Let us all be on guard, awake, watchful, and enthusiastically expecting the return of our precious Lord and Savior, Jesus!

Are you ready?

TODAY'S CHALLENGE:

Tell the Father you look forward to the soon appearing of His Son, Jesus. Ask the Holy Spirit what Kingdom business you should be accomplishing today.

Dive Deeper: Study 1 Thessalonians 4:13 – 5:11; 2 Thessalonians 2:1-12; 1 Corinthians 15:51-58.

July 26

DON'T BE ALARMED

2 Thessalonians 2:1-3
"Concerning the coming of our Lord Jesus Christ and our being gathered to him, we ask you, brothers and sisters, ² not to become easily unsettled or alarmed... ³ Don't let anyone deceive you in any way..."

Although the times we are living in are perilous, troubling and seem to be growing darker by the day, we are exhorted "not to become easily unsettled or alarmed". These are exciting days for the Body of Christ who long for the appearing of our great God and Savior, Jesus Christ!

Here Paul warns again of possible deception, and Jesus Himself emphasized it as we learned on July 24, and more particularly on February 11. Jesus told us that if it were possible, even "the elect" would be deceived (Matthew 24:24). Praise God, it is not possible for the very elect to be deceived, and we want to be sure we are part of "the elect", or the remnant of true believers!

As we see Biblical prophecy being fulfilled right before our very eyes every week, it should encourage us to be about our Father's business. We should be praying for our family members and friends who do not have an intimate personal relationship with Jesus. Be bold about sharing your testimony of what God has done in your life.

I believe God wants us to focus one day at a time on the plan He gives us each morning. Whatever He wants you to do today, do it with a sense of urgency and a pattern of excellence. Tomorrow, receive your instructions from Him again.

TODAY'S CHALLENGE:

Ask the Father what He has in mind for you today that would positively impact the Kingdom.

Dive Deeper: Study 2 Thessalonians 2; Matthew 24:24.

July 27

MAN OF LAWLESSNESS

2 Thessalonians 2:3-4
"Don't let anyone deceive you in any way, for that day will not come until the rebellion occurs and the man of lawlessness is revealed, the man doomed to destruction. ⁴ He will oppose and will exalt himself over everything that is called God or is worshiped, so that he sets himself up in God's temple, proclaiming himself to be God."

Before the Day of the Lord, Paul tells us the "man of lawlessness" will be revealed. Many believe he is referring to "the Antichrist" who will deceive most of the world. I am the first to admit I am not a prophecy expert, but apparently the Antichrist will be aided by the False Prophet.

Endless speculation exists as the whether we see these two on the world stage today, and who they might be. Regardless of specifically who it is, we are warned not to be deceived.

This man will "exalt himself over everything that is called God or is worshiped." There are a few world leaders now that basically assume this position among their own people, but we will see this man have influence on a worldwide basis.

In Israel, there is a specific group of dedicated, religious Jews who have been planning for many years to rebuild the Hebrew Temple. My understanding is that they are preparing the way for the coming of Messiah; but, Christians believe Jesus the Messiah has already come, and is coming again. Apparently, the rebuilt Temple will be the stage for the antichrist to proclaim himself as God.

Don't let anyone deceive you.

TODAY'S CHALLENGE:

Ask the Father for discernment from His Holy Spirit to continue to seek, believe and remain in, the Truth Who is Jesus.

Dive Deeper: Study 2 Thessalonians 2; Daniel 12.

July 28

POWER OF LAWLESSNESS

2 Thessalonians 2:7-8
"For the secret power of lawlessness is already at work; but the one who now holds it back will continue to do so till he is taken out of the way. ^{8} And then the lawless one will be revealed, whom the Lord Jesus will overthrow with the breath of his mouth and destroy by the splendor of his coming."

Jesus told us that before His return wickedness would increase (see July 24). In our scripture today, Paul says "the secret power of lawlessness is already at work". This secret power of lawlessness has been steadily increasing for 2,000 years.

The advance of evil, wickedness and lawlessness can only go so far while "the one who now holds it back" is operating in the earth. Most believe Paul is referring here to the Holy Spirit. Until the Father is ready to send Jesus back for His Bride - the elect remnant - lawlessness cannot have free reign on the earth.

We should remember that Jesus, through the Cross and Resurrection, has been given all authority in Heaven and on earth (see Matthew 28:18). He has given us His authority to make Disciples in the midst of whatever the enemy still tries to do in the earth.

For a time, God's restraint on the enemy will be removed, but the Lord Jesus will have the final say at His Second Coming! Let's keep working while it is day, because night is coming when no man can work (see John 9:4).

TODAY'S CHALLENGE:

Tell the Father you want to be utilized by the Holy Spirit to exercise the authority of Jesus to keep building the Body of Christ. Rededicate your life, and recommit your heart, to Him today.

Dive Deeper: Study 2 Thessalonians 2; Matthew 28:18-20; John 9:4.

July 29

STAND FIRM AND HOLD FAST

2 Thessalonians 2:13-15
"But we ought always to thank God for you, brothers and sisters loved by the Lord, because God chose you as firstfruits to be saved through the sanctifying work of the Spirit and through belief in the truth. ¹⁴ He called you to this through our gospel, that you might share in the glory of our Lord Jesus Christ. ¹⁵ So then, brothers and sisters, stand firm and hold fast to the teachings we passed on to you, whether by word of mouth or by letter."

The Bible tells us that in the last days there will be many false prophets and false teachings. It is crucial for us to "stand firm and hold fast" to sound Biblical instruction and guidance.

The Holy Spirit will continue to sanctify us after we come to faith through belief in the Truth. We must let the Holy Spirit do His work in and through us to set us apart for God's service, and make us progressively more holy. Our role is to be surrendered, submitted and obedient.

The Lord Jesus has called us to serve Him; and, to grow in our faith and in His likeness. The more time we spend prayerfully in the Presence of God daily, the more we will be able to rightly discern the spirits of this age. As we set aside regular time daily for the serious study of His Holy Word, we will correctly understand and apply Truth to our lives.

TODAY'S CHALLENGE:

Ask the Father to give you a heart that hungers for the Truth, and ask the Holy Spirit to empower its application in your life.

Stand firm on the Rock. Hold fast to the Truth.

Dive Deeper: Study 2 Thessalonians; Matthew 7:24-27.

July 30

SEARED CONSCIENCES

1 Timothy 4:1-2
"The Spirit clearly says that in later times some will abandon the faith and follow deceiving spirits and things taught by demons. ² Such teachings come through hypocritical liars, whose consciences have been seared as with a hot iron."

As believers, the Holy Spirit wants to train our conscience to choose holiness which glorifies God, and reject deceitful philosophies that glorify self. Paul warns Timothy that some Christians will abandon their faith in the last days.

Having once investigated "new age" philosophies before I came to Christ, as well as Hinduism and Buddhism, I remember that they had in common the appeal to self; for example, self-improvement, self-enlightenment, self-image, and self-consciousness.

This prideful focus on self begins to sear the conscience towards the things of God. Someone who is self-conscious cannot at the same time be God-conscious. Hypocritical teachers with a seared conscience will tend to elevate "self", and misapply scripture to provide for self-justification of sin. Beware.

Jesus tells us His Way is to deny self, and let the Holy Spirit sanctify us. He provides enlightenment through His Word. We are to let the Holy Spirit conform us to the image of Christ, rather than trying to improve our naturally sinful image of self. Walking in humility rather than pride gives us the proper perspective of our new life in Christ.

Trying to improve our "old man" and becoming more self-dependent, rather than depending on the Holy Spirit to mold our "new man" in Christ, is emphasizing worldly principles suggested by deceiving spirits and taught by demons.

TODAY'S CHALLENGE:

Tell the Father you want to maintain a good conscience properly led by His Holy Spirit.

Dive Deeper: Study 1 Timothy 4.

July 31

LOVERS OF THEMSELVES

2 Timothy 3:1-5
"But mark this: There will be terrible times in the last days. ²People will be lovers of themselves, lovers of money, boastful, proud, abusive, disobedient to their parents, ungrateful, unholy, ³without love, unforgiving, slanderous, without self-control, brutal, not lovers of the good, ⁴treacherous, rash, conceited, lovers of pleasure rather than lovers of God— ⁵having a form of godliness but denying its power. Have nothing to do with such people."

It is important to point out that Paul was writing to the Pastor of a body of believers, not to a group of unbelievers. These are apparently signs of conditions in the Church in the last days. The elevated focus on self we learned about yesterday (see July 30) could play into the deception of uninformed and unwary believers.

It is disheartening to see how many have become self-focused and selfish. The emphasis and widespread growth of social media has fueled this very disturbing downward trend. It is easier to judge and criticize others because it is done from a safe distance. The opportunities to stir up division and strife, even among family members, is without precedent.

Crass commercialism, hedonistic comparisons, inflammatory disparagement, and morally deviant normalization all combine to make the sinfulness of all this seem normal. Yet, many falsely believe their "religion" is intact. Having a "form of godliness but denying its power", in my opinion, is true of those who do not acknowledge the power of the Holy Spirit to convict them of sin and strengthen their conscience.

The power of godliness is obedience to the Holy Spirit.

TODAY'S CHALLENGE:

Ask the Father to identify areas where you could be described in today's verse. Repent and surrender to the Holy Spirit for Him to change you. Be obedient.

Dive Deeper: Study 2 Timothy 3; Galatians 5:19-21.

August 1

JESUS IS COMING BACK

John 14:1-3

"Do not let your hearts be troubled. You believe in God; believe also in me. ² My Father's house has many rooms; if that were not so, would I have told you that I am going there to prepare a place for you?³ And if I go and prepare a place for you, I will come back and take you to be with me that you also may be where I am."

Jesus is coming back for His people. The signs of His soon return are increasing. See devotionals for February 13 and July 24 for more information. We are not to be in anxiety, fear or turmoil about this. We know we can trust Jesus, and He says He is coming back.

In the Jewish marriage custom, once the couple was betrothed (similar to engagement, but more binding), the man would go home to his father's house to prepare a place for he and his bride to honeymoon. When everything was completed, furnished, and ready, only the father of the groom could proclaim all was ready, and that it was time for the groom to go get His bride. Until then when asked about the date, the groom responded, "only my father knows."

The bride had to be ready because she did not know when her bridegroom would return, but she knew without doubt that he would come. Jesus uses this sacred custom so that His followers would understand the importance and surety of His return.

TODAY'S CHALLENGE:

Tell the Father you are anticipating the return of Jesus for you as part of His Bride, the Church. Ask His Holy Spirit to help you ready yourself, and your loved ones, for this day.

Jesus is coming back!

Dive Deeper: Study John 14; 1 Thessalonians 4:13-18.

August 2

JESUS IS COMING QUICKLY

Matthew 24:27
"For as lightning that comes from the east is visible even in the west, so will be the coming of the Son of Man."

1 Thessalonians 5:3
"While people are saying, 'Peace and safety,' destruction will come on them suddenly, as labor pains on a pregnant woman, and they will not escape."

The return of our Lord will happen suddenly, as quick as lightning flashes across the sky! Also, Paul tells us that it will be in the twinkling of an eye (1 Corinthians 15:52)!

So, how fast is the twinkling of an eye? Scientists say this is the amount of time that it takes light to enter the eye, reflect off the retina and be seen. Light travels at 186,000 miles per second, so a twinkle is estimated to be about a billionth of a second.

It is also reported that a flash of lightning travels at 200,000,000 miles per hour! That's fast! A person will not have time to make things right with the Lord when He comes. One moment we will be here, but in the next moment we will be with Him!

Brothers and Sister in Christ, we must always live in such a way that we are ready for His return. Let us pray diligently for those who don't know Jesus, and let's live expectantly looking for Him!

TODAY'S CHALLENGE:

Ask the Father to help you reflect on your life to be sure you are living in such a way that you will be ready for the return of Jesus. Ask the Holy Spirit to bring to your mind the loved ones and friends who may not yet be ready, so you can be praying for them diligently.

Dive Deeper: Study Matthew 24; 1 Thessalonians 5:1-11; 1 Corinthians 15:51-58.

August 3

JESUS IS COMING ANY DAY NOW

Revelation 22:12-13
Jesus said, "Look, I am coming soon! My reward is with me, and I will give to each person according to what they have done. ¹³ I am the Alpha and the Omega, the First and the Last, the Beginning and the End."

What an exciting time in which we live! Jesus Himself says He is coming soon. As we have discussed on February 13, and July 24, we are witnessing the prophetic signs happening right before our eyes.

Everything is contained in Jesus – all knowledge, all priority, and all time. We can trust Him to fulfill His Word. He encourages us not to be anxious, but when we see these things happening we are to "Look up for our redemption is near" (Luke 21:28).

Many of the prophetic signs, especially in chapters of Ezekiel 37-39, Zechariah 12-14, Psalm 83, and Daniel 11-12, are centered around Israel. Many believe the miraculous return of the Jews to the land Israel in 1948 began a prophetic clock that is quickly winding down ending in the return of Jesus our Messiah.

Never before have we seen the military and political alliance of nations like Turkey, Russia and Iran combining against Israel. Even the Chinese are in the Middle East. Almost all the nations of the earth rage against Israel and God. See Psalm 2.

Study the above-referenced chapters, and be ready, because Jesus is coming soon – any day now!

TODAY'S CHALLENGE:

Ask the Father to show you how to pray for Israel. Ask the Holy Spirit to help you pray for Jesus Christ, their true Messiah, to be revealed to them, and that a great end-times revival would happen among His original children, as well as the Body of Christ.

Dive Deeper: Study Revelation 22; Luke 21:28; Psalm 2.

August 4

KEEP WATCH

Matthew 24:42-44
Jesus said, "Therefore keep watch, because you do not know on what day your Lord will come. ⁴³ But understand this: If the owner of the house had known at what time of night the thief was coming, he would have kept watch and would not have let his house be broken into. ⁴⁴ So you also must be ready, because the Son of Man will come at an hour when you do not expect him."

One of my prison ministry evangelist friends said they could tell me exactly when Jesus was coming. I said they couldn't know that precisely because Jesus said, "only the Father knows". They said, "He is coming at an hour when you do not expect Him!" Well, that is sure right!

Today's verse emphasizes that very fact. For more information on this see devotional for July 25. Jesus warns us to be alert and keep watch, and uses the analogy of a thief trying to break into a house.

As I consider this, I am reminded that Jesus said in John 10:10 that "the thief comes to steal, kill and destroy". The enemy wants to steal the plan God has for your life, kill your Christian witness, and, thereby, destroy your Kingdom effectiveness.

As we look forward to the return of our King, we must be diligent to use the talents and abilities God has given us to fulfill the work we have been assigned.

Guard your heart, and keep watch. We have important work to do.

TODAY'S CHALLENGE:

Tell the Father you want to fulfill all of His plans for your life. Surrender today to the Holy Spirit's desire to impact the world around you.

You are His vessel. Be obedient and expectant.

Dive Deeper: Study Matthew 24; 1 Thessalonians 5:1-11; 1 Corinthians 15:51-58.

August 5

HE IS GREATER

1 John 4:4-5
"You, dear children, are from God and have overcome them, because the one who is in you is greater than the one who is in the world. ⁵ They are from the world and therefore speak from the viewpoint of the world, and the world listens to them."

The complete context of today's verse can be understood more fully by reading the passages of 1 John 4:1-5 altogether. John is warning the church about discerning the spirits because of false prophets who were teaching against the incarnation, that is, saying that Jesus did not really come in the flesh. He says this is the spirit of anti-Christ and it was already happening in the late first century.

In the current times, this spirit of anti-Christ has only been spread more widely. The viewpoint of much of the world is to deny or downplay the life and redeeming work of Jesus. Christians are marginalized, mocked, and persecuted. The world seems be "tolerant" of all religions and beliefs except for those of true Christians who believe the Bible and try to walk it out in their daily lives.

We must remember we have the Holy Spirit living inside us. He is Greater than any other spirit in the world. He is the One Who gives us discernment, and enables us to be bold and courageous in standing strong in Christ Jesus against those who dispute the Truth.

Do not be intimidated. You and God comprise the majority!

TODAY'S CHALLENGE:

Thank the Father that He is Greater; and, for the fact that He lives in you by His Holy Spirit. Ask His Holy Spirit to sharpen your discernment of false teachers and the spirit of anti-Christ.

Be bold and courageous.

Dive Deeper: Study 1 John 4; Romans 8:31; Psalm 34:7; 2 Chronicles 32:7; 2 Kings 6:16.

August 6

THE SECRET OF CONTENTMENT

Philippians 4:12-13
"I know what it is to be in need, and I know what it is to have plenty. I have learned the secret of being content in any and every situation, whether well fed or hungry, whether living in plenty or in want. ¹³ I can do all this through him who gives me strength."

A study of Paul's life reveals a man whose experiences had run the entire spectrum. Having once been a man of financial means, a leader among the most religious Jews, and having held positions of status and authority; he ended up being severely persecuted, beaten, imprisoned, ridiculed, without material possessions, abandoned, and eventually martyred.

Yet, even as he wrote this particular letter from prison, he says he has learned to be content in all circumstances. For those of who have been imprisoned, I think we know at that particular time and place he was not "well fed", and was not "living in plenty". In fact, I am sure the prisons 2,000 years ago were much worse than today.

With society's current obsession with materialism, and the bombardment of every kind of enticing advertisement, we are constantly influenced to want more of everything - newer, better, faster. Fortunately, those of us in Christ have access to the same secret as Paul – the Holy Spirit Who empowers us within!

As long as we trust wholly in God, He will be our Source of peace and contentment in every circumstance.

TODAY'S CHALLENGE:

Thank the Father for giving you His Holy Spirit to empower you, and that He gives you His peace. Ask the Holy Spirit to show you any areas in your life today where you are not manifesting contentment and peace. Choose to trust Him.

Dive Deeper: Study Philippians 4; Philippians 1:6, 2:13; Psalm 138:8; 1 Thessalonians 5:24; John 3:21.

August 7

THROUGH THE POWER OF THE SPIRIT

Romans 15:17-19
"Therefore I glory in Christ Jesus in my service to God. ¹⁸ I will not venture to speak of anything except what Christ has accomplished through me in leading the Gentiles to obey God by what I have said and done— ¹⁹ by the power of signs and wonders, through the power of the Spirit of God..."

Of all the New Testament saints, Paul probably had the most reasons to speak highly of himself and his accomplishments. Yet, in every case, Paul defers to the work of Christ in and through him. He remained humble. In fact, the Bible says he learned to glory in his weaknesses knowing that it was in those very weaknesses that Christ would show Himself strong (see 2 Corinthians 12:9-11).

Paul only speaks of "what Christ has accomplished through me", not what Paul himself has done. Yet, notice how he expands upon this statement when he mentions "the power of signs and wonders, through the power of the Spirit of God."

Paul's life was an example to the Gentiles that inspired them to obey God. Our lives ought to be examples to all those with whom we come into contact that would inspire them to want what they see in us. Yet, like Paul, we must realize it is not us, but the Holy Spirit in us that empowers our walk in Christ.

Let's glory only in Christ Jesus for what He is doing by and through His Holy Spirit in us.

TODAY'S CHALLENGE:

Tell the Father how grateful you are for Jesus and the power of the Holy Spirit in your life. Think about how the Spirit has positively influenced others through you, and give Him the credit.

Dive Deeper: Study Romans 15; 2 Corinthians 12:9-11.

August 8

ACCORDING TO HIS POWER

Ephesians 3:16-18, 20
"I pray that out of his glorious riches he may strengthen you with power through his Spirit in your inner being, [17] so that Christ may dwell in your hearts through faith. And I pray that you, being rooted and established in love, [18] may have power... [20] Now to him who is able to do immeasurably more than all we ask or imagine, according to his power that is at work within us..."

In these few verses, Paul refers three times to the power of God through the Holy Spirit. As we have been learning, we find this emphasized in many of Paul's writings. He realizes how very important it is and he tries to share this magnificent truth with everyone.

Notice that Christ dwells in our hearts, through faith, by the power of the Holy Spirit in our inner being. Jesus Himself does not literally dwell there as He is seated in Heavenly places with the Father (Ephesians 2:6); rather, the Holy Spirit dwells there.

I love how Paul says that we will have power as we are "rooted and established in love". Jesus said we must love God and love others. In fact, we are to love each other the way Jesus loves us (John 13:34-35).

Finally, Paul tells us how it is that God "is able to do immeasurably more than all we ask or imagine". How? According to His power at work within us!

We must let the Holy Spirit work in us.

TODAY'S CHALLENGE:

Thank the Father, and Jesus, for sending their Holy Spirit to reside in you with power. Ask the Holy Spirit to reveal more of His love and tell Him you want to be firmly established in it.

Dive Deeper: Study Ephesians 3; Ephesians 2:6; John 13:34-35.

August 9

STRIVING WITH HIS ENERGY

Colossians 1:28-29, AMP
"Him we preach and proclaim, warning and admonishing everyone and instructing everyone in all wisdom (comprehensive insight into the ways and purposes of God), that we may present every person mature (full-grown, fully initiated, complete, and perfect) in Christ (the Anointed One). [29] For this I labor [unto weariness], striving with all the superhuman energy which He so mightily enkindles and works within me."

In verse 27, Paul had disclosed the mystery which is "Christ in you the hope of Glory". Then, Paul summarizes here, in verse 28, the responsibilities we all share after we come to faith in Christ. What a marvelous truth he uses to introduce us to the things we can and should do in Christ Jesus.

As we have discovered in the last several days' devotionals, Paul knows it is not in his own power that he is who he is in Christ, and here today he tells us how he does it. Surely, he worked hard to advance the Gospel, and to disciple those who were coming into faith in the cities where he traveled.

He says he labors unto weariness and strives, but it is not by his human energy or wisdom, but by the superhuman energy kindled within him by the power of the Holy Spirit. This is how he is able to proclaim the Gospel; and, warn, admonish and instruct in wisdom those he wants to help to mature in Christ Jesus.

Let us follow his example to labor and strive by the power of the Holy Spirit, and not our own human energy.

TODAY'S CHALLENGE:

Ask the Father to help you set aside your own works, and submit, rather, to the work of the Holy Spirit in and through you.

Dive Deeper: Study Colossians 1.

August 10

SHAPING FROM THE CLAY

Jeremiah 18:1-6
"This is the word that came to Jeremiah from the Lord: [2] *"Go down to the potter's house, and there I will give you my message."* [3] *So I went down to the potter's house, and I saw him working at the wheel.* [4] *But the pot he was shaping from the clay was marred in his hands; so the potter formed it into another pot, shaping it as seemed best to him.* [5] *Then the word of the Lord came to me.* [6] *He said, "Can I not do with you, Israel, as this potter does?" declares the Lord. "Like clay in the hand of the potter, so are you in my hand, Israel."*

I love this story. Are you allowing God to shape you? Are you trusting Him to make of you what He wants - what He sees in His mind's eye - so you can know and fulfill the plan He has for you? (Review January 11 and 12)

As I think about "the potter's house" I think it may have a couple of meanings for us today. We know we are the house of the Holy Spirit, so I believe it can be to us in our private time with God where He says, "I will give you My message." But I also think of corporate worship in the house of God, where we assemble with other believers, that can also be the place where He can and will speak to us.

But do we listen? We have all been "marred" in life by our sin, and the sins of others. Are you patiently trusting Him to re-make you?

TODAY'S CHALLENGE:

Ask the Father to make of you what He wants. Let Him mold and shape you.

Dive Deeper: Study Jeremiah 18; Romans 9:20-21.

August 11

PREDESTINED TO CONFORM

Romans 8:29
"For those God foreknew he also predestined to be conformed to the image of his Son, that he might be the firstborn among many brothers and sisters."

One of the primary purposes of God as "The Potter" (see January 11 & 12, and August 10 devotionals) is to conform us to the image of His Son, Jesus. The Word today tells us that Jesus is the "firstborn among many brothers and sisters."

The Father's ultimate intention is for the family of God to bear a striking resemblance to the firstborn in the family, Jesus, the "second man" (see 1 Corinthians 15:45-48). Part of the Holy Spirit's work in us through the ongoing process of sanctification is to remove anything that does not look like Christ.

When Michelangelo was asked how he did his statues, he said, "The sculpture is already complete within the marble block, before I start my work. It is already there, I just have to chisel away the superfluous material."

When we are reborn into the family of God, we are born of incorruptible seed by faith in the Son through the Word of God (see 1 Peter 1:22-24); so the source material is there for the Holy Spirit to work with to start the process of conforming us to the image of Jesus!

Our job, as we previously learned about being moldable clay for the potter, is to submit to and cooperate with the Holy Spirit. Try to make His job easier!

TODAY'S CHALLENGE:

Thank the Father for taking you into His family. Tell Him you want to be more like Jesus today, and listen for the Holy Spirit's guidance.

You are predestined to conform!

Dive Deeper: Study Romans 8; 1 Corinthians 15:45-49; 1 Peter 1:22-25; Jeremiah 18:1-6.

August 12

PARTICIPATE IN THE DIVINE NATURE

2 Peter 1:3-4
"His divine power has given us everything we need for a godly life through our knowledge of him who called us by his own glory and goodness. ⁴ Through these he has given us his very great and precious promises, so that through them you may participate in the divine nature, having escaped the corruption in the world caused by evil desires."

Sometimes, to better understand a verse, it is helpful to examine it from bottom up. So, beginning at the end, let's back up through the verse and unpack some of this magnificent truth.

As we progressively escape the corruption in the world caused by evil desires, we are able to participate in the Divine Nature of God. We are allowed to participate in His nature through the very great and precious promises the Father has given us in His Son, and in His Word, after we are born again.

We are eligible to meet the conditions for these promises, should we choose to be obedient, because Jesus has called us by His own grace, glory and goodness as a result of His work at the Cross and Resurrection. But how can we possibly meet these conditions on our own?

We have already been given everything we need for a godly life in Christ by His divine power, the Holy Spirit!

So, God Himself has empowered us to live a godly life; benefit from His promises; and, participate in the Divine Nature, through the progressive, sanctifying work of the Holy Spirit. It is God Who does this start to finish!

TODAY'S CHALLENGE:

Thank the Father for His amazing plan, promises, and empowerment for a godly life, by the Holy Spirit, in Christ Jesus!

Dive Deeper: Study 2 Peter 1; Hebrews 6:11-12.

August 13

BE HOLY IN ALL YOU DO

1 Peter 1:14-16
"As obedient children, do not conform to the evil desires you had when you lived in ignorance. ¹⁵ But just as he who called you is holy, so be holy in all you do; ¹⁶ for it is written: 'Be holy, because I am holy.'"

I suggest you read 1 Peter 1:3-16, which is the important passage leading into, and including, today's verses. This is one section you ought to take your time with and really absorb in your spirit.

Sometimes it is hard for me to believe the incredible transformation (brought on at Pentecost by the Baptism of the Holy Spirit) in Peter, an unlearned fisherman, to such an extent that he could later write such beautiful and meaningful letters as 1 and 2 Peter.

Today's extended passage is a powerful presentation of our blessedness in Christ, such that we are supernaturally inspired, challenged and empowered to live a holy life as a natural outflow of this remarkable truth in our lives. Peter says, in verse 12, that all this is so spectacular and unique that, "Even angels long to look into these things".

God is Holy. As humans, we could never approach His Holiness. Peter does not say we are to be holy "as" He is Holy; rather, he is careful to say "because" He is Holy. There is an immeasurable difference in the two.

I believe the Holy Spirit will help us "be holy in all we do" if we let Him lead us, and are obedient.

TODAY'S CHALLENGE:

Consider and meditate upon the absolute Holiness of God. Thank the Father that through Jesus and His Holy Spirit, you are able to be holy in all you do today.

Dive Deeper: Study 1 Peter 1; Romans 12:1-2.

August 14

MAKE THE MOST OF OPPORTUNITY

Ephesians 5:15-17
"Be very careful, then, how you live—not as unwise but as wise, making the most of every opportunity, because the days are evil. Therefore, do not be foolish, but understand what the Lord's will is."

In these very challenging last days, it is clear that the Lord's will is for more souls to be saved. Time is short, and certainly the days are growing progressively more evil and darker very quickly.

It is especially imperative now for true believers to be careful to "walk their talk". As we do, unbelievers will be drawn by the Holy Spirit to the Father, in part, by their attraction to the fruit they see being produced in your life.

I believe it may have been St. Francis of Assisi who said, "We should preach the Gospel at all times and, if necessary, use words." So, be very careful how you live.

We must also look for opportunities to share our testimony of what the blood of Jesus has done in our lives. We should pray for more boldness and courage because there are, in fact, many opportunities for us to conversationally share with others the hope we have found in Christ.

Daniel 12:3 says that those who are wise will lead many to righteousness and will shine like the stars forever and ever! Surely, then, this is the Lord's will.

In these dark days, let Isaiah 60:1 encourage you to, *"Arise, shine, for your light has come, and the glory of the Lord rises upon you."*

TODAY'S CHALLENGE:

Thank the Father for allowing you to be a light to the world around you. Ask the Holy Spirit to help you make the most of every opportunity today to share the Gospel.

Dive Deeper: Study Ephesians 5; Daniel 12:3; Isaiah 60:1.

August 15

ABSTAIN FROM SINFUL DESIRES

1 Peter 2:11
"Dear friends, I urge you, as foreigners and exiles, to abstain from sinful desires, which wage war against your soul."

Whether you are in prison or in the free world, after we are born again, we are to view ourselves as citizens of another Kingdom. We are no longer "of this world"; rather, we are "foreigners and exiles" just passing through on the way to our permanent home.

While we are still on this earthly plane, we should separate ourselves from "old people, places and things" so that we are not so easily surrounded and tempted by former sinful desires. Because we are a new creation in Christ Jesus (see 2 Corinthians 5:17), it is very possible to abstain from sinful desires and no longer practice sin (see 1 John 5:18-19). This is only achieved by choosing to be led by the Spirit instead of the flesh, and by the power of the Holy Spirit living in us.

Our soul, that is, our mind, will and emotions, must choose continuously between our flesh and our human spirit which, when we are born again, is influenced by the Holy Spirit. So, in a sense, our soul is subject to be in a constant "tug of war". We must decide to follow the Leadership of the Holy Spirit who will empower us to say "no" to temptation.

God will not let us be tempted beyond that which we can bear, but will always provide a way of escape (1 Corinthians 10:13), and that way is always Christ.

TODAY'S CHALLENGE:

Tell the Father that you want to abstain from sinful desires. Ask the Holy Spirit to help you say "no" to temptation today. Follow His leadership.

Dive Deeper: Study 1 Peter 2; 2 Corinthians 5:17; 1 John 5:18-19; 1 Corinthians 10:13.

August 16

CLEANSED BY GOD

1 John 1:9, AMP
"If we [freely] admit that we have sinned and confess our sins, He is faithful and just (true to His own nature and promises) and will forgive our sins [dismiss our lawlessness] and [continuously] cleanse us from all unrighteousness [everything not in conformity to His will in purpose, thought, and action]."

In Christ Jesus, we have the righteousness of God (2 Corinthians 5:21). When we give in to temptation or sin of any kind, we fall back under our own righteousness, which, to God, is as disgusting, filthy rags (Isaiah 64:6). That's when the devil really comes in against us as "the accuser".

The enemy is really experienced at trying to get us to buy into his accusations, and he wants us to start accusing ourselves. He uses feelings like shame, guilt, and embarrassment to harshly condemn us. Trying to convince us that "I have gone too far", and "God couldn't love me or forgive me", he wants us too ashamed to repent and seek God's cleansing.

We must choose to believe the Bible; and, listen to the still, small voice of the Holy Spirit gently convicting us that we were wrong and encouraging us to go to the Father to repent and confess (see March 9 devotional). God is Faithful and True. Jesus has paid the price for our forgiveness, so the Father can justly assign our sin to Jesus and the work of the Cross, and thereby cleanse us of all unrighteousness.

Then we are immediately possessing again the righteousness of God in Christ!

TODAY'S CHALLENGE:

Talk to the Father about any unconfessed sin. Repent, turn from the sin, and follow the Holy Spirit's leadership today, and every day, in Christ Jesus.

Dive Deeper: Study 1 John 1; 2 Corinthians 5:21; Isaiah 64:6; 1 Corinthians 1:30.

August 17

APPOINTED TO MINISTRY

1 Timothy 1:12, AMP
"I give thanks to Him Who has granted me [the needed] strength and made me able [for this], Christ Jesus our Lord, because He has judged and counted me faithful and trustworthy, appointing me to [this stewardship of] the ministry."

Regardless of your past, God still has a unique, perfect plan designed specifically for you. I personally know former murderers, gang leaders, drug dealers, addicts, kidnappers, robbers and sex offenders who truly repented, and turned their lives completely over to God.

Many of these people came to faith in prison, and now have successful ministries of their own. It seems God specializes in using former outcasts and rebels to showcase His grace, mercy and forgiveness to give others hope. It doesn't matter what you've done in the past, God really is ready, willing and able to make you a totally new creation in Christ Jesus.

As a former sex offender, I am still amazed at how God has been able to use my testimony to help and encourage so many others. If God can change me, and He has, He can change anyone! In 2009, when I came to faith in prison, I had no idea what God had in mind for me.

I am so very grateful and humbled that He placed me under Don Castleberry as my mentor and accountability partner. For several years now I have had the honor and privilege of running the prison ministry Don started over 35 years ago, which is now one of the most active prison ministries in Texas. I was ordained into the Gospel ministry under Don in 2012.

What an awesome God we serve!

TODAY'S CHALLENGE:

Seek God with all your heart. Worship Him in spirit and truth. Fully surrender.

Dive Deeper: Study 1 Timothy 1.

August 18

IGNORANCE IN UNBELIEF

1 Timothy 1:13-14, AMP
"Though I formerly blasphemed and persecuted and was shamefully and outrageously and aggressively insulting [to Him], nevertheless, I obtained mercy because I had acted out of ignorance in unbelief. [14] And the grace (unmerited favor and blessing) of our Lord [actually] flowed out super-abundantly and beyond measure for me, accompanied by faith and love that are [to be realized] in Christ Jesus."

Although I grew up in a Christian home, and in the Baptist church, once I went to college I turned my back on God. I think I chose not to remember what I had learned of His mercy, love and forgiveness, and for all practical purposes defaulted to "ignorance" of Him.

Though I still asserted belief in God and salvation in Jesus, nothing in my life supported this assertion in any way. I had the foulest mouth of almost anyone I knew, and blasphemed God by my words and actions. The outward evidence in my life screamed "unbelief" to others. I am certain my shamefully immoral life was insulting to God in every way.

Of all people, I certainly did not deserve God's grace, favor and blessing that resulted when I finally came to the stark truth that I could not run my own life, truly repented to God, humbled myself, and turned over my life entirely to Him. I held nothing back; thankfully, He didn't either!

His grace towards us will, in fact, flow out superabundantly; and, He exchanges His wisdom and faith for our ignorance and unbelief. Now that's a great deal!

TODAY'S CHALLENGE:

Tell the Father how thankful you are for His superabundant grace, love, mercy and forgiveness towards you. Ask the Holy Spirit if there is anything you are holding back. Give it to God today.

Dive Deeper: Study 1 Timothy 1.

August 19

FOREMOST OF SINNERS

1 Timothy 1:15-16, AMP
"The saying is sure and true and worthy of full and universal acceptance, that Christ Jesus (the Messiah) came into the world to save sinners, of whom I am foremost. ¹⁶ But I obtained mercy for the reason that in me, as the foremost [of sinners], Jesus Christ might show forth and display all His perfect long-suffering and patience for an example to [encourage] those who would thereafter believe on Him for [the gaining of] eternal life."

Earlier in this book, underneath the picture of my long and scraggly-haired, "old man" before Christ, are a lot of embarrassingly transparent descriptions of sin and shame. Actually, I have been reminded of some that aren't even on there. In the face of that man I am certain you can see regret, embarrassment, remorse, depression, rejection, shame, hopelessness and despair. Earlier in life, I had been filled with pride, greed, arrogance, selfishness, conceit, manipulation, deceitfulness and control.

Knowing everything I had done, or thought about doing, I thought I was beyond salvaging or redemption. Surely there was no blacker heart than mine. But, God…

I am so very thankful for His mercy. I totally agreed with Paul about being the "foremost of sinners". The remarkable transformation God has done in me has since given many people genuine hope for their eternal future, and encourages them to seek Him with all their heart.

Jesus Christ has surely displayed "His perfect long-suffering and patience", along with His mercy, towards us all!

TODAY'S CHALLENGE:

Spend a few minutes with the Father thanking Him for His patience, love, mercy and forgiveness. Ask the Holy Spirit to help you list your sins and circumstances from which you are free.

Dive Deeper: Study 1 Timothy 1.

August 20

DEATH AND LIFE

Proverbs 18:21, AMP
"Death and life are in the power of the tongue, and they who indulge in it shall eat the fruit of it [for death or life]."

James 3:9-10
"With the tongue we praise our Lord and Father, and with it we curse human beings, who have been made in God's likeness. ¹⁰ Out of the same mouth come praise and cursing. My brothers and sisters, this should not be."

Until I came to faith in Christ Jesus, I never considered how powerful my own words (and thoughts) were relative to success or failure in every area of life. Yet, for over 2,000 years the Word of God warned whoever would listen that "death and life are in the power of the tongue".

Spoken word curses, whether unintentional or not, have great power to negatively impact the life of the person to whomever they are directed, especially towards ourselves. The negative things we speak over ourselves reinforce the bad thoughts that created them. We were made in the image of God, and like Him, when we speak all kinds of things are set in motion.

When God spoke in Creation He declared everything "good", but in our case, many of our words do not result in anything we could ever classify as "good". We can powerfully influence for good everything and everyone around us when we declare truth and hope over ourselves and others in the form of the Word of God.

Start a practice of confessing God's Word aloud over your life daily. Make it a habit.

TODAY'S CHALLENGE:

Tell the Father you are thankful for His Word, and for its inherent power to positively impact your life. Ask the Holy Spirit to help you confess good things when you speak.

Dive Deeper: Study Proverbs 18; James 3:1-11.

August 21

WISDOM AND TRUTH

John 16:13
"But when he, the Spirit of truth, comes, he will guide you into all the truth. He will not speak on his own; he will speak only what he hears, and he will tell you what is yet to come."

James 1:5
"If any of you lacks wisdom, you should ask God, who gives generously to all without finding fault, and it will be given to you."

The Word of God is alive and powerful. When we confess it and apply it to our lives, we can expect to see positive measureable results. Today's verses promise that God makes available to us truth and wisdom. We do not have to beg Him for them.

The Spirit of Truth, the Holy Spirit, abides in every born again follower of Jesus. He will always be available to guide us into all truth, but He will not force it upon us. We should ask God about everything we do. Even what we consider small decisions can have large consequences.

We should seek God's wisdom to help us properly apply the principles in His Word along with truth being revealed by His Holy Spirit. The Word says Jesus has become for us wisdom from God (1 Corinthians 1:30), so as we live in Christ, we have access to all wisdom.

God's promises are real. Believe them, confess them, and expect them to bear fruit.

TODAY'S CHALLENGE:

Put the Word of God deep into your heart. Confess this aloud, and repeat it often today:

"The Spirit of Truth abides in me and teaches me all things, and He guides me into all truths. Therefore, I confess I have perfect knowledge of every situation and circumstance I come up against for I have the wisdom of God."

Dive Deeper: Study John 16; James 1:5-8.

August 22

TRUST IN THE LORD

Proverbs 3:5-6, AMP
"Lean on, trust in, and be confident in the Lord with all your heart and mind and do not rely on your own insight or understanding. ⁶ In all your ways know, recognize, and acknowledge Him, and He will direct and make straight and plain your paths."

Our trust and confidence in the Lord, as well as our daily dependence on Him, grows in direct proportion to us humbly admitting that our own insight or understanding is inferior to His. This recognition, for a believer, causes us to seek Him first for direction and guidance daily.

Many of us previously thought we had all the answers; but after coming to Christ, we realize how prideful it was to think we could run our lives without God's help. Frankly, I find it a relief to seek His will and guidance in everything first (Matthew 6:33). Without His direction, I sit still (Psalm 46:10).

We should humbly give God credit for every good thing, and boldly proclaim, to ourselves and others, His goodness, favor and grace over our lives. The more we thank Him for leading us in even the smallest areas, the more the Holy Spirit will direct us, and clear the path ahead of us.

Personally, I find it useful to give the Holy Spirit grateful recognition for every positive thing throughout the entire day, no matter how small a matter it may seem to me. He is so wise and gracious; everything matters to Him!

TODAY'S CHALLENGE:

Put the Word of God deep into your heart. Confess this aloud, and repeat it often today:

"I trust in the Lord with all my heart and I do not lean on my own understanding. In all my ways I acknowledge Him, and He directs my path."

Dive Deeper: Study Proverbs 3; Matthew 6:33; Psalm 46:10.

August 23

GOD COMPLETES HIS WORK

Psalm 138:8
"The Lord will perfect that which concerns me; Your mercy and loving-kindness, O Lord, endure forever—forsake not the works of Your own hands."

Philippians 1:6
"...being confident of this, that he who began a good work in you will carry it on to completion until the day of Christ Jesus."

God never leaves anything undone. Whatever He starts, He finishes.

God has a plan for each and every one of His children. He wants to see us walk in the fullness of His intention for us. The most amazing part of this truth is that He has given us His Spirit to accomplish the work in us; we merely have to surrender to Him daily and submit to His leadership.

The Holy Spirit's work in us is ongoing and progressively fruitful as He conforms us to the image of Christ Jesus, and leads us in the paths God in His Wisdom has ordained for us. As the world around us sees the fruit of His labor in our lives, others will naturally be drawn to Him.

God has said He will never leave us or forsake us (Hebrews 13:5-6). He will not abandon us or leave us as orphans (John 14:18). God works in us to will and to act to fulfill His good purpose (Philippians 2:13).

TODAY'S CHALLENGE:

Put the Word of God deep into your heart. Confess this aloud, and repeat it often today:

"The Lord will perfect that which concerns me, and fulfill His purpose for me. He Who began a good work in me will complete it! God works in me, and will never leave me or forsake me."

Dive Deeper: Study Psalm 138; Hebrews 13:5-6; John 14:18; Philippians 2:13; Ephesians 2:9.

August 24

LET THE WORD DWELL RICHLY

Colossians 3:16
"Let the message of Christ dwell among you richly as you teach and admonish one another with all wisdom..."

2 Timothy 3:16
"All Scripture is God-breathed and is useful for teaching, rebuking, correcting and training in righteousness..."

God's Word never returns to Him without accomplishing exactly what He intended (Isaiah 55:10-11). We must put it in our hearts, and meditate continuously on its meaning and application for our lives. We must let the Word live in us.

Since the Word is alive (Hebrews 4:12), it adds life to our whole being – spirit, soul and body. God's Words are "life to those who find them and health to one's body" (Proverbs 4:20-22).

The Word becomes more and more active in our lives as we confess it aloud and meditate on it. In so doing, the Word becomes available to the Holy Spirit to bring out of us at the proper time and for the correct purpose. The Spirit uses the Word to encourage, teach, rebuke, correct and train us. As He trains us, we are able to help and encourage others.

The Spirit will always guide us in ways that align with the Word. We more easily discern His voice and leadership by how well we know and understand His Word. Fervently praying God's Word back to Him makes our prayers powerfully effective (James 5:16).

TODAY'S CHALLENGE:

Put the Word of God deep into your heart. Confess this aloud, and repeat it often today:

"I let the Word of Christ dwell in me richly in all wisdom. His Word is alive and active in me. It teaches me, rebukes me, corrects me, and trains me in righteousness. His Word always accomplishes in me what He intends!"

Dive Deeper: Study Colossians 3; Isaiah 55:10-11; Hebrews 4:12; Proverbs 4:20-22; James 5:16.

August 25

SHEEP LISTEN AND FOLLOW

John 10:4-5
Jesus said, "When he has brought out all his own, he goes on ahead of them, and his sheep follow him because they know his voice. ⁵ But they will never follow a stranger; in fact, they will run away from him because they do not recognize a stranger's voice."

John 10:27
"My sheep listen to my voice; I know them, and they follow me."

Jesus always taught using examples even the most common of people would understand. In that day, shepherds were very numerous and people often saw them with their flocks. They knew that sheep were not "herded" in the sense we think of it today. The shepherd did not walk behind his sheep tying to move them forward.

Instead, his voice alone would be used to lead the sheep. They recognized their shepherds voice and would respond to no other voice.

It was common during certain times of the year to bring the flocks together at night in a pen, a sheepfold. Several flocks were mixed together. At daylight, each shepherd would stand at the gate and call for his sheep. Only his sheep would listen and follow him out to pasture for the day. They trusted him, and knew they would be safe in his care.

The primary time a sheep would encounter trouble was when they stopped listening for the voice of their shepherd, and thus wandered off on their own. That ought to be a lesson for us.

TODAY'S CHALLENGE:

Put the Word of God deep into your heart. Confess this aloud, and repeat it often today:

"I do follow the Good Shepherd. I listen for Him. I know His voice, and I obey. The voice of a stranger I will not follow."

Dive Deeper: Study John 10.

August 26

WISDOM AND RIGHTEOUSNESS

1 Corinthians 1:30
"It is because of him that you are in Christ Jesus, who has become for us wisdom from God—that is, our righteousness, holiness and redemption."

2 Corinthians 5:21
"God made him who had no sin to be sin for us, so that in him we might become the righteousness of God."

What a marvelous plan the Father had to reconcile the world back to Himself through the sacrifice of Jesus and the power of the Holy Spirit! Everything we need for all of time and eternity is available to us in Christ Jesus.

Paul had an exceptionally powerful revelation from God about a born again believer's position "in" Christ Jesus. In the New Testament, primarily in the writings of Paul, the terms "in Christ", "in Him", and "in Whom" are used over 130 times.

All the passages in which Paul uses these terms are important for us because Paul is encouraging us to see ourselves as a totally new creation in Christ Jesus, and he uses these terms to teach us something more about how God sees us once we are born again.

Jesus Himself is the wisdom of God, and in Him we are wise. Jesus Himself is the righteousness of God, and in Him we are righteous. Jesus is Holy, and in Him we are progressively made more holy by the Holy Spirit. Our redemption from sin is only through the Blood and Life of Jesus.

TODAY'S CHALLENGE:

Put the Word of God deep into your heart. Confess this aloud, and repeat it often today:

"Jesus is made unto me wisdom, righteousness, sanctification, and redemption. Therefore, I confess I have the wisdom of God, and I am the righteousness of God in Christ Jesus."

Dive Deeper: Study 1 Corinthians 1.

August 27

KNOWLEDGE OF THE LORD'S WILL

Colossians 1:9-10
"...We continually ask God to fill you with the knowledge of his will through all the wisdom and understanding that the Spirit gives, [10] so that you may live a life worthy of the Lord and please him in every way..."

I imagine each of us reading this would say we want to have the knowledge of the Lord's will for our lives. Am I right?

Notice in this scripture that this knowledge is available "through all the wisdom and understanding that the Spirit gives". The Holy Spirit of God is the One who gives us wisdom, knowledge and understanding. We must continually be in fellowship, and communicating with, the Holy Spirit (see 2 Corinthians 13:14).

Something I do often in my prayers is to ask God for the following through His Holy Spirit in me: wisdom, knowledge, understanding, truth, discernment, revelation and application to my life. I also ask Him for more boldness and courage so I can serve Him better.

I believe all these are crucially important for me to seek and receive daily so that I "may live a life worthy of the Lord and please Him in every way".

We should bathe our mind in the Word daily. Romans 12:2 says that we are transformed by the renewing of our mind so that we can know what the Lord's will is, His good, pleasing and perfect will. Let's seek His will today. Do it.

TODAY'S CHALLENGE:

Put the Word of God deep into your heart. Confess this aloud, and repeat it often today:

"I am filled with the knowledge of the Lord's will in all wisdom and spiritual understanding. I want to live a life worthy of the Lord Jesus and please Him in every way."

Dive Deeper: Study Colossians 1; 2 Corinthians 13:14.

August 28

THE MIND OF CHRIST

Ephesians 2:10
"For we are God's handiwork, created in Christ Jesus to do good works, which God prepared in advance for us to do."

1 Corinthians 2:15-16
"The person with the Spirit makes judgments about all things, but such a person is not subject to merely human judgments, [16] for, 'Who has known the mind of the Lord so as to instruct him?' But we have the mind of Christ."

One thing we must remember daily is the truth that 2 Corinthians 5:17 reveals, *"Therefore, if anyone is in Christ, the new creation has come: The old has gone, the new is here!"* In Christ, we are a totally new creation, one that never existed before!

In Him, we are created by God to do good works. Our good deeds do not save us, but anyone who is truly saved will, by the Holy Spirit, certainly accomplish good things which help present Jesus to the world. We are always to "re-present" Him. Over and over, the world should see Jesus in us.

The Word says, by and through the Holy Spirit, we are now able to make good judgments about all things because we have the mind of Christ! For me, making sound decisions was not something I had been doing in the midst of my sin and addictions. Do I have a witness?

What refreshing, important truths these are today! Walk in them.

TODAY'S CHALLENGE:

Put the Word of God deep into your heart. Confess this aloud, and repeat it often today:

"I am a new creation in Christ. I am His workmanship created in Christ Jesus. Therefore, I confess I have the mind of Christ and the wisdom of God is formed within me."

Dive Deeper: Study 1 Corinthians 2; Ephesians 2.

August 29

WISDOM AND REVELATION

Ephesians 1:17-18
"I keep asking that the God of our Lord Jesus Christ, the glorious Father, may give you the Spirit of wisdom and revelation, so that you may know him better. [18] I pray that the eyes of your heart may be enlightened in order that you may know the hope to which he has called you..."

Romans 12:2
"Do not conform to the pattern of this world, but be transformed by the renewing of your mind. Then you will be able to test and approve what God's will is — his good, pleasing and perfect will."

Because of our faith in Jesus, God the Father is pleased to give us "the Spirit of wisdom and revelation" so that we may know Him better. The God of the universe wants to have an intimate personal relationship with us!

All our hope is in Him, and He gives us enlightened hearts to realize and walk in His hope-filled calling for us. He longs for us to know His will, and we are encouraged to transform and renew our minds through His Word so that the allurements of the world will not entrap us.

With a renewed mind, we are able to better discern the voice of the Holy Spirit apart from the competing voices of the world, the flesh, and the devil. Then we can be led in His will!

TODAY'S CHALLENGE:

Put the Word of God deep into your heart. Confess this aloud, and repeat it often today:

"I receive the Spirit of wisdom and revelation in the knowledge of Him, the eyes of my understanding being enlightened. I am not conformed to this world but I am transformed by the renewing of my mind. My mind is renewed by the Word of God."

Dive Deeper: Study Ephesians 1.

August 30

SAVED AND FORGIVEN

Ephesians 2:8
"For it is by grace you have been saved, through faith—and this is not from yourselves, it is the gift of God..."

Colossians 1:13-14
"For he has rescued us from the dominion of darkness and brought us into the kingdom of the Son he loves, [14] in whom we have redemption, the forgiveness of sins."

Knowing very well who I used to be when I followed the ways of the world, I remain in awe at the magnificence of God's Plan of Salvation through Jesus Christ. He has made it so simple. Why do we make it so hard, or think we need to add anything to it in and of ourselves?

What a relief it is to know that I do not have to work for my salvation. Christianity is the only world religion where this is true. It is for freedom that Christ has set us free (see Galatians 5:1). Unlike the rest of the people who follow other faiths, we are not in bondage to rule-keeping and good works necessary, in their view, to attain Heaven.

We are forgiven of all our sins – past, present and future – through the Blood-bought price of redemption by the precious sacrifice of our Savior, Jesus Christ. I thank God that He rescued me for the dominion of darkness! How about you?

TODAY'S CHALLENGE:

Put the Word of God deep into your heart. Confess this aloud, and repeat it often today:

"I am saved by grace through faith, and this is a gift of God. I did not earn my salvation. I have been rescued from the dominion of darkness, and I now live in the Kingdom of Light in Christ Jesus. I am redeemed, set free, and forgiven of all my sins!"

Dive Deeper: Study Ephesians 2; Colossians 1.

August 31

CHILDREN OF GOD

John 1:12
"Yet to all who did receive him, to those who believed in his name, he gave the right to become children of God..."

Romans 8:14
"For those who are led by the Spirit of God are the children of God."

We often hear unbelievers say, "we are all God's children". That is not true. In fact, it is a great deception of the enemy. We are all "created" by God, but not everyone is a "child" of God.

Before I came to Christ, I was a child of my father, the devil (see John 8:44), and I only did his works. Like a slave, I was led around by the world, the flesh and the devil.

In prison, when I finally gave in to the relentless, overwhelming love of God in Christ Jesus, my Savior, I became a child of the One True God. I received Jesus and I believe in His Name.

I am now led by the Holy Spirit of God! Because I have been adopted into the family of God, I am a joint heir with Christ, and now able to share with Him all the marvelous, abundant inheritance from Our Father.

This is all available to you. Do you believe? Have you received? Are you led by the Holy Spirit? Are you a true child of God?

TODAY'S CHALLENGE:

Put the Word of God deep into your heart. Confess this aloud, and repeat it often today:

"I am a child of God. I receive the work of Jesus at the Cross and in the Resurrection done on my behalf. I trust in, rely on and call on His Name. I am led by the Spirit of God, and I know I am one of God's children!"

Dive Deeper: Study Romans 8.

September 1

SAFE AND SECURE

Psalm 91:11-12
"For he will command his angels concerning you to guard you in all your ways; ¹² they will lift you up in their hands, so that you will not strike your foot against a stone."

Psalm 27:1
"The Lord is my light and my salvation — whom shall I fear? The Lord is the stronghold of my life — of whom shall I be afraid?"

I have never counted them, but I have heard there are 365 references in the Bible telling us, "Do not fear", "Do not be afraid", or "Fear not". If correct, this would be interesting and significant, in part, because it would be one admonition (warning) for each day of the year.

The Word of God is filled with verses that build trust in God; and, inspire confidence, courage, and boldness in us. We have the Holy Spirit of God with us at all times, and He promises never to leave us or forsake us.

A stronghold is a fortress, or an embattlement position. For us as true believers, the Lord Himself is our fortress and our refuge (Psalm 91:2). He is our Light to penetrate every darkness, and He is forever our salvation.

I believe we have angels watching over us, and keeping us out of harm's way. I can think of a number of specific times where, in hindsight, I know I was supernaturally protected from harm, and even death. Can you think of some?

TODAY'S CHALLENGE:

Put the Word of God deep into your heart. Confess this aloud, and repeat it often today:

"I am kept in safety wherever I go. I will not fear because the Lord is my light and my salvation. The Lord is the stronghold of my life, of whom shall I be afraid?"

Dive Deeper: Study Psalm 27; Psalm 91.

September 2

ALL YOU NEED

Philippians 4:19
"And my God will meet all your needs according to the riches of his glory in Christ Jesus."

2 Corinthians 9:8
"And God is able to bless you abundantly, so that in all things at all times, having all that you need, you will abound in every good work."

It is interesting to note that the context of the Philippians passage leading up to verse 19 has to do with Paul thanking, and further exhorting, believers for their gifts supporting his Gospel ministry (Philippians 4:15-19). So, in some sense, God's provision of our personal needs is directly related to our personal giving.

Many correctly point out that Philippians 4:19 applies to our true "needs" not necessarily our desires. Yet, Psalm 37:4 says as we delight in the Lord He will give us the desires of our heart. I believe this means as we sincerely seek intimacy of relationship with God, He puts appropriate, Godly desires in our hearts, and then sets about to fulfill them!

We can trust our Father to know exactly what we need at all times in every situation. He will not withhold anything from us that we need to fulfill His will and plan for our life. His grace, love and generosity is abundant to reward those who diligently seek Him (Hebrews 11:6).

Let's choose to trust God daily for even the smallest of our needs, and continuously express our gratitude!

TODAY'S CHALLENGE:

Put the Word of God deep into your heart. Confess this aloud, and repeat it often today:

"I am getting all my needs met by Jesus. I am blessed abundantly at all times. For all things, I have all I need, so that I am supplied for every good work God has planned for me."

Dive Deeper: Study Philippians 4.

September 3

DO NOT BE ANXIOUS

1 Peter 5:6-7
"Humble yourselves, therefore, under God's mighty hand, that he may lift you up in due time. ⁷ Cast all your anxiety on him because he cares for you."

Philippians 4:6
"Do not be anxious about anything, but in every situation, by prayer and petition, with thanksgiving, present your requests to God."

In 1 Peter 5:7 above, the word translated as "cast" comes from a Greek word that means "to throw over". In <u>The Merriam-Webster Dictionary</u> "cast" is defined as "to throw out or away, to fling, or toss". God does not want us carrying burdens; if we throw them over onto Him we can trust His caring, loving hands to catch them.

Psalm 55:22 says to "Cast your cares on the Lord and He will sustain you; He will never let the righteous fall." He not only bears you up and sustains you, but He will bear your cares for you!

When we are trusting God, we will be grateful that He hears and responds to our prayerful requests and petitions. For example, if you were ever too "altered" to drive home, and you tossed your car keys over to your sober friend, you could trust Him to help you.

But you have to be wise enough to let go of the keys, and don't take them back!

TODAY'S CHALLENGE:

Put the Word of God deep into your heart. Confess this aloud, and repeat it often today:

"I humble myself before God, and He cares for me. I throw all my anxious cares over upon Him, and He will carry them for me. I am not anxious about anything because I talk to God about everything that concerns me. I always express my thanks and gratitude to Him."

Dive Deeper: Study 1 Peter 5; Psalm 55:22; Psalm 68:19; Matthew 6:25-34; Matthew 11:28-30.

September 4

BE STRONG IN THE LORD

Ephesians 6:10
"Finally, be strong in the Lord and in his mighty power."

Philippians 4:13
"I can do all this through him who gives me strength."

In these exciting days, more than ever, we will be called on to "be strong in the Lord"; and we must know that "His mighty power" resides in us by His Holy Spirit. When prophesying about the last days, the prophet Daniel wrote, *"...the people who know their God shall be strong, and carry out great exploits."* (Daniel 11:32, NKJV)

God wants us to be certain that He will empower us and give us strength from within so that we can do all things He asks us to do. He does not expect us to operate out of our own strength.

Many people exercise their bodies regularly to build up their muscles and tone their body so that they become stronger physically. I noticed this is especially true in prison. This builds their self-confidence for the occasion when they need to carry out an arduous task, or defend themselves.

Similarly, when we exercise our spirit and soul by spending regular time in the Word and in the Presence of God, we will build God-confidence for the times when we are performing Kingdom work, or defending ourselves in spiritual warfare from the attacks of the enemy. God will never give us a task we can't handle, and the enemy is already a defeated foe by Christ Jesus!

TODAY'S CHALLENGE:

Put the Word of God deep into your heart. Confess this aloud, and repeat it often today:

"I am strong in the Lord and in His mighty power by the Holy Spirit. I am doing all things through Christ Who strengthen me."

Dive Deeper: Study Ephesians 6; Micah 3:8; Zechariah 4:6; 2 Corinthians 12:9-10.

September 5

BLESSED IN OBEDIENCE

Deuteronomy 28:6
"You will be blessed when you come in and blessed when you go out."

Deuteronomy 28:13
"The LORD will make you the head, not the tail. If you pay attention to the commands of the LORD your God that I give you this day and carefully follow them, you will always be at the top, never at the bottom."

God honors obedience. Even though we are not perfectly obedient all the time, God longs to see a heart whose desire, aim and purpose is to be obedient to Him. If this is our heart, we will pay attention to God's commands and we will try to carefully follow them.

When King Saul disobeyed God and let his soldiers keep some of the plunder instead of destroying everything, Saul tried to justify his actions to the Prophet Samuel by saying they were going to sacrifice the best to God. Samuel makes it clear that to God, *"To obey is better than sacrifice"* (1 Samuel 15:22).

Sacrifices were often made for disobedience. It cost the person something valuable to them as a result of their disobedience. God would have accepted Saul's obedience, but his sacrifice for disobedience was rejected; and, Saul was rejected as King.

Our obedience may sometimes be costly in a worldly sense, but it will always result in God's blessing. Will you pay attention to God's commands and carefully follow them?

TODAY'S CHALLENGE:

Put the Word of God deep into your heart. Confess this aloud, and repeat it often today:

"I am observing and doing the Lord's commandments, so I am always blessed coming in, and I am blessed going out! By obedience, I am the head, and not the tail; I am at the top, and never at the bottom!"

Dive Deeper: Study Deuteronomy 28.

September 6

EVERY SPIRITUAL BLESSING

Ephesians 1:3
"Praise be to the God and Father of our Lord Jesus Christ, who has blessed us in the heavenly realms with every spiritual blessing in Christ."

What a marvelous statement of truth for Paul to make! We have every spiritual blessing in Christ Jesus. All, I repeat, all spiritual blessings God has ever made available to His people are forever found in Christ Jesus; and, they are never to be withdrawn or diminished in any way. They are eternal.

I suggest you study the passage immediately following today's verse, that is, Ephesians 1:3-14. In this passage, Paul enumerates many of these spiritual blessings:

God chose us in Christ before the foundation of the world to be holy and blameless in His sight. Out of His limitless love, He predestined us to be adopted in the family of God through (and only through) Jesus Christ. He did this because He wanted the pleasure of extending His superabundant grace to those who could never deserve or earn it, if only they would receive it in Christ Jesus.

In Christ, we have redemption, forgiveness, wisdom and understanding. God made known to us His ultimate intention to bring all things together in Heaven and on earth under One Head, Christ Jesus.

God has made us trophies of His grace for the praise of His Glory. When we were born again, God marked us as His own with a seal, the promised Holy Spirit, Who is a down payment guaranteeing our inheritance until our ultimate redemption for all of eternity, again, to the praise of His Glory!

TODAY'S CHALLENGE:

Put the Word of God deep into your heart. Confess this aloud, and repeat it often today:

"I am blessed with ALL spiritual blessings in Christ Jesus."

Dive Deeper: Study Ephesians 1.

September 7

YOU HAVE BEEN HEALED

1 Peter 2:24
"He himself bore our sins in his body on the cross, so that we might die to sins and live for righteousness; 'by his wounds you have been healed.'"

Psalm 107:20
"He sent out his word and healed them; he rescued them from the grave."

In the Great Exchange of the Cross, one of the many blessings that Jesus Christ provided was healing for us who believe, through His stripes and wounds.

In our verse today, Peter is referring to what we know now as Isaiah 53, where 700 years before Jesus' sacrificial death, Isaiah prophesies with pin-point accuracy the "Suffering Servant", our Messiah, Jesus. He enumerates there what Jesus would accomplish on our behalf at the Cross and Resurrection (see Isaiah 53:1-12).

Even earlier, in the Psalms, it was prophesied that God "sent out his word and healed them", and we know Jesus was the Living Word. Psalm 103:3, says God "heals all our diseases".

The enemy knows these truths but attacks believers anyway with illnesses, diseases and other afflictions. Most Christians either do not know these truths, or will not, in faith, proclaim them over their lives at the first signs of attack.

I have personally seen God's miraculous response to prayers for healing in many instances. Is it every instance? No, and I do not know why. But I trust His Word and I proclaim it over myself and others, in faith, believing!

TODAY'S CHALLENGE:

Put the Word of God deep into your heart. Confess this aloud, and repeat it often today:

"God sent His Word and healed me; He has rescued me from the grave. By the wounds and stripes of Jesus I have been healed. Praise the Lord, oh my soul, God heals all my diseases."

Dive Deeper: Study Isaiah 53; Psalm 30:2; Psalm 103:1-5; Matthew 8:17.

September 8

OVERCOMER AND CONQUEROR

Romans 8:35, 37
"Who shall separate us from the love of Christ? Shall trouble or hardship or persecution or famine or nakedness or danger or sword?... [37] No, in all these things we are more than conquerors through him who loved us."

Revelation 12:11
"They triumphed over (overcame) him by the blood of the Lamb and by the word of their testimony; they did not love their lives so much as to shrink from death."

Jesus is the ultimate Overcomer and Conqueror. In Him, we are also overcomers and conquerors. In the spiritual battles that rage around us in unseen realms we are not fighting "for" victory, rather, we fight "from" victory!

When we are "in Christ" nothing can separate us from Him, and every victory He achieved. Paul says, in Romans 8:39-40, that absolutely nothing can separate us from the love of Christ – *"neither death nor life, neither angels nor demons, neither the present nor the future, nor any powers,[39] neither height nor depth, nor anything else in all creation."*

One of my favorite teachers, Derek Prince, taught that Revelation 12:11 can also be translated as, "We overcome when we testify of what the Blood of Jesus has done in our lives!" Yes, we must testify to others, but sometimes we need to testify to ourselves. We should always be quick to thank God for what He has done in our lives.

There should never be heard the description "defeated Christian". It is an oxymoron!

TODAY'S CHALLENGE:

Put the Word of God deep into your heart. Confess this aloud, and repeat it often today:

"I am more than a conqueror. I am an overcomer by the Blood of the Lamb and the word of my testimony. Nothing by shall any means harm me."

Dive Deeper: Study Romans 8.

September 9

LIVING BY FAITH

2 Corinthians 5:7
"For we live by faith, not by sight."

2 Corinthians 4:8-9
"We are hard pressed on every side, but not crushed; perplexed, but not in despair; ⁹persecuted, but not abandoned; struck down, but not destroyed."

We must not let our perception of circumstances or events dictate how we respond to them. We must do our best to imitate "…God, who gives life to the dead and calls those things which do not exist as though they did" (Romans 4:17).

We trust in the Creator Who, by His Word and Spirit, brought forth everything out of nothing. Our eyes must be set firmly, confidently and assuredly on Him and His promises. Faith is trusting in God in and through all circumstances; and this faith enables us to persevere and overcome as we remain loyal to Him. God is Who He says He is, and He does what He says He will do!

In Christ, our sins are forgiven and we are justified by His grace; in Him we are "righteous". Hebrews 10:38 quotes God as saying, *"But my righteous one will live by faith. And I take no pleasure in the one who shrinks back."*

We must always remember who we are "in Christ". All the promises and protections of God are always available to us in Christ Jesus. Are you living by faith?

TODAY'S CHALLENGE:

Put the Word of God deep into your heart. Confess this aloud, and repeat it often today:

"I am walking and living by faith and not by sight. I am not moved by what I see. I proclaim things that do not exist as though they do. I trust in the Lord with all my heart and I do not rely on my own understanding."

Dive Deeper: Study 2 Corinthians 4; Hebrews 11; Romans 4:17; Hebrews 10:38.

September 10

OVERCOME THE DEVIL

2 Corinthians 10:4-5
"The weapons we fight with are not the weapons of the world. On the contrary, they have divine power to demolish strongholds. [5] We demolish arguments and every pretension that sets itself up against the knowledge of God, and we take captive every thought to make it obedient to Christ."

1 John 4:4
"You, dear children, are from God and have overcome them, because the one who is in you is greater than the one who is in the world."

Every day we come up against some sort of resistance from the enemy in the form of worldly ideas, sinful temptations, false teaching, and other challenges to our Christian beliefs. As these enter our minds through our five senses, we must be proactive in using the weapons we have in Christ to counter and reject them.

Joyce Meyer says, "We must think about what we are thinking about!" This means we must always be consciously aware of what is going through our minds, getting down into our hearts, and coming out of our mouths. We have the ability to examine every thought and make it obedient to Christ.

We have the most powerful weapons in the universe in the Word of God, prayer, and the Holy Spirit. These are not the weapons of the world. Do you use them?

TODAY'S CHALLENGE:

Put the Word of God deep into your heart. Confess this aloud, and repeat it often today:

"I am daily overcoming the devil, because the One in me is greater than the one in the world. My weapons have Divine Power to demolish strongholds, vain imaginations and pretensions, and everything that sets itself up against the knowledge of God. I take captive every thought to make it obedient to Christ!"

Dive Deeper: Study 2 Corinthians 10; Psalm 119:11; Luke 4:1-13.

September 11

PRAISE THE LORD

Psalm 34:1
"I will extol the LORD at all times; his praise will always be on my lips."

Colossians 3:16
"Let the message of Christ dwell among you richly as you teach and admonish one another with all wisdom through psalms, hymns, and songs from the Spirit, singing to God with gratitude in your hearts."

As believers, the love, peace and joy produced inside us by the Holy Spirit should naturally bubble up from deep within us in praises to our God. Our heart should always be in a continual state of thankfulness for all our many blessings.

Think about all the many ways God has blessed you and your family. How do you feel about being delivered from the bondage that once enslaved you?

Even if a person doesn't think they can sing well, the Bible says to make a joyful noise unto the Lord. I may not sing on key but I am loud and can make a joyful noise to glorify God. Are you like me? Although we may be embarrassed to sing loudly in public, we can praise God in any number of ways in a less public setting.

After all, we should not be concerned about criticism from others. I am certain that even our weakest attempts to express gratitude and praise warm the Heart of God! Can you imagine how He feels when we are enthusiastic and exuberant? Don't be shy, praise the Lord!

TODAY'S CHALLENGE:

Put the Word of God deep into your heart. Confess this aloud, and repeat it often today:

"I am blessing the Lord at all times and continually praising the Lord with my mouth. With psalms, hymns and songs from the Spirit I will sing to God with gratitude in my heart!"

Dive Deeper: Study Psalm 34; Colossians 3.

September 12

PRAYING THE SCRIPTURES

Personalized Prayers from Scripture:

Personalizing scripture and repeating them back to God can be very effective. As you pray God's Word back to Him, He is pleased, for He has told us to put Him in remembrance of His Word. Do you think He needs to be reminded? Like He forgot?

No, we are the ones who need to be reminded. We claim these awesome promises for ourselves. Pray these prayers from your heart several times today. You will be richly blessed in doing so.

Psalm 103:1-5
I praise you Lord from my soul. From my inmost being I praise your Holy name. I praise you Lord from my soul. I will not forget all your benefits – you forgive all my sins and heal all my diseases. You redeemed my life from the pit and crowned me with your love and compassion. You satisfy my desires with good things so that my youth is renewed like an eagle's. In the Name of Jesus, Amen.

Isaiah 54:17
No weapon forged against me will prevail and I will refute every tongue that accuses me. This is my heritage as a servant of the Lord, and this is my vindication from you. In the Name of Jesus, Amen.

Philippians 1:9-11
This also is my prayer: that my love may abound more and more in knowledge and depth of insight, so that I may be able to discern what is best and may be pure and blameless until the day of Christ, filled with the fruit of righteousness that comes through Jesus Christ – to the glory and praise of you, God. In the Name of Jesus, Amen.

TODAY'S CHALLENGE:

Ask the Holy Spirit to bring to your mind a favorite scripture of yours. Personalize it for yourself.

Dive Deeper: Study Psalm 103.

September 13

PRAYING PROTECTION

Claim these awesome personalized, scriptural promises of protection in prayer!

Psalm 91
As I dwell in the shelter of the Most High I will rest in the shadow of the Almighty. I will say of you Lord, "You are my refuge and my fortress. You are my God and I will trust in you." Surely you will save me from the fowler's snare and from the deadly pestilence. You will cover me with your feathers, and under your wings I will find refuge; your faithfulness will be my shield and rampart.

I will not fear the terror of night nor the arrow that flies by day, nor the pestilence that stalks in the darkness, nor the plague that destroys at midday. A thousand may fall at my side, ten thousand by my right hand, but it will not come near me.

I will observe with my eyes and see the punishment of the wicked. I will make the Most High my dwelling – the Lord is my refuge – so that no harm will befall me, no disaster will come near my tent. God, you will command your angels concerning me to guard me in all my ways; they will lift me up in their hands, so that I will not strike my foot against a stone. I will tread upon the lion and the cobra; I will trample the great lion and the serpent.

Lord, you said because I love you, you will rescue me. You will protect me, for I acknowledge your name. I will call upon you and you will answer me; you will be with me in trouble, you will deliver me and honor me. With long life will you satisfy me and show me your salvation. In the Name of Jesus, Amen.

TODAY'S CHALLENGE:

Pray this prayer from your heart several times today. You will be richly blessed in doing so.

Dive Deeper: Study Psalm 91.

September 14

PETITIONING GOD

Pray these awesome personalized, scriptural petitions to our Father God!

Ephesians 1:17-23
I keep asking that you, God of my Lord Jesus Christ, my glorious Father, may give me the Spirit of wisdom and revelation that I may know you better. I pray also that the eyes of my heart may be enlightened in order that I may know the hope to which you have called me, the riches of your glorious inheritance in the saints, and your incomparably great power for us who believe.

That power is like the working of your mighty strength, which you exerted in Christ when you raised Him from the dead and seated Him at your right hand in heavenly realms, far above all rule and authority, power and dominion, and every title that can be given, not only in the present age but also in the one to come.

And you, God, placed all things under His feet and appointed Him to be over everything for the church, which is His body, the fullness of Him who fills everything in every way. In the Name of Jesus, Amen.

Colossians 1:9-11
I pray that you fill me with the knowledge of your will through all spiritual wisdom and understanding. I pray this in order that I may live a life worthy of the Lord Jesus and please Him in every way: bearing fruit in every good work, growing in the knowledge of you, God, so that I may be strengthened with all power according to your glorious might so that I may have great endurance and patience and joyfully give you thanks. In the Name of Jesus, Amen.

TODAY'S CHALLENGE:

Pray these prayers from your heart several times today. You will be richly blessed in doing so.

Dive Deeper: Study Ephesians 1; Colossians 1.

September 15

PRAYERS FOR POWER

Pray these personalized prayers for power to our Father God!

Ephesians 3:16-21

I pray that out of your glorious riches you may strengthen me with power through your Spirit in my inner being, so that Christ may dwell in my heart through faith. And I pray that as I am rooted and established in love, I may have power, together with all the saints, to grasp how wide and long and high and deep is the love of Christ, and that I may know this love that surpasses knowledge – that I may be filled to the measure of all your fullness.

Now to you, God, who is able to do immeasurably more than all I ask or imagine, according to your power that is at work within me, to you be glory in the church and in Christ Jesus throughout all generations, forever and ever! In the Name of Jesus, Amen.

Luke 4:18-19

I pray that the Spirit of the Lord is on me with power, because he has anointed me to proclaim good news to the poor. I thank you that you have sent me to proclaim freedom for the prisoners and recovery of sight for the blind, to set the oppressed free, to proclaim the year of the Lord's favor. In the Name of Jesus, Amen.

Acts 10:38

I pray that you would anoint me like Jesus of Nazareth with the Holy Spirit and power, so that I could also go around doing good and healing all who are under the power of the devil, because God is with me. In the Name of Jesus, Amen.

TODAY'S CHALLENGE:

Pray these prayers from your heart several times today. You will be richly blessed in doing so.

Dive Deeper: Study Ephesians 3.

September 16

LET NOTHING MOVE YOU

1 Corinthians 15:58
"Therefore, my dear brothers and sisters, stand firm. Let nothing move you. Always give yourselves fully to the work of the Lord, because you know that your labor in the Lord is not in vain."

Going "all in" for Jesus means that we will put Him first in every area of our life – His character, His love, His compassion, His mercy, His forgiveness.

We must stand firm against the world, the flesh and the devil. They will always be pushing against the principles of Christ. The assault on the Biblical worldview and Christians is increasing daily. Paul exhorts us to be focused, tireless, and totally devoted to our mission.

We are all ambassadors for Christ, and we are to represent His Kingdom to the world around us wherever we are every day. Each of us is charged to fulfill the great commission to spread the Good News of Jesus in our particular environments.

This is best done by letting our lives shine forth the love, peace, joy, kindness, goodness, faithfulness, gentleness, self-control, and patience produced as fruit by the Holy Spirit in our totally surrendered lives. We must submit to the Lordship of Jesus and the Leadership of the Holy Spirit.

We will not fully realize the impact on others of our work for the Lord until we stand in front of Jesus in Heaven. But, our labor will be rewarded magnificently in eternity.

TODAY'S CHALLENGE:

Ask the Father to show you an area in your life where there is compromise between your Christian principles and the world's ways of living. Tell Him you want to stand firm for Jesus and do the right thing. Ask the Holy Spirit to make the necessary changes as you re-surrender to Him today.

Dive Deeper: Study 1 Corinthians 15; Hebrews 6:10-12.

September 17

PUT IT INTO PRACTICE

Philippians 4:9
"Whatever you have learned or received or heard from me, or seen in me—put it into practice. And the God of peace will be with you."

James 1:22
"Do not merely listen to the word, and so deceive yourselves. Do what it says."

From prison, Paul teaches and encourages the believers in Philippi to actually do what he has been teaching them and modeling in his own life. Paul freely admits weakness and imperfection, but his personal revelation and relationship with Christ Jesus have so profoundly changed his life that he wants everyone to experience what he has.

James, the half-brother of Jesus, did not have the full revelation of Christ until after His Resurrection, but once he encountered the Truth of the Living Word, James shares his revelation that listening to the Word is not enough; rather, we must obey it.

My personal experience after coming to faith in prison was first to begin to learn the Word – what it says, and what it means. But the active, living nature of the Word (Hebrews 4:12) requires that it be believed and acted upon. As I began to actually "do what it says" my whole life shifted into an entirely new and more powerful realm!

At first I tried to do this in my own strength, but found it impossible to do consistently and completely without surrendering to the Holy Spirit daily, and asking Him to do it in and through me. There is abundant peace and contentment in obedience.

TODAY'S CHALLENGE:

Tell the Father you want to learn to apply scripture in your daily life. Jesus exemplified obedience. Ask the Holy Spirit to teach you how to be obedient. You will see great results and experience His peace.

Dive Deeper: Study James 1.

September 18

YOU WERE DEAD

Ephesians 2:1-3

"As for you, you were dead in your transgressions and sins, ² in which you used to live when you followed the ways of this world and of the ruler of the kingdom of the air, the spirit who is now at work in those who are disobedient. ³ All of us also lived among them at one time, gratifying the cravings of our flesh and following its desires and thoughts. Like the rest, we were by nature deserving of wrath."

Before we began to follow Jesus, we followed the enemy. Before we were given eternal life in Christ Jesus, we were dead in sin and hopelessness. All our ways were disobedient and rebellious.

Satan always makes the world and its ways look attractive and promising. The vacuum of emptiness we all felt deep inside was impossible to fill, but we kept trying out every temptation the enemy threw towards us. For the most part, we gave in to every fleshly desire, and our minds were full of impure thoughts and motives.

Like most of the people we associated with, we lived our lives for the next high, the next thrill, or the next midnight encounter. But nothing ever satisfied. It was never enough. We were left empty still. That hole deep inside grew larger. We deserved the condemnation and wrath of a Holy God.

We had living and breathing bodies, but our souls were dead men walking. Notice please in today's verse that Paul is speaking of who we used to be, not who we are now. Tomorrow, we learn God's remedy for bringing us to life!

TODAY'S CHALLENGE:

Thank the Father that He is filling every empty space in you with His Spirit because of the finished work of Jesus.

Dive Deeper: Study Ephesians 2.

September 19

GOD MADE US ALIVE

Ephesians 2:4-6
"But because of his great love for us, God, who is rich in mercy, ⁵ made us alive with Christ even when we were dead in transgressions—it is by grace you have been saved. ⁶ And God raised us up with Christ and seated us with him in the heavenly realms in Christ Jesus..."

Yesterday we learned we were dead men walking. We deserved God's judgment and wrath. But because of God's great love for us, in Christ Jesus He showed us mercy and compassion instead!

It is by, through, and because of God's magnificent grace that we were made alive with Christ even while we were still dead in our trespasses and sins. In truth, God did not have an obligation to save us, but loved us so very much that He opened the way for us to find and experience true life. This life in His Son who said, "I am the way, the truth and the life".

God snatched us from the jaws of death when we finally cried out to Him in brokenness and true repentance. He has rescued us from the dominion of darkness and transferred us into His Kingdom of Light. In Christ, we have redemption and the forgiveness of sins. See Colossians 1:13-14.

Even though we are physically still in this world, we are to accept the truth of our current spiritual position as our Father God having already seated us with Christ in Heavenly realms. Though we live "in" this world, we are no longer "of" this world! That's Good News!

TODAY'S CHALLENGE:

Tell the Father how thankful you are for His unconditional love, mercy and forgiveness. Thank Jesus for receiving you into His Kingdom of Light after having rescued you from darkness!

Dive Deeper: Study Ephesians 2; Colossians 1:13-14; Hebrews 2:7-9.

September 20

THE GIFT OF GOD

Ephesians 2:8-10
"For it is by grace you have been saved, through faith—and this is not from yourselves, it is the gift of God— ⁹ not by works, so that no one can boast. ¹⁰ For we are God's handiwork, created in Christ Jesus to do good works, which God prepared in advance for us to do."

The primary difference between Christianity and every other "religion" is revealed is this passage today. The rest of the religious world believes you can, in some measure and in various ways, do things to "earn" the good favor of God, and thereby be able to live in Heaven with Him.

In other words, they say your good works must outweigh your bad deeds. Unfortunately, there is no way to know how it all balances out before your death. There is no assurance of salvation, and very little real hope for eternity. Sincere seekers live daily under condemnation of the enemy and their own conscience.

But our Father God knows we can never be good enough to approach Him in His Holiness. Nothing we can ever do on our own in the way of good deeds or works can offset our natural sinfulness. Sin produces death.

But, praise Jesus, He came in the form of a man, lived the perfect, sinless life and died in our place. He paid the price for all our sin. Our faith in Him, and Him alone, results in salvation and redemption only because of God's wonderful grace. Our "works" do not save us, but being truly saved results in us doing good.

TODAY'S CHALLENGE:

Ask the Father for a deeper revelation of the Gift of His grace; and, the salvation, rest and empowerment to do good works available only in Jesus.

Dive Deeper: Study Ephesians 2; Matthew 5:16; Romans 4:4-5; Titus 3:14; James 2:26; 1 Peter 2:9-10.

September 21

GOD IS NOT UNJUST

Hebrews 6:10
"God is not unjust; he will not forget your work and the love you have shown him as you have helped his people and continue to help them."

Doing good does not earn salvation as we learned yesterday. However, good works naturally flow from a truly repentant, born-again lifestyle.

Crowns and other rewards await us in Heaven for our earthly works bearing eternal fruit, but I believe we will be so overtaken with love and gratitude for Jesus that we will adoringly present our own rewards back to Him by laying them at His feet.

Our challenge daily is to serve the Lord with all our heart by properly representing Him to all those with whom we come into contact. Most of the time, we may not see any immediate positive results, nor receive positive feedback. But, God instantly knows and sees everything, and He appreciates even the smallest act of kindness.

We have already been given so much in what Jesus has done for us who deserve nothing, that we are not really even concerned with future rewards. Because we have been forgiven, we want to forgive others. Since we have received love, mercy, and grace so abundantly, we want to give it to others freely. Since Jesus sacrificed His life for us, we should willingly deny ourselves and sacrifice for others.

Don't give up. Don't be discouraged. Keep serving God with all your heart. You are pleasing the Lord Jesus by helping His people.

TODAY'S CHALLENGE:

Tell the Father you are thankful He allows you to serve Him by serving His people. Ask the Holy Spirit to let you see others the way Jesus sees them, and surrender to the Holy Spirit's desire and ability to help them through you.

Dive Deeper: Study Hebrews 6; 1 Corinthians 15:58.

September 22

BUILD OTHERS UP

Ephesians 4:29
"Do not let any unwholesome talk come out of your mouths, but only what is helpful for building others up according to their needs, that it may benefit those who listen."

The Holy Spirit is grieved when we speak in ungodly ways. See March 30, and April 18. We are able to choose our words, so we should not let the wrong ones out.

This is possible when we become more successful in changing our hearts and taking the wrong thoughts captive to the obedience of Christ (2 Corinthians 10:3-5). Out of the abundance of the heart the mouth speaks (Matthew 12:34).

The world is full of negativity, and the enemy is constantly telling depressing lies to everyone around us. People always need hope and encouragement, and there is little, if any, available to them in the natural. As spirit beings, we are able to impact others in ways the rest of the world can't.

As we read, study and meditate upon scripture daily, we are depositing into our hearts hope, light and encouragement that the Holy Spirit will be able to bring up out of us at the right time to speak into the ears and hearts of those trying to survive in a hopeless, dark, discouraged world.

Before we speak, let us anticipate the impact of our words upon those within the sound of our voice. We like to be encouraged and strengthened. We enjoy positive words of reinforcement. It benefits us. Speak words that benefit others today.

TODAY'S CHALLENGE:

Tell the Father you want to choose your words carefully today. Ask the Holy Spirit to teach you how to better anticipate the effect of your speech on those around you today. Consider how Jesus would say things, and imitate Him.

Dive Deeper: Study Ephesians 4; 2 Corinthians 10:3-5; Matthew 12:34; Proverbs 18:21.

September 23

OUT OF PLACE

Ephesians 5:4
"Nor should there be obscenity, foolish talk or coarse joking, which are out of place, but rather thanksgiving."

Diving deeper into what we learned yesterday and on March 30, today's verse might step on some toes! Ouch! Yes, even my own. All of us can learn something from Paul's instruction to us.

Those of us who have been in prison know there is special, very negative significance to the words "out of place". Being in the wrong place at the wrong time generally has bad consequences. Similarly, there is a kind of talk the world participates in that should not be a part of a Christian's life. For us, that kind of talk would be out of place.

Our lives are a constant sermon to those around us. Our words and actions demonstrate where we are in our Christian maturity and how we are progressing in being renewed by the Word, the Spirit, and Christ Jesus.

While it may seem natural to complain, joke and talk foolishly like the world does around us, we must desire to please God rather than try to "fit in". In fact, while we are still "in" the world, as Christians, we are no longer "of" this world. People should hear and see that we are indeed different, and they should be attracted to Christ as a result.

Let us be voluntarily accountable to our Christian brothers and sisters for the words we speak. Let's ask someone to privately and lovingly point out any unwholesome speech.

TODAY'S CHALLENGE:

Tell the Father you want to properly represent Him and His Kingdom in the way you converse with others. Ask the Holy Spirit to help you find someone to whom you will be accountable, and ask them for their help.

Dive Deeper: Study Ephesians 5.

September 24

WHAT PLEASES THE LORD

Ephesians 5:8-10
"For you were once darkness, but now you are light in the Lord. Live as children of light ⁹ (for the fruit of the light consists in all goodness, righteousness and truth) ¹⁰ and find out what pleases the Lord."

This is a very revealing verse. Not only did we once live and walk in darkness, we actually were darkness! At that time, we were "of our father, the devil." (John 8:44)! Our fruit was sinful deeds of the flesh.

However, now we are "children of light"; that is, we are born again of the "Father of Heavenly Lights" (James 1:17), and, in the Spirit, we are brothers and sisters of Jesus, the "Light of the World" (John 8:12)!

Light and water are essential to fruit-bearing. Paul tells us that the fruit of the light is "all goodness, righteousness and truth". Our Living Water, the Spirit of Christ, brings forth this kind of fruit in the lives of those who walk and live as children of light.

We have previously learned about the fruit of the Spirit (see April 30 and June 2) – love, joy, peace, patience, kindness, goodness, gentleness, faithfulness and self-control - and it is this fruit the world needs to see in our lives. This pleases the Lord!

For many years I lived to please others, didn't you? But now, as we find out more about the fruit of the light, and the fruit of the Spirit, let us become more intentional about pleasing the Lord.

TODAY'S CHALLENGE:

Thank the Father for changing you from darkness to light. Tell Him you want to live today in such a way that will please Him. Ask the Holy Spirit to help you live as a child of the light today.

Dive Deeper: Study Ephesians 5; John 8:12, 44; James 1:17.

September 25

BECOME A LIGHT

Ephesians 5:11-14
"Have nothing to do with the fruitless deeds of darkness, but rather expose them. ¹² It is shameful even to mention what the disobedient do in secret. ¹³ But everything exposed by the light becomes visible—and everything that is illuminated becomes a light. ¹⁴ This is why it is said: 'Wake up, sleeper, rise from the dead, and Christ will shine on you.'"

Yesterday we learned that we were once darkness, but now we are light. The light bears fruit – goodness, righteousness and truth. I imagine we can all list many "fruitless deeds of darkness" from our many years before we were born again as children of light.

I do not believe it is helpful to our Christian witness to keep re-hashing to ourselves and others the many sordid, explicit details of our past. We must use discretion in sharing our testimonies so that we are not glorifying the devil.

However, I believe great benefit comes when we are honest and transparent about our weaknesses, past and present. His strength is perfected in our weaknesses (2 Corinthians 12:9), but we must be willing to admit them, and let Him work in our lives to change us. We should always do this in such a way that God gets the Glory for our transformation.

Done in the proper way, exposing our past to the light illuminates our present walk in Christ and provides for future opportunities for His Light to shine through us to positively impact others.

TODAY'S CHALLENGE:

Tell the Father you want your life illuminated by His Truth, Jesus. Ask the Holy Spirit for wisdom and discernment to live your life, and share your testimony, in such a way that it glorifies God.

Become a light.

Dive Deeper: Study Ephesians 5; 2 Corinthians 12:9.

September 26

SERVE WHOLEHEARTEDLY

Ephesians 6:7-8
"Serve wholeheartedly, as if you were serving the Lord, not people,[8] because you know that the Lord will reward each one for whatever good they do..."

Reading this verse should remind us how Jesus humbled Himself to serve mankind. This was in part illustrated as He washed the feet of His disciples the night before He knew He would give up His life for us all. He did this as an example for all of us that we should serve one another. See John 13:12-17.

Even though Jesus was clearly their Master and Teacher, He very intentionally humbled Himself and became their servant. By all rights, they should have been washing His feet. This very same evening, Jesus tells His disciples, "As I have loved you, so you must love one another." (John 13:34-35). He was showing His love for them.

One of the greatest demonstrations of love is to serve someone else willingly, unexpectedly, and wholeheartedly. It is important to do this without expecting recognition, or even gratitude. We serve out of a heart of love for our Savior who first loved and served us. Human recognition and rewards are temporary, but the reward from our Lord is eternal.

Every day we should be looking for ways to serve others out of love with our whole heart. The world needs to see something distinctive about those who follow Jesus. Let them see it in our love and service for others.

TODAY'S CHALLENGE:

Ask the Father to give you ideas and opportunities how to serve someone today. Make a decision to represent Jesus today by demonstrating to others His example of service with a pure and whole heart by His Holy Spirit.

Serve wholeheartedly.

Dive Deeper: Study Ephesians 6; 1 Corinthians 10:31; Colossians 3:17; John 13:12-17, 34-35.

September 27

WORTHY OF YOUR CALLING

Ephesians 4:1-3
"As a prisoner for the Lord, then, I urge you to live a life worthy of the calling you have received. ² Be completely humble and gentle; be patient, bearing with one another in love. ³ Make every effort to keep the unity of the Spirit through the bond of peace."

Paul wrote a number of his letters from prison. His letter to the Ephesians is one of them. He considered Himself a "prisoner for the Lord". He was unfairly treated, falsely accused, and unjustly imprisoned; yet, he was determined he would use his time "for" the Lord Jesus.

Paul knew He was called by the Lord, and even behind bars he wanted to live a life worthy of his calling. Therefore, I believe Paul shares with the believers in Ephesus, and us, the secrets he has learned in His journey with the Lord.

Wherever we find ourselves in life, we can consider our life to be "for" the Lord Jesus. We all have spheres of influence among people right where we are who need to see us living our life in a manner worthy of our Lord.

When we allow the Holy Spirit to bring forth His fruit in our lives, we will exhibit humility, gentleness, patience, forbearance, love and peace. As we read today's exhortation and teaching from Paul, we see these are the very qualities that will demonstrate the unity of the Spirit for all the world to observe and be attracted to Christ.

TODAY'S CHALLENGE:

Tell the Father you are thankful for His forgiveness, and the calling of the Lord Jesus on your life. Tell Him you want to be absolutely surrendered to His Holy Spirit today to bring forth fruit that will attract the world to Jesus.

Dive Deeper: Study Ephesians 4.

September 28

GROWING TO MATURITY

Ephesians 4:14-15
"Then we will no longer be infants, tossed back and forth by the waves, and blown here and there by every wind of teaching and by the cunning and craftiness of people in their deceitful scheming. [15] Instead, speaking the truth in love, we will grow to become in every respect the mature body of him who is the head, that is, Christ."

Yesterday we discussed living a life worthy of our calling. After we respond to the call of the Holy Spirit for salvation and a new life in Christ Jesus, we are called to be ambassadors for Christ (see 2 Corinthians 5:17-20). In this capacity, we are expected to grow daily in Christ so we will "no longer be infants."

Today's passage is in the context of Paul relating how Jesus Himself gave apostles, prophets, evangelists, pastors and teachers so that we in the body of Christ could be equipped for works of service so that the Body of Christ could be built up in unity and fullness (see Ephesians 4:11-13).

As ambassadors in the Body of Christ, we should desire to study the Word daily so we can properly hear our leaders, and apply truth to our lives. In so doing, the Holy Spirit will give us discernment so we will not be led astray by false teachers. In these last days, Jesus warned us to be careful we are not deceived (Matthew 24:4-5).

We must be growing daily in maturity in Christ so we can speak the truth in love to others.

TODAY'S CHALLENGE:

Thank the Father for calling you to be an ambassador for Jesus Christ. Tell Him you want to grow daily towards full maturity in Christ. Ask the Holy Spirit to teach you and give you discernment.

Dive Deeper: Study Ephesians 4; 2 Corinthians 5:17-20; Matthew 24:4-5; Ephesians 4:11-13.

September 29

A NEW WAY OF LIVING

Ephesians 4:17-19
"So I tell you this, and insist on it in the Lord, that you must no longer live as the Gentiles do, in the futility of their thinking. ¹⁸ They are darkened in their understanding and separated from the life of God because of the ignorance that is in them due to the hardening of their hearts. ¹⁹ Having lost all sensitivity, they have given themselves over to sensuality so as to indulge in every kind of impurity, and they are full of greed."

After we have become a new creation in Christ Jesus, our old life is gone, and we are called to a new way of living (see 2 Corinthians 5:17). We are also told we cannot continue to conform to the world and its way of doing things; rather, we are to be transformed by the renewing of our mind (see Romans 12:1-2).

I am so very thankful I no longer think and act the way I used to before I was saved. Surely, today's verse applied to me in that prior life – futile thinking, darkened understanding, separated from God, ignorant, greedy, and with a hardened heart. I gave myself over to "sensuality so as to indulge in every kind of impurity". Can you too relate?

Recognizing who we used to be, we must be deliberate and intentional about separating ourselves from the same old people, places, and things we were around before salvation. If we don't, it becomes almost impossible to experience the new way of life to which we are called.

TODAY'S CHALLENGE:

Tell the Father you desire to experience all of the new life He has planned for you. Thank Jesus for making it possible, and ask the Holy Spirit to help you today.

Dive Deeper: Study Ephesians 4; 2 Corinthians 5:17; Romans 12:1-2.

September 30

PUT ON THE NEW SELF

Ephesians 4:22-24
"You were taught, with regard to your former way of life, to put off your old self, which is being corrupted by its deceitful desires;²³ to be made new in the attitude of your minds; ²⁴ and to put on the new self, created to be like God in true righteousness and holiness."

Yesterday, Paul reminded us of our old self. Today, he continues by commanding us to "put off our old self", and to "put on the new self". This is something we must remind ourselves daily.

The enemy will be constantly trying to tempt us to act out of our old nature, "our old self". We must be wise to his tricks, and take every thought captive to the obedience of Christ. We must "be made new in the attitude of our minds". This occurs progressively as we are being transformed by the renewing of our minds (Romans 12:2) through the Word of God.

Because Jesus took all our sin upon Himself, our new man received the righteousness of God (see 2 Corinthians 5:21). In Christ, we can walk in His righteousness and holiness, which is the Father's intention for us. We are able to achieve this more every day to the extent we learn to surrender absolutely to the Holy Spirit as He sanctifies us in Christ and sets us apart for service to the Father.

Every day, I remind myself I am altogether a new person. I often express my deep gratitude to the Father that my old self is gone! Do you?

TODAY'S CHALLENGE:

Thank the Father for making you a totally new person in Christ Jesus. Ask the Holy Spirit to show you more completely how to put off the old self and put on the new.

Dive Deeper: Study Ephesians 4; Romans 12:2; Colossians 3:9-10; Titus 2:11-14.

October 1

NO GRUMBLING OR ARGUING

Philippians 2:14-16
"Do everything without grumbling or arguing, [15] so that you may become blameless and pure, 'children of God without fault in a warped and crooked generation.' Then you will shine among them like stars in the sky [16] as you hold firmly to the word of life..."

God does not want us to grumble and complain, or argue. It promotes strife and discord within the body of Christ, and gives a very bad witness to unbelievers. Read Numbers 14 to see what happened to the Israelites as a result of their grumbling and complaining.

With regard to arguing, in 2 Timothy 2:23-24, Paul instructs us, "Don't have anything to do with foolish and stupid arguments, because you know they produce quarrels. And the Lord's servant must not quarrel..."

Although the way of the world is certainly to complain and argue, as believers we will stand out in a positive way when we refuse to give in to these devices of the enemy. We must remember that although we are "in" the world, we are no longer "of" the world.

The Father wants us to become blameless and pure, without fault, so that His Love demonstrated in us will allow us to shine like stars. As we surrender more every day to the Holy Spirit, He is able to teach us and help us hold firmly to the Word of Life, Christ Jesus, in the midst of an angry, sinful, grumbling, and arguing world.

TODAY'S CHALLENGE:

Tell your Heavenly Father that you desire to go through this day without complaining or arguing. Ask the Holy Spirit to help you quickly take wrong thoughts captive so that you do not hinder your Christian witness by being lured into the enemy's trap.

Dive Deeper: Study Philippians 2; Numbers 14; 2 Timothy 2:23-24.

October 2

GOD IS WITH YOU

Joshua 1:5
"No one will be able to stand against you all the days of your life. As I was with Moses, so I will be with you; I will never leave you nor forsake you."

Matthew 28:20
Jesus said, "… and surely I am with you always, to the very end of the age."

There are plenty of times in our lives where we have felt alone. In the middle of the night we may have shed tears wondering who we could turn to for comfort and companionship.

Sometimes our families and friends have abandoned us as a result of our lives of sin negatively impacting their own lives. Loneliness is now considered one of society's biggest maladies plaguing a large percentage of people in the world.

As Christians, we are promised that although the world may abandon us, forsake us, and leave us, God never will! Jesus and the Father have sent us a "Comforter" in the Holy Spirit. He wants us to see Him as our constant companion and true friend. He is also called our Teacher and Counselor, and someone who comes along and stands beside us in every situation of life. I have heard it said, one person with God is the majority!

Paul writes in Romans 8:31, "If God is for us, who can be against us?" In Psalm 27:1, David wrote, "The Lord is my light and my salvation, whom shall I fear?"

With God, you are never alone, and nobody will be able to stand against you!

TODAY'S CHALLENGE:

Talk to the Father about any sense of loneliness you may have today. Ask His Holy Spirit to help you see that in Christ Jesus you are never alone! Thank the Father for His everlasting presence.

Dive Deeper: Study Joshua 1; Deuteronomy 31:8; Zephaniah 3:17; Romans 8:31; Psalm 27:1.

October 3

BE PROSPEROUS AND SUCCESSFUL

Joshua 1:7-8

"Be strong and very courageous. Be careful to obey all the law my servant Moses gave you; do not turn from it to the right or to the left, that you may be successful wherever you go. ⁸ Keep this Book of the Law always on your lips; meditate on it day and night, so that you may be careful to do everything written in it. Then you will be prosperous and successful."

Here we have the secret to success and prosperity in life – faithful obedience to, and meditating continually upon, God's Word!

God Himself gave these instructions to Joshua before he led the children of Israel into the Promised Land. Notice that he urged Joshua to "Be strong and courageous". In fact, God told him this three times in four verses. In the times in which we now live, it certainly takes courage and strength to serve God and obey His Word. But as we learned yesterday, we are never alone.

The Bible is filled with examples of how blessings from God always follow obedience to God. In this passage today, God tells us to adhere closely to the Word because in doing so faithfully we will find success.

My own experience in prison led me to begin to memorize verses, and meditate upon their meaning and daily application to my life. The more I have read, memorized and meditated upon the Word, the more success and prosperity have come my way as I have sincerely tried to obey it daily.

Try it yourself!

TODAY'S CHALLENGE:

Thank the Father for His Word. Tell Him you want to be able to memorize it and meditate upon its meaning. Ask the Holy Spirit to help you obey, and to use His Word to guide your life today.

Dive Deeper: Study Joshua 1; Deuteronomy 29:9; Isaiah 59:20-21; Psalm 1:1-3.

October 4

BE STRONG AND COURAGEOUS

Joshua 1:9
*"Have I not commanded you? Be strong and courageous. Do not be afraid; do not be discouraged, for the L*ORD *your God will be with you wherever you go."*

Over the years after having been saved in prison, this verse has been one of my very favorites. Jehovah God Himself is talking to Joshua just before he is to lead the Israelites into the promised land.

I believe God is purposefully reminding Joshua that it has actually been God commanding them while they were in the wilderness. I believe God wants them to remember His faithfulness to them as He led them. In His faithfulness and ability, we can be strong and courageous.

Of our own selves, it is hard to consistently have faith in our own strength or courage. In fact, as we continue our Christian journey, we really learn the truth of what Jesus told Paul, that is, "His strength is made perfect in weakness!" See 2 Corinthians 12:9.

The more we learn to believe and receive God's unconditional love for us, we will have increasingly greater success overcoming the fear with which the enemy wants to attack us. The Bible says perfect love casts out fear! See 1 John 4:18.

God urges us to remember Who has been leading us, and how much He loves us. We do not have to be afraid or discouraged. In Him, we have great strength and courage! We can trust Him to be with us wherever we go and whatever we do.

TODAY'S CHALLENGE:

Tell the Father any areas of fear, anxiety or concern you have today. Think about how faithful He has been. Remember that you have the Father, Son and Holy Spirit with you wherever you go today.

Dive Deeper: Study Joshua 1; 2 Corinthians 12:9-10; 1 John 4:18; Ephesians 6:10; Micah 3:8; Zechariah 4:6.

October 5

CHOOSE WHOM YOU WILL SERVE

Joshua 24:14-15
"Now therefore, fear the Lord, serve Him in sincerity and in truth, and put away the gods which your fathers served on the other side of the River and in Egypt. Serve the Lord! ¹⁵ And if it seems evil to you to serve the Lord, choose for yourselves this day whom you will serve, whether the gods which your fathers served that were on the other side of the River, or the gods of the Amorites, in whose land you dwell. But as for me and my house, we will serve the Lord."

In these last hours of the last days before the soon return of our King Jesus, it has never been more important to decide once and for all who you will serve in sincerity and truth. Now is certainly NOT the time to be "lukewarm", "on the fence", or "playing with God".

This choice has eternal consequences, not just for you, but potentially for your family and other loved ones. God has so very much in store for all those who will seek Him and serve Him with all their hearts.

We must forever turn our backs on our past and destroy all the idols to which we once bowed. This should be a once and for all event. It is a decision to serve God with all of our hearts in spite of what the world may think about us.

Whom will you serve? Decide today to serve God forever in sincerity and truth.

TODAY'S CHALLENGE:

Tell the Father you are choosing to serve Him with all of your heart for all of your days in sincerity and truth. Ask the Holy Spirit to help you identify any idols left over from your past.

Dive Deeper: Study Joshua 24; Deuteronomy 30:15-20; 1 Kings 18:21; Revelation 3:14-19.

October 6

CHOOSE LIFE

Deuteronomy 30:19-20
"This day I call the heavens and the earth as witnesses against you that I have set before you life and death, blessings and curses. Now choose life, so that you and your children may live [20] and that you may love the Lord your God, listen to his voice, and hold fast to him. For the Lord is your life..."

I recommend you stop and take a few minutes to read the entire chapter 30 of Deuteronomy from which today's passage is selected. Go ahead, I'll wait.

Moses makes it exceedingly clear for the Israelites what Jehovah is asking of them. Tremendous promises lie in store for anyone who will follow the Lord in the manner laid out by Moses to the children of Israel.

Many of us, for a long time before we were saved, participated in the devil's schemes to kill, steal and destroy our lives and those of our families. In contrast, Jesus told us in John 10:10, that He came to give abundant life!

We are given a choice between blessings or curses, life or death. We must choose life! This is a choice for ourselves and our families. Deciding to wholeheartedly serve and follow the Lord opens the way for us to love Him completely, listen to Him closely, obey Him faithfully, and cling to Him and His promises tenaciously.

You will never regret your decision to choose life. Life with the Lord is so much more rewarding, fulfilling, and satisfying than anything I ever experienced when I was serving the devil.

TODAY'S CHALLENGE:

Tell your Heavenly Father you are thankful that Jesus sacrificed His life for you. Talk to the Father about any reservations you have in committing wholeheartedly to serve and follow Christ Jesus. Choose life!

Dive Deeper: Study Deuteronomy 30; John 10:10; Jeremiah 21:8; Isaiah 1:18-20.

October 7

NOTHING'S TOO HARD FOR GOD

Jeremiah 32:27
"I am the LORD, the God of all mankind. Is anything too hard for me?"

Genesis 18:14
"Is anything too hard for the Lord?"

These are simple but amazing passages! God Himself is speaking in both cases. Sometimes I imagine Him saying it with a little bit of a sarcastic tone like, "Really???"

As we continue to learn more about God's Power, Presence and Preeminence, we begin to really trust Him with everything about us and our lives. The more we exercise our faith, our confidence in Him and His promises continues to increase.

There is absolutely nothing beyond His control. He has absolute power in all of the universe. He has no need of anything, yet He desires an intimate relationship with us. That almost blows my mind. He is everywhere present all the time, and knows everything completely and perfectly.

All time and eternity is contained in Him. Nothing exists outside of Him. He knows everything about us and loves us anyway! His grace, mercy, kindness, goodness and love are endless and without measure.

In spite of how hopeless things seem to us, and how helpless we are to work out for ourselves the most important matters of life, we must remember God is Able, Faithful and True! In spite of how negatively we view ourselves or our circumstances, we must know that God can bring something positive out of any bad situation. See Genesis 50:20, and Romans 8:28. Remember, this is God our Creator we are talking about!

TODAY'S CHALLENGE:

Spend some time quietly in His Presence considering all you have just read. Express to Him your awe and amazement for Who He is, and thank Him for desiring a relationship with you.

Trust Him completely.

Dive Deeper: Study Jeremiah 32; Genesis 50:20; Proverbs 3:5-6; Romans 8:26-28.

October 8

GOD INTENDS IT FOR GOOD

Genesis 50:20
"You intended to harm me, but God intended it for good to accomplish what is now being done, the saving of many lives."

Christians are not promised lives free of trouble and tragedy. Jesus Himself said, *"In this world you will have trouble. But take heart! I have overcome the world."* (John 16:33)

Paul tells us in Romans 8:28, *"And we know that in all things God works for the good of those who love him, who have been called according to his purpose."*

In our passage today, Joseph gives his brothers a most hopeful and helpful truth – even the bad things they meant for harm to Joseph were used for good by God to save their very lives!

We can take great comfort in this truth. In many of our lives we have been on what we felt was the losing end of trials and tribulations. Loved ones have been lost, and hopes have been shattered. Families have been separated, and material possessions have disappeared.

But when true repentance brings us back to God, He has the amazing desire and capacity to bring good out of hopeless situations. When all our love, faith and expectations are set firmly on Him and His abilities, He is free to work on our behalf in ways we could never have imagined.

By working miracles in our personal lives God is also able to positively impact our families. Further, He can use our testimonies to affect others for their own eternal salvation!

TODAY'S CHALLENGE:

Talk to God about the situations in your life that you are convinced are hopeless. Re-commit yourself today to trust Him completely to work however He sees fit. Take your eyes off your circumstances and keep them on Him.

Dive Deeper: Study Genesis 50; John 16:33; Romans 8:26-28; Psalm 40:1-5.

October 9

NO MORE EXCUSES

Exodus 4:10-12

"Moses said to the LORD, 'Pardon your servant, Lord. I have never been eloquent, neither in the past nor since you have spoken to your servant. I am slow of speech and tongue.' [11] The LORD said to him, 'Who gave human beings their mouths? Who makes them deaf or mute? Who gives them sight or makes them blind? Is it not I, the LORD? [12] Now go; I will help you speak and will teach you what to say.'"

Moses tried every excuse he could think of to try to avoid God's call on his life. I can relate to Him in several ways. I ran from God for many years before I finally surrendered to His call on my life. Have you been running from God?

In Exodus 3 and 4, Moses has one of the most amazing and interesting encounters with God found anywhere in the Bible. I recommend you read both chapters.

At first, in Exodus 3:11, Moses questions his identity, *"Who am I that I should go to Pharaoh and bring the Israelites out of Egypt?"* Sort of like, "Are you sure you have the right guy?"

Then, Moses says things like, "What if they ask me a question I don't know?" or, "What if they do not believe me or listen to me?" Finally, Moses tries the excuse we see in our passage for today, but God was ready for him!

I have heard it said that God is not so interested in our ability as He is our availability! Are you making excuses to God why you can't fulfill the plan He has for your life?

TODAY'S CHALLENGE:

Tell God you surrender to His plan for your life, and trust Him to make it happen.

Dive Deeper: Study Exodus 3:1 – 4:17.

October 10

THE BLOOD WILL BE A SIGN

Exodus 12:12-13
"On that same night I will pass through Egypt and strike down every first-born of both people and animals, and I will bring judgment on all the gods of Egypt. I am the LORD. [13] The blood will be a sign for you on the houses where you are, and when I see the blood, I will pass over you. No destructive plague will touch you when I strike Egypt."

The children of Israel protected their households from the death of their firstborn by applying the blood of a sacrificed lamb to the doorposts of their homes. Very specific instructions and details were given by God so that the sacrifice and application of the blood would be effective thereby enabling the death angel to pass over their home.

For us, this is a picture of the sacrifice of the Lamb of God, Jesus. He voluntarily gave up his life so we could live. His death, burial and resurrection proclaimed absolute and total victory over death, hell and the grave for all time. His Blood represents His Life.

Like the children of Israel during the first Passover, we must recognize the sacrifice of Jesus and the effectiveness of His Blood being poured out on our behalf. There is nothing more precious or powerful than the Life of our Lord and Savior, Jesus; and, the Blood represents His sacrifice.

Have you applied the Blood of Jesus to the doorposts of your heart? Are you eternally protected from the power of death, hell and the grave?

TODAY'S CHALLENGE:

Tell the Father you are thankful for His love so completely expressed in the sacrifice of His Son, Jesus. Ask the Holy Spirit to reveal to you the power of applying the Blood to your life.

Dive Deeper: Study Exodus 12; Leviticus 17:11; Hebrews 7:18-28; Hebrews 10:1-12.

October 11

YOU NEED ONLY TO BE STILL

Exodus 14:13-14
"Moses answered the people, 'Do not be afraid. Stand firm and you will see the deliverance the Lord will bring you today. The Egyptians you see today you will never see again. ¹⁴ The Lord will fight for you; you need only to be still.'"

As the children of Israel were leaving Egypt under the leadership of Moses at the instruction of God, they found themselves in what appeared to them to be an impossible situation. In the natural, all their circumstances seemed stacked totally against them, and they were convinced there was no hope for a way of escape. Have you ever felt this way?

The Israelites were terrified as they saw Pharaoh's armies approaching. They felt trapped and feared for their death, but they did not know that it was actually God's plan to trap and destroy their pursuers.

Moses knew God had not brought them this far to abandon them. He exhorted the people not to be afraid, rather, that they should stand still and see the deliverance of the Lord. In response to God's instructions, Moses exercised his faith, raised his staff and stretched out his arm above the sea and the waters parted so the Israelites could pass through safely!

How many times have you been convinced of a hopeless situation? Maybe your circumstances seem impossible to you even now – a mountain too big, or an ocean too deep? Exercise your faith. Stand firm and see the Lord's deliverance.

TODAY'S CHALLENGE:

Talk to the Father about how you view your circumstances and why they seem impossible to you. Ask the Holy Spirit to give you peace in the storm and the patience to wait on God. Believe.

You need only to be still.

Dive Deeper: Study Exodus 14; Joshua 1:9; Psalm 46:10; Jeremiah 1:19.

October 12

HELP WIN THE BATTLE

Exodus 17:11-13
"As long as Moses held up his hands, the Israelites were winning, but whenever he lowered his hands, the Amalekites were winning. [12] When Moses' hands grew tired, they took a stone and put it under him and he sat on it. Aaron and Hur held his hands up—one on one side, one on the other—so that his hands remained steady till sunset. [13] So Joshua overcame the Amalekite army with the sword."

What a powerful illustration and lesson we have in this scripture passage today. The Israelites had come under an intense attack by the Amalekites. The man of God, Moses, gave instructions to Joshua to take some men and go out to fight them. He assured Joshua that he would take the "staff of God" to the top of the hill overlooking the battle.

As long as Moses held up the staff of God the Israelites were winning, but whenever he lowered the staff in weakness the battle shifted to the enemy. The man of God was anointed for leadership, and he had the wisdom to exercise his faith with the staff of God, but on his own he did not have the strength to prevail. He needed others to help him.

Wherever you find yourself involved in the body of Christ today, make it your aim to humbly serve the leaders God has provided you. They were never meant to carry the entire burden of leadership alone. Make yourself useful and help win the victory.

TODAY'S CHALLENGE:

Tell the Father you want to be utilized in any way He sees fit to help His appointed leaders. Ask the Holy Spirit to help you see where you can lend a hand to make a difference.

Help win the battle.

Dive Deeper: Study Exodus 17.

October 13

DISTINGUISHED BY THE PRESENCE

Exodus 33:15-16
"Then Moses said to him, "If your Presence does not go with us, do not send us up from here. ¹⁶ How will anyone know that you are pleased with me and with your people unless you go with us? What else will distinguish me and your people from all the other people on the face of the earth?"

Moses knew very well that he could not lead the people alone. He asked God in Exodus 33:13 to "teach me your ways so I may know you and continue to find favor with you." The Lord replied in verse 14, "My presence will go with you, and I will give you rest."

Moses recognized how helpless he was without God. In true humility, he submitted himself totally to God because he realized the importance of God's favor, and he desired above all else to learn His ways. God's answer was to give Moses Himself.

As true followers of Jesus, we must admit that without Him we can do nothing (John 15:5), but with Him all things are possible (Matthew 19:26). God has given us His Presence to remain with us at all times. The Holy Spirit is our Helper, Teacher, Counselor, Friend and Guide.

For the Israelites, the Presence of God went before them in a flame of fire. Today, we have the fire of God residing in us! Surely, the world sees a difference in those who host His Presence well. Does this distinguish you from those around you?

TODAY'S CHALLENGE:

Tell the Father you want to learn His ways and receive His favor. Ask the Holy Spirit to show you how to host His Presence effectively every day. Make a choice to seek the Spirit's direction in everything you do today.

Dive Deeper: Study Exodus 33; Matthew 19:26; John 14:25-27; John 15:5.

October 14

UNRESTRICTED ACCESS

Leviticus 16:2
"The Lord said to Moses: "Tell your brother Aaron that he is not to come whenever he chooses into the Most Holy Place behind the curtain in front of the atonement cover on the ark, or else he will die. For I will appear in the cloud over the atonement cover."

In the Tabernacle, and later in the Temple, the actual presence of God was manifested in the Most Holy Place. Access to it was severely restricted. A very thick, heavy curtain enclosed the Most Holy Place.

There were strict limitations regarding specifically who could enter the Most Holy Place and also when, and under what conditions, they may safely enter. The most severe consequence – death – awaited anyone who did not precisely adhere to the limitations and abide by the conditions.

When Jesus gave up His Spirit on the cross, the Word tells us that the curtain in the Temple was torn open from the top to the bottom to show it was not opened by man. The Father Himself was recognizing the finished work of Jesus, and showing the world that it is only through Him that we may now enter into God's Presence.

As Christians, Hebrews 10:19-20 tells us, *"...we have confidence to enter the Most Holy Place by the blood of Jesus, by a new and living way opened for us through the curtain, that is, his body..."*. Hebrews 4:16 tells us we can, *"...approach God's throne of Grace with confidence..."*.

You now have unrestricted access to God! Be confident. Go on in.

TODAY'S CHALLENGE:

Thank the Father for making the Way through Jesus for you to find Truth and Life in His Presence by His Holy Spirit. Take time today to prayerfully consider these implications.

Dive Deeper: Study Leviticus 16; Matthew 27:51-54; Hebrews 4:16; Hebrews 10:19-20.

October 15

BLOOD ATONEMENT

Leviticus 17:11
"For the life of a creature is in the blood, and I have given it to you to make atonement for yourselves on the altar; it is the blood that makes atonement for one's life."

God teaches us here that the life force of a creature is in their blood. Pouring out the blood is taking the life of the creature and results in death. Paul tells us the wages of sin is death (Romans 6:23), and the old testament sacrificial system used blood sacrifice to achieve atonement for sin.

Sin requires reparation, or payment, in order to reconcile the guilty party back to God. This is what is meant by "atonement". The writer of Hebrews teaches us that it is impossible for the blood of bulls and goats to take away sins, they were only temporarily covered for another year, and the worshipers still felt guilty.

In Jesus Christ, the final perfect sacrifice, we learn that the old testament sacrifices were a foreshadowing of the only atonement that will satisfy God the Father – the lifeblood of the Son, willingly offered by Jesus. By His one sacrifice, "He has made perfect forever those who are being made holy." (Hebrews 10:14)

Sins were only deferred from one year to the next under the old system. But, in Jesus, forgiveness of sin is achieved forever, not deferred. Where sins have been forgiven, "sacrifice for sin is no longer necessary." See Hebrews 10:1-18.

Our permanent reconciliation back to God the Father, and our restoration of relationship, was achieved once for all, finally and forever, through the blood atonement of Jesus.

TODAY'S CHALLENGE:

Praise the Father for providing the perfect plan, and thank Jesus for executing the plan, that through the Holy Spirit brings you forever into right relationship with God.

Dive Deeper: Study Leviticus 17; Romans 6:23; Hebrews 10:1-18.

October 16

POSSESS THE PROMISE

Numbers 13:30, 14:7-8, 24
"Then Caleb silenced the people before Moses and said, 'We should go up and take possession of the land, for we can certainly do it...[7] The land we passed through and explored is exceedingly good. [8] If the Lord is pleased with us, he will lead us into that land, a land flowing with milk and honey, and will give it to us.'...[24](God said) 'But because my servant Caleb has a different spirit and follows me wholeheartedly, I will bring him into the land he went to, and his descendants will inherit it.'"

How very important it is to present a good report, confess it in faith, and believe God will deliver on what He has promised! The Bible is full of promises for His people who meet the specific conditions.

Joshua and Caleb were the only ones who came back with a good report out of the twelve men sent by Moses to explore the promised land. They believed God was able to deliver on His promise to give them the land, and they were bold in their confession. Even though theirs was the minority report, they did not cower in unbelief. They wanted to please God and were unafraid of men.

As Christians today, we ought to always want to please God, not man. We should always have a spirit of faith and courage, boldly state God's promises, meet His conditions, and follow God with all our heart. Like Caleb, we should have a "different spirit" from the world.

Don't agree with any negative report. Have faith!

TODAY'S CHALLENGE:

Ask the Father to give you a spirit of faith, boldness and courage. Thank Him for the many promises He has made available to you though Jesus.

Possess the promise.

Dive Deeper: Study Numbers 13:1 – 14:45; Hebrews 10:38-39.

October 17

THE MAJORITY REPORT

Numbers 14:37-38
*"...these men who were responsible for spreading the bad report about the land were struck down and died of a plague before the L*ORD*. *[38]* Of the men who went to explore the land, only Joshua son of Nun and Caleb son of Jephunneh survived."*

Yesterday we learned about the minority report given by Caleb and Joshua. Today, we learn the rest of the story.

Ten of the twelve spies sent by Moses into the promised land returned in fear and gave a negative report of sure defeat. In spite of the fact that God had promised to safely deliver them into the land, these ten spoke out of hopelessness and unbelief. They let their own perception of "reality" overwhelm God's reality for them.

These ten men looked at their situation and circumstances, and became fearful and defeated, instead of keeping their eyes on God and His promised victory. In spite of how many times they had already seen God move on their behalf in their journey from Egypt, they thought this was too big a job for God.

Isn't it silly to even think there could be anything too hard for God? See Jeremiah 32:27. These men should have taken their eyes off the problem and focused instead on God. But because they didn't, and they believed the negative report they heard themselves confess from their own mouths, these ten men were struck down and died of a plague.

"The tongue has the power of life and death, and those who love it will eat its fruit." (Proverbs 18:21)

TODAY'S CHALLENGE:

Tell the Father you want to see things from His perspective. Ask the Holy Spirit to teach you how to increase your faith by proclaiming God's Word and promises over every situation.

Dive Deeper: Study Numbers 14; Jeremiah 32:27; Proverbs 18:21.

October 18

A SNAKE ON A POLE

Numbers 21:8-9
"The Lord said to Moses, 'Make a snake and put it up on a pole; anyone who is bitten can look at it and live.' ⁹ So Moses made a bronze snake and put it up on a pole. Then when anyone was bitten by a snake and looked at the bronze snake, they lived."

In the wilderness, the Israelites often expressed impatience with God by grumbling and complaining against their leaders, Moses and Aaron, as well as God Himself. As we learned on October 1, God is not pleased when we do this. For example, see Numbers 14:20-23.

In this instance, the people had said, *"Why have you brought us up out of Egypt to die in the wilderness? There is no bread! There is no water! And we detest this miserable food!"* (Numbers 21:5). God responded by sending venomous snakes among them that bit the people and many died.

In response to the people's repentance, and the prayer of Moses, God instructs Moses as we see in verses 8-9 of today's passage. Anyone who, in faith, looked upon the upraised bronze snake, lived.

Before Jesus went to the cross, he twice referred to this very story in declaring that the Son of Man would be lifted up, and everyone who believes would have eternal life (John 3:14-15). He said when He is lifted up He would draw all men to Himself (John 12:32).

All of humanity has a sentence of death upon them due to their sin, and their only hope is to gaze with faith upon the One Who is lifted up, Jesus.

TODAY'S CHALLENGE:

Speak to the Father about your faith in His Son, Jesus, Who was lifted up for you. Look upon Him and live forever.

Dive Deeper: Study Numbers 21; Numbers 14:20-23; John 3:14-15; John 12:32.

October 19

SHEEP WITHOUT A SHEPHERD

Numbers 27:16-17
"May the Lord, the God who gives breath to all living things, appoint someone over this community ¹⁷ to go out and come in before them, one who will lead them out and bring them in, so the Lord's people will not be like sheep without a shepherd."

In the verses preceding today's passage (verses 12-14), Moses is instructed by God to go up to the mountain overlooking the promised land and see the land God had given to the Israelites. He could look, but he could not enter in due to his earlier disobedience, and after seeing it, God said he too "would be gathered to your people as your brother Aaron was."

Moses did not argue, nor did He complain. Instead, his first concern was for the people he had been leading the past forty years in the wilderness. He knew how very important it was for them to have a leader chosen by God Himself, someone who would be anointed with the same kind of spirit as Moses. He did not want them to be as sheep without a shepherd.

In your own sphere of influence among your family, work environment, or wherever else you spend the majority of your time, is God calling you to be a leader, an influencer, or a shepherd? If not, are you assisting the ones in these roles?

In these very challenging times, it is more important than ever for the body of Christ to come together to protect, feed, nurture and lead the flock. How will you help?

TODAY'S CHALLENGE:

Ask the Father how you can help shepherd His sheep. Like Peter, will you commit to Jesus to feed His lambs, and tend His sheep? Ask the Holy Spirit to empower you for service.

Dive Deeper: Study Numbers 27; Ezekiel 34; John 10:1-30; John 21:15-19.

October 20

SEEK THE LORD YOUR GOD

Deuteronomy 4:29-31

"But if from there you seek the Lord your God, you will find him if you seek him with all your heart and with all your soul. ³⁰ When you are in distress and all these things have happened to you, then in later days you will return to the Lord your God and obey him. ³¹ For the Lord your God is a merciful God; he will not abandon or destroy you or forget the covenant..."

In the verses preceding today's passage (verses 21-28), Moses is speaking to the Israelites not long before they are to enter into the promised land without him. He cautions them not to forget the covenant the Lord had made with them, and warned them not to "make for yourselves an idol in the form of anything the Lord your God has forbidden" (verse 23).

Then, as if Moses knew they would not obey, he warns them of the severe consequences of disobedience – they would be scattered among the nations and only a few of them survive. But even with this disturbing truth, he reminds them of the goodness, faithfulness and mercy of God. If, among those who survive, there are those who will again seek Him with all their hearts, God will be merciful and receive them when they return to Him.

Even though I knew the Lord in my teens, my many idols and disobedience over the next forty years took me far from Him. How very grateful I am that when I began to seek Him with all my heart He lovingly received me. Have you experienced this too?

TODAY'S CHALLENGE:

Tell the Father how very grateful you are that He lovingly accepts you in spite of how far, or how long, you were away. Seek Him today with all your heart and soul.

Dive Deeper: Study Deuteronomy 4.

October 21

THERE IS NO OTHER

Deuteronomy 4:39-40
"Acknowledge and take to heart this day that the Lord is God in heaven above and on the earth below. There is no other. ⁴⁰ Keep his decrees and commands, which I am giving you today, so that it may go well with you and your children after you and that you may live long in the land the Lord your God gives you for all time."

Over many years I encountered many gods. Yes, gods of self, success, money, sex, and drugs. I heard about Norse gods, Greek gods, Hindu gods, and gods of the underworld. Some of these I had personal experience with, others I only read about.

I was nearly 57 when I truly encountered the LORD Who is God. Now, I know there is no other. My only son, who was adopted, then abandoned by me at age 2, was already an adult before I really met the one and only "God in heaven above and on the earth below. There is no other."

Since I began an intimate relationship with Him, I have learned by experience the truth of the Biblical principle that blessings follow obedience. It is not the other way around. In doing my best to be obedient, it surely has gone well with me. I only wish, for the sake of my son and ex-wife, I had truly repented and actually known God earlier in life.

My passion is to share the truth in today's passage with many young people, and help them implement it in their lives for the sake of their current and future families.

Have you truly met God?

TODAY'S CHALLENGE:

Ask God the Father to help you, by His Holy Spirit, keep His decrees and commands for the good of you and your children.

Dive Deeper: Study Deuteronomy 4.

October 22

LOVE THE LORD YOUR GOD

Deuteronomy 6:4-5
"Hear, O Israel: The Lord our God, the Lord is one. [5] Love the Lord your God with all your heart and with all your soul and with all your strength."

When Jesus was asked what is the most important commandment, He quoted this very passage from the Jewish Torah which we have included in what we refer to as our Old Testament. His emphasis deserves very serious consideration.

In a time when all the rest of the world worshiped more than one god, the fact that the Jews professed One God alone was remarkably unique. We believe our One God has manifested Himself to us in three persons – the Father, Son, and Holy Spirit – but they are all One.

The emphasis Jesus made in Matthew 22:37 was primarily one of absolute love and devotion with every fiber of being. When we refer to "loving God with all our heart", we mean from the deepest most significant part of us which is our spirit - the part of us that is in the very likeness of God Himself Who is Spirit.

"Loving Him with all our soul" refers to our mind, will and emotions. We make a definite decision to love Him in our thought life and to invest our emotional energy in worship. "Loving God with all our strength" involves our physical lives being directed towards service and obedience.

The use of the word "all" in front of heart, soul, and strength is perhaps the most significant part of this command. Are you "all" about loving God? Is He first in every area of your life?

TODAY'S CHALLENGE:

Tell God you want to make Him first priority in every part of you. Ask the Holy Spirit to help you.

Dive Deeper: Study Deuteronomy 6; Matthew 22:37-40.

October 23

DIVINE DISCIPLINE

Deuteronomy 8:2,5
"Remember how the Lord your God led you all the way in the wilderness these forty years, to humble and test you in order to know what was in your heart, whether or not you would keep his commands... ⁵ Know then in your heart that as a man disciplines his son, so the Lord your God disciplines you."

As I look back over my life, I see now there were a number of very difficult stages I believe God actually used for my good to discipline me; although at the time, I did not recognize them as having any useful longer term purpose. Going to prison certainly qualifies as one of these periods. Can you relate?

With hindsight, I see the truth that God disciplines those He loves; those He treats as sons (see Proverbs 3:11-12; and Hebrews 12:5-13). He does not want us to be discouraged; rather, He desires for us to learn lessons from these tests.

For example, an important life lesson is that decisions have consequences – good decisions have good consequences, and bad decisions have bad consequences.

Disobedience to God's principles and commands will always have bad consequences. This is a natural law. God does not cause the outcomes, but our decisions have natural consequences. If we are humble and repentant, God can use these circumstances to teach and strengthen us.

It is important also to understand that God already knows our hearts, but testing shows us what is in our heart. When we acknowledge our heart condition, wisdom and understanding come to help us make necessary changes.

TODAY'S CHALLENGE:

Thank the Father for times of testing and discipline. Ask the Holy Spirit to give you wisdom and insight from your trials to know your own heart and make adjustments.

Dive Deeper: Study Deuteronomy 8; Proverbs 3:11-12; Hebrews 12:5-13; Job 5:17-18; Psalm 94:12-13.

October 24

WHAT GOD ASKS OF US

Deuteronomy 10:12-13
"And now, Israel, what does the Lord your God ask of you but to fear the Lord your God, to walk in obedience to him, to love him, to serve the Lord your God with all your heart and with all your soul, ¹³ and to observe the Lord's commands and decrees that I am giving you today for your own good?"

At first glance, today's passage may be intimidating; but it answers the question many of us have asked – what does God want from me? What is my proper response to God's overwhelming grace, mercy and love?

If we truly understood and met the first requirement – "to fear the Lord your God" – I believe everything else would naturally follow with little effort. This is not the kind of fear that makes one want to run and hide, or freezes one from any action at all. Rather, this is to approach the Lord God in holy reverence, childlike awe, and ultimate respect.

This is the proper attitude we need to begin to comprehend the unlimited, unconditional love God has for each and every one of us as His unique sons and daughters. The more we are able to progressively believe and receive this incredible gift, the more we will naturally want to please Him with our entire being.

It is from this love that we learn it is for our own ultimate good that we observe the Lord's commands and decrees, walk in obedience to Him, and serve Him with all our heart and soul.

TODAY'S CHALLENGE:

Thank the Father for His unconditional love expressed in the sacrifice of His Son, Jesus. Ask the Holy Spirit to teach you the fear of the Lord, and empower you to serve Him obediently.

Dive Deeper: Study Deuteronomy 10; Micah 6:8.

October 25

A PROPHET LIKE MOSES

Deuteronomy 18:15, 18-19
"(Moses said) ¹⁵The Lord your God will raise up for you a prophet like me from among you, from your fellow Israelites. You must listen to him... (God said) ¹⁸ I will raise up for them a prophet like you from among their fellow Israelites, and I will put my words in his mouth. He will tell them everything I command him. ¹⁹ I myself will call to account anyone who does not listen to my words that the prophet speaks in my name."

The people of Israel were told to expect a prophet like Moses in their future. There was no question that this prophet would be sent to them by God Himself. This is who they were referring to when they asked John the Baptist, "Are you the prophet?", to which John replied, "No." See John 1:21 and 25.

Most scholars believe this scripture passage is a prophecy of Jesus Christ of Nazareth. It is reported that about 25% or more of Scripture was prophetic at the time it was written. The fact that most of these prophecies have already been fulfilled over the years with pinpoint-like accuracy distinguishes the Bible from every other book in the world.

God the Father clearly assigns great importance and authority to this prophet He raises up. Jesus repeated often that He only said what He heard the Father say. At the Transfiguration, the Father said, "This is my Son, listen to Him".

Jesus is called the "Living Word" by John; and, Peter said, "You have the words of life."

Are you listening to Jesus?

TODAY'S CHALLENGE:

Tell the Father you want to hear Jesus better. Ask the Holy Spirit to help you learn to hear and obey Jesus more all the time.

Dive Deeper: Study Deuteronomy 18; John 1:21.

October 26

SECRET THINGS

Deuteronomy 29:29
"The secret things belong to the Lord our God, but the things revealed belong to us and to our children forever, that we may follow all the words of this law."

I am convinced for all of eternity we will be learning more about God – His love, His thoughts, His ways, His character, His creation, and His plans. Even then, we will never be able to fully comprehend Him.

Yet, for now, He has revealed much of Himself through His Word. He knows our feeble brains cannot understand much of His majesty, but He has disclosed enough for us to be able to decide whether we want to have an intimate, personal relationship with Him in this world and extending throughout all of eternity.

Until one is born again, the Bible does not make a lot of sense to most people. But after the Spirit of God indwells the believer, the Holy Spirit begins to reveal precepts, promises, and principles that, when applied to our lives, bless us with genuine wisdom, knowledge and understanding.

Jesus said that those who hunger and thirst for righteousness shall be filled (Matthew 5:6), and it is the Spirit of God who gives us a hunger for the Word so we can learn increasingly more about God and His plans for our life.

Are there plenty of situations and concepts in life that we do not understand, and perhaps never will comprehend? Certainly, there are "secret things that belong to the Lord our God".

TODAY'S CHALLENGE:

Tell the Father you trust Him to reveal as much to you about Himself as you are able to comprehend. Ask the Holy Spirit give you a hunger for the Word like you have never had before, and to help you apply it.

Dive Deeper: Study Deuteronomy 29; Proverbs 25:2; Isaiah 55:8-9; Ecclesiastes 3:11, 11:5; Daniel 2:22.

October 27

CONSECRATE YOURSELF

Joshua 3:5
"Joshua told the people, 'Consecrate yourselves, for tomorrow the LORD will do amazing things among you.'"

2 Corinthians 6:17-18
"Therefore, 'Come out from them and be separate, says the Lord. Touch no unclean thing, and I will receive you.' [18] And, 'I will be a Father to you, and you will be my sons and daughters, says the Lord Almighty.'"

Here is an important truth for everyone who is born again. Applying this diligently in your life results in great rewards. The Bible is clear that God is a rewarder of those who diligently seek Him (see Hebrews 11:6). You will see the Lord do many amazing things!

The word "Consecrate" means to separate yourself for a holy purpose. It also means to be set apart as dedicated to God; set aside as sacred; and, to devote solemnly to a purpose.

This is not a "religious" activity; rather, it is increasingly a way of life for those who love God, and are diligently seeking Him. If you want to go deeper in God, this is a lifestyle choice. The day-to-day activities of life naturally require our attention; but setting aside more time with God instead of allowing worldly activities to dominate our "free" time is part of what we mean by separating yourself. It is not going off somewhere to live in a monastery, or giving up every worldly responsibility.

An important part of consecrating yourself is guarding what you allow to enter you mind, eyes and ears. We must be deliberate about the things we allow to influence our thinking, speech or actions.

TODAY'S CHALLENGE:

Tell the Father you desire to seek Him diligently and you will dedicate yourself to Him.

Dive Deeper: Study Joshua 3; Hebrews 11:6; 2 Corinthians 6:14-7:1; Romans 12:1; James 4:4-5, 8-9; Romans 8:5-7; 1 John 2:15-17; John 15:19; 1 John 5:19, 21; 1 Peter 1:13-17; 1 Peter 2:11-12.

October 28

THROW AWAY FOREIGN GODS

Joshua 24:22-23
"Then Joshua said, 'You are witnesses against yourselves that you have chosen to serve the LORD.' 'Yes, we are witnesses,' they replied. ²³ 'Now then,' said Joshua, 'throw away the foreign gods that are among you and yield your hearts to the LORD, the God of Israel.'"

Our passage today is best understood after a review of all of Joshua 24. I recommend you take a few minutes to read it. For further insight, see October 5 devotional.

After the promised land was conquered and possessed by all the Israelite tribes, Joshua assembled them for his final address to the people. Joshua reminds them how God worked through His covenant with their forefathers Abraham, Isaac and Jacob over many years to finally settle them as a large, victorious nation in the promised land.

He reminded them that God gave them a productive, fruitful land they did not have to toil over; vineyards and orchards they did not plant; and, cities they did not have to build (verse 13).

As born again believers, we too have access to many similar blessings after we choose to be "all in" about our daily Christian walk. A review of the preceding devotionals for the last week or so speaks of dedication and consecration that results when we really love and obey God.

However, part of that renewed commitment involves purging our lives of all "the foreign gods" we served previously. They might also be called "idols", which is really anything we value or "worship" more than God.

Where do you invest your time, energy and resources?

TODAY'S CHALLENGE:

Ask the Holy Spirit to help you honestly consider any "foreign gods" or "idols" in your life. Tell the Father you will yield your heart completely to Him.

Dive Deeper: Study Joshua 24.

October 29

DON'T FORSAKE THE LORD

Judges 2:10-12
"After that whole generation had been gathered to their ancestors, another generation grew up who knew neither the Lord nor what he had done for Israel. [11] Then the Israelites did evil in the eyes of the Lord and served the Baals. [12] They forsook the Lord, the God of their ancestors, who had brought them out of Egypt...'"

Our passage today is best understood after reading the broader surrounding text of Judges 2:6-23. I recommend you take a few minutes to read it.

After the promised land was conquered and possessed by all the Israelite tribes, Joshua died. Yesterday's devotional disclosed some of the background for his last message to them. Today we learn what happened in the years which followed, and the repeated disturbing patterns of disobedience, rebellion and apostasy.

The key to the repetitive cycles of national sin was that the Israelites "forsook the Lord, the God of their ancestors". The generation who witnessed the Lord's miraculous deliverance, and who served the Lord, died off without training up the next generation in the ways and character of God.

Much of our worst societal ills today are the result of generations of children who are not being trained to honor, serve and worship God. In America, we have removed God and prayer from our schools, courthouses, public events, and sadly, even some "churches".

I assume you've been born again; and, if you are studying these devotionals daily you must already be serious about going deeper in God. Be careful to continue pressing in to God daily, and make it your lifelong goal to inspire the next generation to do the same.

TODAY'S CHALLENGE:

Talk to the Father about your commitment to Him. Ask the Holy Spirit to train you to inspire the generation behind you.

Dive Deeper: Study Judges 2.

October 30

MIGHTY WARRIOR

Judges 6:12, 14-16
"When the angel of the Lord appeared to Gideon, he said, 'The Lord is with you, mighty warrior.'... [14] *The Lord turned to him and said, 'Go in the strength you have and save Israel out of Midian's hand. Am I not sending you?'* [15] *'Pardon me, my lord,' Gideon replied, 'but how can I save Israel? My clan is the weakest in Manasseh, and I am the least in my family.'* [16] *The Lord answered, 'I will be with you, and you will strike down all the Midianites, leaving none alive.'"*

The story of Gideon is a fascinating, inspiring story and I suggest you read it all in Judges 6 and 7. The passage today is a great illustration of how God sees us fulfilling His plan for our lives. Gideon thought he was too weak, too unimportant and uncourageous. But, God saw Him as a "Mighty warrior"!

God uses the weak things of this world to shame the strong, and He chooses the lowly and despised to change the world, so that man himself cannot boast (1 Corinthians 1:27-29). Actually, the best place in humility for us to be is the realization that when we are weak, then He is strong (2 Corinthians 12:10).

God will not unveil his plan all at once. He expects us to trust Him one day at a time. He wants us to see ourselves the way He sees us. This comes progressively as we study His Word and choose to believe what He says, instead of what the world and the enemy wants us to believe about ourselves. Seek and follow God's plan for your life. He will be with you!

TODAY'S CHALLENGE:

Ask the Father to help you see yourself the way He does. Trust Him to be with you.

Dive Deeper: Study Judges 6:1–7:25; 1 Corinthians 1:27-29; 2 Corinthians 12:10.

October 31

LESS IS MORE

Judges 7:2, 7-8
"The Lord said to Gideon, 'You have too many men. I cannot deliver Midian into their hands, or Israel would boast against me, 'My own strength has saved me.''...⁷ The Lord said to Gideon, 'With the three hundred men that lapped I will save you and give the Midianites into your hands. Let all the others go home.' ⁸ So Gideon sent the rest of the Israelites home but kept the three hundred..."

Continuing today with the story of Gideon, we learn how with God less is more. Gideon started out with 32,000 men to go against the Midianites and Amalekites who were too numerous to count. Already, we know that Gideon is far outnumbered.

God wants to make the odds even more impossible, and whittles down Gideon's force to 22,000, but God says that is still too many. So then he reduced it to only 300! God wanted to be sure that the people of Israel knew beyond the shadow of a doubt that it was only the Lord's work that made the overwhelming victory possible.

We often find ourselves in what seems to be an absolutely hopeless situation against overwhelming odds. In the natural, we do not see any chance of victory. It may be homelessness, illness, imprisonment, unemployment or any of a hundred other situations. But, we must remember God has the final say, ultimate authority, all power, and perfect timing.

We must call out to Him, trust Him, and do what He is leading us to do. Victory is His!

TODAY'S CHALLENGE:

Talk to the Father about the mountains you are facing that seem insurmountable. Thank Him that Jesus has overcome everything in this world. Ask the Holy Spirit to help you put aside everything that might be delaying God's deliverance.

Dive Deeper: Study Judges 6 and 7.

November 1

WEAK MOMENTS

Judges 16:19-21

"After putting him to sleep on her lap, she called for someone to shave off the seven braids of his hair, and so began to subdue him. And his strength left him. [20] Then she called, 'Samson, the Philistines are upon you!' He awoke from his sleep and thought, 'I'll go out as before and shake myself free.' But he did not know that the Lord had left him. [21] Then the Philistines seized him, gouged out his eyes and took him down to Gaza. Binding him with bronze shackles, they set him to grinding grain in the prison."

The story of Sampson in Judges 13-16 offers a number of great illustrations for us, and today's passage is no exception. Samson had the anointing of the Holy Spirit on his life, and supernatural strength. But he let the temptations of the world, and his pride, destroy him.

It would seem Samson had everything going his way in spite of several poor decisions along the way. But he knew where his strength came from, walked in repentance, and didn't let the world hold him down. That all changed when he met Delilah, the prostitute.

Those of us who have been saved in prison, and sought the Lord diligently while incarcerated, realize the enemy is waiting outside upon release. The devil knows what temptations we use to fall for, and it isn't long before he starts tempting us.

Three things often lead back to prison: sexual involvement outside of marriage, mind-altering substances, and pride. All of these took Samson to prison, and soon death. Be sure this does not happen to you.

TODAY'S CHALLENGE:

Ask the Father to reveal His overwhelming love to you more every day. Ask the Holy Spirit, in response to God's love, to strengthen you daily to walk in obedience.

Dive Deeper: Study Judges 13:1 – 16:31.

November 2

A LISTENING SERVANT

1 Samuel 3:10-11
"The Lord came and stood there, calling as at the other times, 'Samuel! Samuel!' Then Samuel said, 'Speak, for your servant is listening.' [11] And the Lord said to Samuel: 'See, I am about to do something in Israel that will make the ears of everyone who hears about it tingle.'"

Samuel was a very young boy in service to the priest Eli. We learn in 1 Samuel 3:7, that Samuel did not yet know the Lord, and the Word of the Lord had not yet been revealed to him.

While Samuel was lying down, and Eli had already gone to bed, Samuel hears a voice calling his name. Three times this happens and each time when he goes to Eli, he was told that it wasn't Eli calling him. The third time, Eli tells him it must be God, and instructs him how to answer if it happens again.

This time, the Lord actually appeared in a visitation to Samuel, and Samuel responded as instructed, "Speak, for your servant is listening." The Lord shares important future events with him for the first time, and Samuel goes on to be one of the foremost of God's prophets who was instrumental in the crowning of Israel's first two Kings, Saul and David.

We can learn a few things from this short story. Many times I think the Lord tries to speak with us through His Holy Spirit, but we do not recognize His voice. We must put aside the distractions of life and listen for His voice. God is wanting to do dramatic things in our lives, one day at a time, if we will only listen and obey.

TODAY'S CHALLENGE:

Tell the Father you will try to set aside distractions so you can better hear His voice. Allow the Holy Spirit to lead you today, and be obedient to His call.

Dive Deeper: Study 1 Samuel 3.

November 3

OBEDIENCE IS BETTER THAN SACRIFICE

1 Samuel 15:22-23
"But Samuel replied: 'Does the Lord delight in burnt offerings and sacrifices as much as in obeying the Lord? To obey is better than sacrifice, and to heed is better than the fat of rams. ²³ For rebellion is like the sin of divination, and arrogance like the evil of idolatry. Because you have rejected the word of the Lord, he has rejected you as king.'"

God spoke through His prophet, Samuel, to the first King of Israel, Saul. Saul understood that the Word of the Lord came to him in this manner. In 1 Samuel 15, Samuel gives Saul very specific instructions from God about an attack Saul was to undertake upon the Amalekites on God's behalf.

Against God's instructions to destroy everything and everybody, Saul allowed his men to keep the best of the herds of sheep and cattle. Saul knew better, but he was afraid of his own people and gave in to their desires. They tried to justify their actions by promising to sacrifice some of them to the Lord.

By the time Samuel confronted Saul, he was erecting a monument in his own honor in Carmel. Rebellion, pride and arrogance, along with fear of the people, caused Saul to disobey the Word of the Lord.

Witchcraft and divination deliberately circumvent God's law and natural order. Rebellion does too. Arrogance and pride are compared to idolatry because we are essentially making ourselves god in our lives.

God values obedience over religious rites, and punishes rebellion and pride.

Will you obey?

TODAY'S CHALLENGE:

Ask the Father to show you areas of your life where you are rebellious, disobedient or prideful. Ask the Holy Spirit to reveal where you are more concerned with what men think rather than God.

Dive Deeper: Study 1 Samuel 15.

November 4

GOD LOOKS AT THE HEART

1 Samuel 16:7
"But the Lord said to Samuel, "Do not consider his appearance or his height, for I have rejected him. The Lord does not look at the things people look at. People look at the outward appearance, but the Lord looks at the heart.""

After God rejected Saul as king, He sent Samuel to Bethlehem to the house of Jesse, saying that He had chosen one of Jesse's sons to be king. Samuel is concerned because this could be viewed as an act of sedition or treason, but God reassures him that He is in control.

When Samuel sees the first son, Eliab, he assumes he is the one. He must have had an impressive appearance and a great track record of accomplishments. Samuel is impressed, and thinks his work is done, but the Lord teaches him something very important in today's passage.

God is not impressed with most of the things the world sees as important. Outward appearances and past accomplishments mean nothing if a person's heart is not right. Interestingly, 1 Samuel 9:1-2, says that Saul had an impressive appearance, but yesterday we read more about the condition of his heart. The people wanted a king, and God gave them what they wanted. His replacement would be different.

Often times, we get too caught up in appearances and accomplishments, and miss the uniqueness of those around us with plenty to offer in the Kingdom. Let's try to look deeper. Many priceless jewels go undiscovered. David was a prime example of one who the world would have overlooked.

TODAY'S CHALLENGE:

Tell the Father you desire a heart of discernment and love towards others. Ask the Holy Spirit to help you be considerate and inclusive of those around you the world might be rejecting.

Dive Deeper: Study 1 Samuel 16; 1 Samuel 9:1-2.

November 5

IN THE NAME OF THE LORD ALMIGHTY

1 Samuel 17:45-46
"David said to the Philistine, 'You come against me with sword and spear and javelin, but I come against you in the name of the Lord Almighty, the God of the armies of Israel, whom you have defied. ⁴⁶ This day the Lord will deliver you into my hands, and I'll strike you down and cut off your head. This very day I will give the carcasses of the Philistine army to the birds and the wild animals, and the whole world will know that there is a God in Israel.'"

Yesterday we learned how God saw the heart of David before He anointed him as Israel's future king. Today's passage shows us something of what God saw in David's heart – courage, faith and leadership.

David's brothers, the more likely-looking candidates for king, were among the many Israelite fighting men who had already been intimidated for forty days by Goliath and the Philistines. Jesse sent David as an errand boy to the front lines with provisions for the brothers and gifts for their commanders, wanting him to return with a report. Little did he know how important this "errand" would be for the battle.

David the shepherd boy knew intimately the God of Israel that Goliath was defiling. He had spent plenty of time getting to know God and His faithfulness out in those lonely fields. When he faced Goliath, it was with great confidence in God that he ran towards his giant declaring aloud God's faithfulness and defending His Name.

TODAY'S CHALLENGE:

Spend time with the Father recalling His faithfulness, power and love. Courageously declare God's Word, in the Name of the Lord Almighty, over the giants in your life today. Let the world know there is a God in Heaven!

Dive Deeper: Study 1 Samuel 17.

November 6

FIND STRENGTH IN GOD

1 Samuel 30:3-4, 6
"When David and his men reached Ziklag, they found it destroyed by fire and their wives and sons and daughters taken captive. ⁴ So David and his men wept aloud until they had no strength left to weep... ⁶ David was greatly distressed because the men were talking of stoning him; each one was bitter in spirit because of his sons and daughters. But David found strength in the Lord his God."

While in waiting many years to become King, David had many trials, discouraging times, and close calls that could have taken his life. Clearly, God's hand was upon him. The passage today describes one of David's darkest days.

David and his 600 men, and their families, had fled Israel to avoid King Saul into the land of the Philistines to live under Achish, the son of the King of Gath. They were turned away from a battle where they would have been helping the Philistines against Saul and his army because the Philistine leaders did not trust their loyalty.

Upon returning to Ziklag they found their village plundered, burned, and their families had been taken captive by a raiding party of Amalekites. They all wept aloud, and talked of killing David. David went off by himself to seek the Lord, and be comforted from the loss of his two wives.

David encouraged himself and found strength in the Lord, recalled His faithfulness, and received instructions to pursue and retrieve all that was lost. They found their enemies and destroyed them. David brought everything back, including their unharmed families.

Are you in a discouraging time of life? You can find strength in God.

TODAY'S CHALLENGE:

Tell God about your situation, and ask Him for direction. Receive the encouragement of the Spirit.

Dive Deeper: Study 1 Samuel 30.

November 7

UNRESTRAINED PRAISE

2 Samuel 6:14-16, 21-22
"Wearing a linen ephod, David was dancing before the Lord with all his might, ¹⁵ while he and all Israel were bringing up the ark of the Lord with shouts and the sound of trumpets.¹⁶ As the ark of the Lord was entering the City of David, Michal daughter of Saul watched from a window. And when she saw King David leaping and dancing before the Lord, she despised him in her heart… ²¹I will celebrate before the Lord. ²² I will become even more undignified than this, and I will be humiliated in my own eyes…"

David put the Lord first in every part of his life. When it was time to bring the Ark of God to the City of David, all of Israel rejoiced with David and his men. There was a great ceremony surrounding the procession, and David was unashamed to dance before the Lord with all his might.

David knew that thanksgiving and praise ushered one into the presence of God. He was celebrating the goodness and faithfulness of God. His worshipful act at the time was all out joyful dancing, and he did not care what others thought, or how undignified it might have been for their king to be without restraint in his praise.

Why should we ever be embarrassed to openly and exuberantly worship and praise our God? Jesus places great importance on acknowledging Him before others, so much so that if we do not, He will not acknowledge us before His Father in Heaven (Matthew 10:32-33).

The Psalms are full of encouragement to sing, shout, and dance before the Lord. Be bold and unashamed!

TODAY'S CHALLENGE:

Tell the Father you will be unafraid to praise Him exuberantly even in front of other people!

Dive Deeper: Study 2 Samuel 6; Matthew 10:32-33; Psalm 100:1-5; Psalm 47:1, 5-6; Psalm 32:11; Psalm 95:1-7; Zechariah 2:10; John 7:37-39; John 11:43.

November 8

SIN HAS CONSEQUENCES

2 Samuel 12:9-11
"Why did you despise the word of the Lord by doing what is evil in his eyes? You struck down Uriah the Hittite with the sword and took his wife to be your own. You killed him with the sword of the Ammonites. [10] Now, therefore, the sword will never depart from your house, because you despised me and took the wife of Uriah the Hittite to be your own. [11] This is what the Lord says: Out of your own household I am going to bring calamity on you..."

King David, honored God, and God honored him. From reading the Psalms, there can be little question that David loved God with all his heart. Yet, he fell into some significant sins through a series of very weak, poor choices.

At a time when he should have been off fighting with his men, he stayed behind in Jerusalem. Could it have been his conscience that left him sleepless and out on his roof at night? He did not avert his eyes when he spotted Bathsheba bathing; and worse, he gave into temptation to send for her and slept with her. When she discovered she was pregnant, David had his very loyal friend, Uriah, killed because he was her husband.

Psalm 51 records David's repentance, and God extended forgiveness. But, sin has consequences. For the rest of David's life his family and his throne was beleaguered with every kind of imaginable trouble. The second half of 2 Samuel records these many tragic consequences.

When tempting thoughts come, we must take them captive, reject them, and make the right decision. The consequences of sin are not worth it.

TODAY'S CHALLENGE:

Ask the Holy Spirit to help you learn how to say "no" to temptation quickly.

Dive Deeper: Study 2 Samuel 12; Galatians 6:7-8.

November 9

DO NOT REMAIN BANISHED

2 Samuel 14:14
"Like water spilled on the ground, which cannot be recovered, so we must die. But that is not what God desires; rather, he devises ways so that a banished person does not remain banished from him."

2 Peter 3:9
"...he (God) is patient with you, not wanting anyone to perish, but everyone to come to repentance."

We are a spirit (our true essence); we possess a soul (mind, will, emotions); and, we live in a physical body. Our spirit will live forever somewhere, but our body is going to die. There is no way around it.

If we went into outer space, we would have to have a "space suit", else we could not maneuver or exist. Similarly, our body is our "earth suit" for our spirit to be able to maneuver and live in this three dimensional temporary world. One day we will lay it aside and return to the spirit world. Our decision whether or not to receive Jesus, and love God, on this earth determines where we will live for all of eternity.

God gives everyone numerous opportunities to choose His Son and pursue an intimate relationship with the Father. He gives us free will, so He will not force us to choose Heaven. The more we understand and receive the unconditional love of the Father, we will want to pursue more intimacy with Him.

Jesus came to give us abundant life, starting right now, and extending throughout all of eternity. Sin separates us from God, and we are banished from His Presence unless we come through Jesus. Pray diligently for those who are still banished.

TODAY'S CHALLENGE:

Talk to someone today who is still banished, and let them know how much God loves them.

Dive Deeper: Study 2 Samuel 14; 1 Thessalonians 5:23; Zechariah 12:1; Acts 7:59.

November 10

THE LORD – HE IS GOD!

1 Kings 18:21, 38-39
"Elijah went before the people and said, 'How long will you waver between two opinions? If the Lord is God, follow him; but if Baal is God, follow him.' But the people said nothing… [38] *Then the fire of the Lord fell and burned up the sacrifice, the wood, the stones and the soil, and also licked up the water in the trench.* [39] *When all the people saw this, they fell prostrate and cried, 'The Lord—he is God! The Lord—he is God!'"*

One of the most interesting and exciting chapters in the Bible is 1 Kings 18. I encourage you to stop and read the entire chapter now.

Elijah exhibited tremendous faith and bravery on Mt. Carmel by facing the 450 prophets of Baal and the 400 prophets of Asherah, who were all supported by the most wicked Queen, Jezebel. This was the time to show all of Israel who was their true, One and Only God, Jehovah, or the false gods of Baal and Asherah. Elijah's life was on the line.

Elijah challenged the other prophets to a demonstration of power. With the same sacrifice on the two altars, whose God would send fire from Heaven to consume the sacrifice?

The false prophets cried out to their gods, cut themselves, and danced feverishly for hours, but nothing happened. Elijah gave them plenty of time, but finally it was his turn.

After drenching the wood and the sacrifice three times with copious amounts of water, Elijah cried out to the Lord one time, and fire fell from Heaven to consume the sacrifice and all the standing water in the trenches! There was no doubt Who was God in Israel and over the whole Earth.

TODAY'S CHALLENGE:

Spend time with the Father contemplating and celebrating His Power and Majesty.

Dive Deeper: Study 1 Kings 18.

November 11

OUTNUMBERED

2 Kings 6:15-17
"When the servant of the man of God got up and went out early the next morning, an army with horses and chariots had surrounded the city. 'Oh no, my lord! What shall we do?' the servant asked. [16] 'Don't be afraid,' the prophet answered. 'Those who are with us are more than those who are with them.' [17] And Elisha prayed, 'Open his eyes, Lord, so that he may see.' Then the Lord opened the servant's eyes, and he looked and saw the hills full of horses and chariots of fire all around Elisha."

At God's instruction, Elijah picked Elisha to succeed him as the Lord's prophet in Israel. Elisha requested and received a double portion of Elijah's anointing! See 2 Kings 2.

In 2 Kings 6, we learn that Elisha was supernaturally intercepting the war plans of the King of Aram. Repeatedly the armies of Israel were warned by Elisha, so every single time the plans of the enemy were thwarted.

The King of Aram was enraged when he learned about Elisha, and finally found out where he was. *"Then he sent horses and chariots and a strong force there. They went by night and surrounded the city."* (verse 14). Elisha only had one servant with him. In the natural, they were outnumbered. Or were they?

The servant panicked when he saw how many of the enemy soldiers were there with all their chariots. But Elisha could see into the spirit realm to see the mighty force of warring angels surrounding the enemy. Who was really outnumbered?

If we could see into the spirit realm all around us where the real battles are always raging (see Ephesians 6:10-18), we would know we are always protected and assisted supernaturally!

TODAY'S CHALLENGE:

Thank the Father for His overwhelming superiority over the enemy! Stay on His side.

Dive Deeper: Study 2 Kings 6; Ephesians 6:10-18.

November 12

SEEK HIS FACE ALWAYS

1 Chronicles 16:8-11
"Give praise to the Lord, proclaim his name; make known among the nations what he has done. ⁹ Sing to him, sing praise to him; tell of all his wonderful acts. ¹⁰ Glory in his holy name; let the hearts of those who seek the Lord rejoice. ¹¹ Look to the Lord and his strength; seek his face always."

After King David prepared a tent to house it, the Ark of God was finally moved to Jerusalem! What a wonderful celebration they had, and David presented gifts to each Israelite man and woman. *"He appointed some of the Levites to minister before the ark of the LORD, to extol, thank, and praise the LORD, the God of Israel."* (verse 4).

David was the first to commit a song of thanks to Asaph and the singers that day. Our passage today is the first part of a wonderful Psalm of thanksgiving and praise that extends through most of Chapter 16. You will be blessed to read and meditate on the entire Psalm.

There is such power, peace and joy in taking time personally to genuinely thank God for all He has done, is doing, and will do in our lives! We should lift up the Name above all names in praise. We ought to celebrate all the ways God is real to us as Provider, Healer, Comforter, Protector, Lifter of our heads, Savior and Deliverer!

We must look to the Lord each day as our strength. All things are possible with God. In every situation of life let us seek His face always.

TODAY'S CHALLENGE:

Spend time with the Father reflecting upon His Mighty Power, His majestic ways, and His unconditional love for you. Seek His counsel for whatever you are facing today.

Dive Deeper: Study 1 Chronicles 16.

November 13

YOU HAVE BROUGHT ME THIS FAR

1 Chronicles 17:16-17
"Then King David went in and sat before the Lord, and he said:
'Who am I, Lord God, and what is my family, that you have brought me
this far? [17] And as if this were not enough in your sight, my God, you have
spoken about the future of the house of your servant. You, Lord God, have
looked on me as though I were the most exalted of men.'"

It bothered David that the Ark of God resided under a tent while he dwelt in a palace. David wanted to build a more permanent, beautiful house for God. At first, the prophet Nathan encouraged him to do whatever he had in mind because the Lord was with him.

However, that very night the Lord came to Nathan in a dream to give him a message for David. The Lord told David He did not want him to be the one to build His house, rather God would let one of his sons build it after David's days were over.

But God surprised David, when He said, instead of David building God a house, God said, "I declare to you that the Lord will build a house for you." (verse 10). God promised to establish the House of David forever.

With that overwhelming surprise and blessing in mind, we have today's passage as David began a long prayer of thanks and praise (verses 16-25). How very humbled He was in front of the Lord.

We must understand that when we set our hearts to follow hard after God for the rest of our lives, God will bless our family now, and for generations to come.

TODAY'S CHALLENGE:

Re-commit your heart to the Father, and thank Him that He has brought you this far.

Dive Deeper: Study 1 Chronicles 17.

November 14

GIVE GENEROUSLY

1 Chronicles 29:9, 14
"The people rejoiced at the willing response of their leaders, for they had given freely and wholeheartedly to the Lord. David the king also rejoiced greatly... (he said) [14] 'But who am I, and who are my people, that we should be able to give as generously as this? Everything comes from you, and we have given you only what comes from your hand.'"

David was not allowed to build the Temple for God because he "was a warrior and have shed blood" (2 Chronicles 28:3). However, the Spirit of God gave David the ideas and ability to draw up all the plans, make all the arrangements, and inspired him to give much of his fortune to pay for it.

When the leaders of Israel heard David's plans and saw his heart to give unto God, they too gave generously in extravagant fashion. We see in today's passage how the people of Israel responded to this great undertaking and the gifts that had been freely given in wholehearted love and honor for God.

In verses 10-13, we are told how David praised the Lord in the presence of the entire assembly of Israel. Oh, how blessed we are to have all the wonderful works of praise of David as examples of how we too ought to honor and praise our God!

David humbly recognizes what a blessing it is to be able to give unto the Lord. After all, everything we have comes from Him, and we are only giving back to Him a portion of what He has given us.

Always be generous with God. You cannot out-give Him!

TODAY'S CHALLENGE:

Ask the Father to give you a heart of generosity towards Him and all His people.

Dive Deeper: Study 1 Chronicles 29; 2 Chronicles 28:3.

November 15

HEAR FROM HEAVEN

2 Chronicles 6:20-21
"May your eyes be open toward this temple day and night, this place of which you said you would put your Name there. May you hear the prayer your servant prays toward this place. ²¹ Hear the supplications of your servant and of your people Israel when they pray toward this place. Hear from heaven, your dwelling place; and when you hear, forgive."

Once Solomon had completed the Temple, there was a big dedication ceremony. After blessing the entire assembly of Israel, Solomon turned back to the altar of the Lord in the Temple, spread out his hands, and prayed his own prayer of dedication (see 2 Chronicles 6 for full text).

Today's passage is just one of the powerfully anointed parts of his prayer, but this section is key for us today. As Christians, we benefit from Jesus tearing down the vail of separation from God through His death and resurrection. We do not go to a particular place like a Temple where God dwells on Earth to offer our prayers through a priest. No, we are the temple!

As New Testament Christians, we are the very dwelling place of God on Earth through His Holy Spirit who resides in us. See 1 Corinthians 6:19. Similar to this passage, we know God's eyes are always open towards us because all of Heaven is attracted to the Spirit of Christ within us. When we lift our voices to Him, with repentant, humble hearts, we know He hears us (1 John 3:21-22):

"Dear friends, if our hearts do not condemn us, we have confidence before God ²² and receive from him anything we ask, because we keep his commands and do what pleases him."

TODAY'S CHALLENGE:

Tell the Father how thankful you are to be His dwelling place on Earth by His Holy Spirit.

Dive Deeper: Study 2 Chronicles 6; 1 Corinthians 6:19; 1 John 3:21-22.

November 16

IF MY PEOPLE

2 Chronicles 7:13-14
"When I shut up the heavens so that there is no rain, or command locusts to devour the land or send a plague among my people, ¹⁴ if my people, who are called by my name, will humble themselves and pray and seek my face and turn from their wicked ways, then I will hear from heaven, and I will forgive their sin and will heal their land."

After Solomon finished praying his dedicatory prayer for the Temple, *"fire came down from Heaven and consumed the burnt offering and sacrifices, and the glory of the Lord filled the Temple."* (2 Chronicles 7:1)

After about two weeks of celebrating the festival and dedication, and after Solomon had done everything he had set out to do regarding the Temple, the Lord appeared to him at night. God said He heard his prayer and had "chosen this place for myself as a temple for sacrifices." (verse 12)

God continues in the passage we have before us today, part of which (verse 14) is very familiar to a lot of Christians. But many people do not realize the full sentence starts in verse 13. God reminds us that it is He, and He alone, who commands nature in order to judge nations or people groups.

When we are beset by trials or judgments, whether caused by God, or by the consequences of poor human choices, we have the responsibility to do four things if we want God to hear, forgive and heal; that is, we must humble ourselves, pray, seek His face, and turn from our wicked ways.

Make sure you do your part when you cry out to Him.

TODAY'S CHALLENGE:

Tell the Father you are humbly repentant, and ask His Spirit to empower you to turn from evil.

Dive Deeper: Study 2 Chronicles 7; 1 Peter 5:5-6; James 4:4-10; Psalm 51:17; Isaiah 57:15; Isaiah 66:1-2.

November 17

FULLY COMMITTED TO GOD

2 Chronicles 16:9
"For the eyes of the LORD range throughout the earth to strengthen those whose hearts are fully committed to him."

Jesus made it pretty clear how He felt about lukewarm Christians in that He would vomit them out of His mouth (Revelation 3:16). God the Father said, *"These people come near to me with their mouth and honor me with their lips, but their hearts are far from me."* (Isaiah 29:13). These are people who are not fully committed to God.

On the other hand, Pastor Mark Batterson exhorts Christians to go "all in, and all out, for the All in All." (Going All In). This is a person who is fully committed to God; and, is the one about whom the scripture passage describes as being strengthened by God.

God promises to bless, strengthen and protect all those who seriously seek Him, and desire to serve Him. Psalm 5:12 says, *"Surely, Lord, you bless the righteous; you surround them with your favor as with a shield."*

When we set our hearts firmly on God, and follow hard after Him daily, it is very encouraging to think about God having His eyes on us to strengthen us in our journey! Why would we ever look outside of Him for any encouragement, fulfillment, or reinforcement?

Let me encourage you to go "all in" with Jesus. Don't be concerned about pleasing men during this temporary stay on Earth; rather, make a decision to serve God wholeheartedly, and unreservedly, for all of your remaining days. You will never regret it.

TODAY'S CHALLENGE:

Tell the Father you are rededicating yourself to serve Him with all your heart in full surrender to whatever His will is for you today. Submit fully to His Holy Spirit leadership.

Dive Deeper: Study 2 Chronicles 16.

November 18

SEEK HELP FROM THE LORD

2 Chronicles 20:2-4, 12
"Some people came and told Jehoshaphat, 'A vast army is coming against you from Edom, from the other side of the Dead Sea. It is already in Haze-zon Tamar' (that is, En Gedi). ³ Alarmed, Jehoshaphat resolved to inquire of the Lord, and he proclaimed a fast for all Judah.⁴ The people of Judah came together to seek help from the Lord; indeed, they came from every town in Judah to seek him… ¹² Our God, will you not judge them? For we have no power to face this vast army that is attacking us. We do not know what to do, but our eyes are on you."

When a superior army of Moabites, Ammonites, and Meunites came to make war on Judah and Jehoshaphat, the King knew just what to do. He proclaimed a fast and assembled the people.

There is considerable supernatural power available to the people of God when they come together in one accord to fast, inquire of God, and seek His help.

The Spirit of the Lord came upon his prophet, Jahaziel, *"…¹⁵ This is what the LORD says to you: 'Do not be afraid or discouraged because of this vast army. For the battle is not yours, but God's… ¹⁷ You will not have to fight this battle. Take up your positions; stand firm and see the deliverance the LORD will give you, Judah and Jerusalem. Do not be afraid; do not be discouraged. Go out to face them tomorrow, and the LORD will be with you."* (2 Chronicles 20:15, 17).

The next day, the King sent out the singers to lead his forces. They did not even fight. The whole enemy army lay dead in front of them!

TODAY'S CHALLENGE:

Tell Father God how amazing He is to respond to the heartfelt prayers and praise of His people.

Dive Deeper: Study 2 Chronicles 20.

November 19

WHOLEHEARTED

2 Chronicles 25:2
"He did what was right in the eyes of the Lord, but not wholeheartedly."

Two days ago, our devotion was about being fully committed to God. Perhaps you could take a few minutes to review the devotional for November 17?

Today's verse takes this idea a little further, but with someone who is an example not fully committed to the Lord. King Amaziah was only 25 when became king, and today's verse is a disturbing introduction to his twenty-nine year reign. *"He did what was right in the eyes of the Lord, but not wholeheartedly."*

As you study the entire chapter 25, you find that Amaziah was prideful in the way he assembled an army. Instead of relying on God's people, he hired mercenaries who ended up betraying him, killing 3,000 people, and carrying off much plunder.

Then, after winning a battle, he was unfaithful to God and brought back the idols of the foreign gods from the defeated people. Amaziah was very stubborn, and would not listen to the counsel of the Lord's prophet (verses 16 and 20). He knew "what was right in the eyes of the Lord", but he wanted to do things his way, with only feeble attempts to follow God.

He was prideful, unfaithful, stubborn, unhearing, halfhearted, and self-centered. Unfortunately, this might describe many who claim to be part of the Body of Christ today.

As the Day of the Lord is fast approaching, let us re-commit ourselves to seeking God wholeheartedly, humbly, faithfully, and attentively in a commitment to our faith that is self-denying and Christ-centered!

TODAY'S CHALLENGE:

Tell Father God you know He is worth your wholehearted devotion. Ask the Holy Spirit to help you identify any areas in your life that are not yet fully committed to God.

Dive Deeper: Study 2 Chronicles 25.

November 20

A HUMBLED PRISONER

2 Chronicles 33:10-12
"The Lord spoke to Manasseh and his people, but they paid no attention. ¹¹ So the Lord brought against them the army commanders of the king of Assyria, who took Manasseh prisoner, put a hook in his nose, bound him with bronze shackles and took him to Babylon. ¹² In his distress he sought the favor of the Lord his God and humbled himself greatly before the God of his ancestors."

Manasseh, son of King Hezekiah, became king when he was only 12 years old, and he reigned in Jerusalem fifty-five years. The Bible said he did more evil than all the nations God destroyed before the Israelites (verse 9).

Today's passage makes the point that God spoke to Manasseh and his people, but they would not listen. Sometimes, God uses cruel and unusual circumstances to get our attention. Generally, something bad happens as a direct consequence of poor choices and sin. God had Manasseh taken prisoner and bound in shackles and chains. For some of us, this seems familiar?

But wait! God's plan must have worked because, from prison, Manasseh turned to God, repented, and prayed. God heard his plea, was moved by his heart, and brought Manasseh back to Jerusalem. 2 Chronicles 33:14-20 describes a totally converted, "sold-out to God", good king, who had truly humbled himself, and then served God the rest of his life.

What a miraculous turn-around! "Jail-House Religion" was "the real thing" for Manasseh.

Can you relate? I can.

TODAY'S CHALLENGE:

Thank the Father for the way He used circumstances to get your attention. Thank Jesus for paying the price to redeem you from the slave market of sin. Ask the Holy Spirit to help you stay humble.

Dive Deeper: Study 2 Chronicles 33.

November 21

THERE WAS NO REMEDY

2 Chronicles 36:15-16
"The Lord, the God of their ancestors, sent word to them through his messengers again and again, because he had pity on his people and on his dwelling place. ¹⁶ But they mocked God's messengers, despised his words and scoffed at his prophets until the wrath of the Lord was aroused against his people and there was no remedy."

God's patience with Judah finally ran out. 2 Chronicles 36 recounts the brief histories of the final four kings of Judah, who served a combined twenty-five years. It is very clear they all did evil in the sight of the Lord.

The final king of the four, Zedekiah, would not listen to God's prophet, Jeremiah, nor humble himself. He became very stubborn and would not turn to the Lord God of Israel (verses 12-13).

Verse 14 continues:
"Furthermore, all the leaders of the priests and the people became more and more unfaithful, following all the detestable practices of the nations and defiling the temple of the Lord, which he had consecrated in Jerusalem."

So finally, God handed over the leaders and people of Judah to King Nebuchadnezzar of Babylon to be taken into captivity for seventy years. The Temple was burned, Jerusalem's wall was torn down, and all the Temple articles of service and all its treasures were plundered.

Sadly, the state of affairs in Jerusalem and Judah in today's passage sounds a lot like our world right now, especially in America. Will we repent and turn back to the Lord before we come under God's judgment? I pray we will.

TODAY'S CHALLENGE:

Ask the Father what you need to do to begin a personal revival for you and your family. Ask the Holy Spirit to empower you to positively influence the world around you before it is too late.

Dive Deeper: Study 2 Chronicles 36.

November 22

A NEW FOUNDATION

Ezra 3:11-12
"With praise and thanksgiving they sang to the LORD: 'He is good; his love toward Israel endures forever.' And all the people gave a great shout of praise to the LORD, because the foundation of the house of the LORD was laid. [12] But many of the older priests and Levites and family heads, who had seen the former temple, wept aloud when they saw the foundation of this temple being laid, while many others shouted for joy."

King Cyrus of Persia captured Babylon after the Israelites had been seventy years in captivity. Cyrus allowed Zerubbabel to lead a large group of about 42,000 Israelites back to Jerusalem to rebuild the Temple that had been destroyed by the Babylonians. This was exactly as prophesied by Isaiah almost two hundred years earlier (see Isaiah 44:28; 45:1, 13).

In the second year after their return to Israel, work was begun on the new Temple foundation. For many of the people this was a grand, historic time of joy and expectation. However, the plans for the new Temple were not near as grand as Solomon's Temple, so when the celebration came for the laying of the foundation, the older priests, Levites and family heads wept aloud.

It is important to put our past behind us, else the enemy can use it against us for depression, or unfair and unrealistic comparisons. Frankly, the "good old days" were never as good as we remember them.

Paul says he "forgets those things that are behind" (Philippians 3:13); and God says, "Forget the former things, do not dwell on the past" (Isaiah 43:18). If we keep living in the past, we cannot enjoy today, and we negatively impact our future.

TODAY'S CHALLENGE:

Tell the Father you are thankful for the present, and glad to be delivered from your past.

Dive Deeper: Study Ezra 3; Isaiah 44:28; Isaiah 45:1, 13; Philippians 3:13; Isaiah 43:18

November 23

WITH THE HELP OF OUR GOD

Nehemiah 6:15-16
"So the wall was completed on the twenty-fifth of Elul, in fifty-two days.
¹⁶ When all our enemies heard about this, all the surrounding nations
were afraid and lost their self-confidence, because they realized that this
work had been done with the help of our God."

About eighty years after Zerubbabel took the first group of exiles back to Jerusalem to rebuild the Temple, Nehemiah, still in Babylon, received a report that "the wall of Jerusalem is broken down and its gates have been burned with fire". It was also reported that the people in Jerusalem were in "great trouble and disgrace" (see Nehemiah 1:3).

When Nehemiah heard all these things he sat down and wept. He mourned, fasted and prayed before the Lord for days (Nehemiah 1:4-11). Nehemiah received the blessing of God and the favor of the King to take some men and supplies to Jerusalem to rebuild the wall.

Without a wall for defense, Jerusalem was very accessible to enemies. After inspecting the wall, and assessing the political situation with competing noble men who had mixed allegiances, Nehemiah got busy. Through prayer, God's protection, good leadership skills, and the resources of the emperor, Nehemiah and his team completed the wall in only fifty-two days. This was accomplished in the face of great cynicism and opposition.

When we are faced with difficulties, tests and trails, if we will follow the example of Nehemiah, we will be overcomers and those around us will give God the glory and recognition He deserves.

After we pray, fast, and seek the Lord's will, God will use the gifts He placed in us to accomplish His purposes.

TODAY'S CHALLENGE:

Thank the Father for the talents and abilities He has given you. Tell Him you want to be utilized!

Dive Deeper: Study Nehemiah 1:3-11; Nehemiah 6.

November 24

SUCH A TIME AS THIS

Esther 4:14
"For if you remain silent at this time, relief and deliverance for the Jews will arise from another place, but you and your father's family will perish. And who knows but that you have come to your royal position for such a time as this?"

The book of Esther contains a tremendous story of protection and deliverance for God's people. There are elements of grandeur, intrigue, deception, cunning, courage, revenge and victory.

Queen Esther is in a unique position to be used of God at a very particular point in the history of His people. In spite of her own personal danger, with even the possibility of losing her very life, she decides to do what God is calling her to do. She sought the wisdom and favor of God, and He utilized her submitted will and surrendered life.

It certainly appeared that she was placed by God in the right place at the right time so she could choose to do the right thing. Her cousin, Mordecai, was an important man in the kingdom and learned of a secret plot hatched at the highest levels to exterminate the Jews. Circumstances had recently made her Queen, and Mordecai urged her to persuade the King to intervene on behalf of the Jews.

Like Esther, Christians find themselves today in a very dangerous, evil world. Time is short before the Day of the Lord comes. Wherever we find ourselves in life at this moment, could it be that each of our lives were planned by God to be right here, right now, "for such a time as this?"

TODAY'S CHALLENGE:

Tell the Father you are ready to be utilized in His Kingdom work today. Thank Him for pre-positioning you in this most critical time.

Dive Deeper: Study Esther 4.

November 25

JOB DID NOT SIN

Job 1:20-22

"At this, Job got up and tore his robe and shaved his head. Then he fell to the ground in worship²¹ and said: 'Naked I came from my mother's womb, and naked I will depart. The Lord gave and the Lord has taken away; may the name of the Lord be praised.' ²² In all this, Job did not sin by charging God with wrongdoing."

The Bible tells us that Job was "blameless and upright; he feared God and shunned evil." (Job 1:1). There are only a handful of people in the Bible that received such a good endorsement of their life. God had richly blessed him, and the Word says, "He was the greatest man among all the people of the East." (verse 3).

God was very pleased with Job, saying, "There is no one on earth like him..." (verse 8). Satan sought God's permission to test Job to try to prove that without all his many blessings he would reject and curse God. God allowed it.

In the space of one afternoon, Job lost all his cattle, sheep and camels; and, even worse, the lives of all of his sons and daughters. Virtually everything that defined his day to day life was taken away. Our passage today records his response to this awful series of tragedies. He did not blame God, and he did not abandon his faith.

God's people are not promised a life without loss or tragedies, but we are assured of help to make it through tests and trials. Too often people want to blame God, and even walk away from Him, when we ought instead to be running to Him.

TODAY'S CHALLENGE:

Talk to God about whatever storm you face today, and take shelter in His goodness and mercy.

Dive Deeper: Study Job 1.

November 26

WE NEED A MEDIATOR

Job 9:32-35
"He is not a mere mortal like me that I might answer him, that we might confront each other in court. [33] If only there were someone to mediate between us, someone to bring us together, [34] someone to remove God's rod from me, so that his terror would frighten me no more. [35] Then I would speak up without fear of him, but as it now stands with me, I cannot."

In today's passage Job acknowledges his great need and desire to meet directly with God Almighty. Since he recognizes and honors the Holiness of God, he knows that he could not approach him because of his own imperfect condition, even if it were physically possible to do so.

It is thought Job lived at least two thousand years before Jesus. Many view today's passage as a prophecy of Jesus our Messiah. Job recognized he needed someone to mediate between God and him. A "mediator" is an intercessor or spokesman. To "mediate" is to act as an intermediary, or to intervene, or interpose.

Though Job did not yet know Jesus in these capacities, he very clearly stated his recognition of the need for the future roles of our Savior. Jesus came to take our place, to interpose Himself into our hopeless situation. He did not come to intervene in our death; He came to die in our place.

Only Jesus could meet the need Job described. *"Therefore he is able to save completely those who come to God through him, because he always lives to intercede for them."* (Hebrews 7:25).

TODAY'S CHALLENGE:

Thank the Father for sending His Son, Jesus, as our ultimate Savior, Mediator and Intercessor.

Dive Deeper: Study Job 9; Hebrews 7.

November 27

MY REDEEMER LIVES

Job 19:25-27
" I know that my redeemer lives, and that in the end he will stand on the earth. [26] And after my skin has been destroyed, yet in my flesh I will see God; [27] I myself will see him with my own eyes –I, and not another. How my heart yearns within me!"

Nowhere else in our Bible is there such a description of the tormenting thoughts of a person in extreme distress and suffering, as there is in this Book of Job.

His so-called friends want to help him, but for the most part they make him feel even worse. Their understanding of God is, in most cases, not even correct. It never helps for someone to say our suffering is our own fault even when it might be caused from our own sin; but in this case, Job had not sinned, and their accusations only made Job more discouraged.

He was very frustrated that he could not defend himself with his friends or God. Job feels absolutely lost, forsaken and abandoned: *"All my intimate friends detest me; those I love have turned against me. [20] I am nothing but skin and bones; I have escaped only by the skin of my teeth."* (Job 19:19-20)

Yesterday's devotional recognized Job's wisdom that he needed a Mediator. Today's passage records Job's faith-filled realization that he has a Redeemer! Job knew he would one day step into Heaven and be completely vindicated. He looked forward to the day when he would see his Redeemer with his own eyes.

What a grand statement of faith from a man who was at the bottom of despair, hopelessness and discouragement! Let's learn from Job how to have faith in desperate situations.

TODAY'S CHALLENGE:

Tell the Father how grateful you are to be redeemed by the Blood of Jesus.

Dive Deeper: Study Job 19; Colossians 1:13-14; Titus 2:14.

November 28

LIFT THEM UP

Job 22:27-29
*"You will pray to him, and he will hear you, and you will fulfill your vows. *
*[28] What you decide on will be done, and light will shine on your ways. *
*[29] When people are brought low and you say, 'Lift them up!' then he will *
save the downcast."

In this section of Chapter 22, Eliphaz is describing a righteous man who has submitted to God, and is at peace with Him, thereby bringing prosperity (verse 21). Someone who repents, turns back to the Almighty, and leaves wickedness behind, can look to God for their reward and treasure (verses 23-24).

We know we can never be righteous on our own merits or actions. But, as born again believers, the Bible says we are the righteousness of God in Christ Jesus (2 Corinthians 5:21). Although we can never achieve our own righteousness, we have the Holy Spirit who progressively sanctifies us so that we begin to live more and more in the righteousness of Christ.

Through Christ and the power of the Holy Spirit, we have been given everything we need for a godly life through the very great and precious promises of God (2 Peter 1:3-4). In the righteousness of Christ, God hears our prayers, and empowers us to live a holy life.

In Christ, God's grace and favor is applied through His Holy Spirit as we are enabled to make good decisions. Our prayers are effective, and we can intercede on someone's behalf and expect God to answer our prayer, and to move on their behalf.

Give someone an encouraging word today, and intercede for them. God will hear and respond.

TODAY'S CHALLENGE:

Admit to yourself and to the Father that you have no righteousness of your own. Thank Jesus for Him crediting you with His righteousness. Be led by His Spirit today.

Dive Deeper: Study Job 22; 2 Corinthians 5:21; 2 Peter 1:3-4.

November 29

MAKE A COVENANT WITH YOUR EYES

Job 31:1
"I made a covenant with my eyes not to look lustfully at a young woman."

Before I gave my life to Jesus while I was in prison, I had many addictions. You may be familiar with my testimony. One of the worst ones was my addiction to pornography. The devil got a big hook in my jaw and drug me around for years.

I felt like I was absolutely helpless to avoid the many temptations the enemy threw like bait in front of a fish. Magazines, adult theatres, on-line porn, adult chat lines, and sexually suggestive conversations occupied an ever larger percentage of my day, every day.

I had descended into reprobation, perversion and depravity of every kind. I participated in almost every form of sexual immorality. Romans 1:18-32 certainly described me, especially verses 24-28. Before Christ, I was filled with shame, regret and embarrassment for the life I was living, but I felt helpless to stop. Have you ever felt this way?

Praise God for freedom! Jesus forgave me for my many sins of yesterday, but He also paid the price to set me free from the power of sin today and tomorrow. But, I have a responsibility to cooperate with His Holy Spirit as He teaches me how to resist temptation and stay free.

We must want to leave our sin, and turn to God. We must choose to take every thought captive to the obedience of Christ (2 Corinthians 10:4-5). Memorizing and quoting scripture specific to the temptation is one of the best ways to accomplish this. Today's verse is still an effective weapon for me.

TODAY'S CHALLENGE:

Tell the Father how thankful you are for Jesus setting you free from the power of sin. Be intentional about staying free.

Dive Deeper: Study Job 31; Romans 1:18-32; 2 Corinthians 10:4-5.

November 30

WILLING AND OBEDIENT

Isaiah 1:19-20
"If you are willing and obedient, you will eat the good things of the land; 20 but if you resist and rebel, you will be devoured by the sword. For the mouth of the Lord has spoken."

One of the Lord's greatest prophets was Isaiah. He lived about seven hundred years before Christ.

A true prophet had a responsibility to speak truth as revealed directly from God, regardless of the consequences. Isaiah certainly knew how to let the people know what God was thinking and saying, and he was unconcerned about what the people thought about him for it.

The first chapter of Isaiah is a stinging indictment of the condition of the country and its people at the time. I recommend you take a few minutes to read it. Actually, it sounds a lot like the state of our world today, even as it regards many within the Body of Christ.

God is not interested in our "religious" activities, He expects our obedience. His Heart is not to see His people struggle, but they are reaping what they sowed in disobedience. When will they learn there are very definite consequences of sin and bad decisions?

Rebellion is such a powerfully useful tool of the enemy, and there are many resulting sins and terrible effects. Heartache, disease, loss, and death are just a few ways we see it destroy people.

Today's passage makes it clear what awaits those who submit willingly to God in obedience; and, unfortunately, what happens to those who insist on resistance and rebellion towards God. A person reaps what they sow.

TODAY'S CHALLENGE:

Ask the Father to forgive you of any areas where you have been disobedient, stubborn or rebellious. Make a decision to allow the Holy Spirit to lead you today to be obedient.

Dive Deeper: Study Isaiah 1.

December 1

CALLING EVIL GOOD

Isaiah 5:20
"Woe to those who call evil good and good evil, who put darkness for light and light for darkness, who put bitter for sweet and sweet for bitter."

We really shouldn't be surprised at how fast the world is sliding into hell. Jesus told us things would get worse and worse as we near the end of the age and the soon coming Day of the Lord. But my heart breaks for how sinful the world has become, especially in America.

In spite of how "progressives" continually want to hide or re-write the history of America, the truth is that our country was founded on Judeo-Christian principles, values and ethics. Yet, today, every semblance of Christian influence in our culture is being attacked and destroyed.

All the values that have been good and loving in our country are now called evil and hateful. Evil deeds formerly done in darkness are now openly celebrated in the light. The enemy is making great inroads in turning everything upside down, substituting counterfeits and perversions for the real and decent things of God.

Judgment is fast approaching. I recommend you study the surrounding context of today's passage, Isaiah 5:8-30. As it was with the people of Israel in Isaiah's day, so it is now in our day. The patience and mercy of God is wearing very thin. His justice and revenge for wickedness and evil is fast approaching.

There has never been a more important time for true Christians to be bold and courageous. We must speak the truth in love. We cannot remain silent.

TODAY'S CHALLENGE:

Pray for a real Holy Ghost revival in our country and this troubled world; and, for people to be overwhelmed with the need for true repentance. Ask the Spirit for courage and boldness.

Dive Deeper: Study Isaiah 5; Ephesians 4:15; Acts 4:29-31.

December 2

SEND ME

Isaiah 6:8
"Then I heard the voice of the Lord saying, 'Whom shall I send? And who will go for us?' And I said, 'Here am I. Send me!'"

Not every Christian is called to be a pastor, teacher or evangelist; but every one of us is called to be an ambassador for Christ. We should all be responding as Isaiah did in today's passage.

An ambassador is generally an official representative of a government; and, an agent of the highest rank appointed for a special assignment. As born again believers, God has officially appointed us to represent His Heavenly Kingdom to the people of earth. See 2 Corinthians 5:20.

As His appointees, we are to represent the message, truth, values and ethics of His Kingdom. We carry His authority everywhere we go every hour of the day. We must always be ready to respond to His leadership by His Holy Spirit, fully expecting Him to provide us with opportunities to positively influence someone with the Kingdom message.

Our most important area of influence and impact is in our day-to-day lives wherever we spend most of our waking hours. The Kingdom of Heaven is not meant to be experienced solely inside the four walls of a building we call a "church" on Sunday morning! In fact, I suggest, it is to be primarily advanced in our workplace and living environments.

I heard it said that, "God does not call the trained; He trains the called!" You are in training every day as you pray, study the Word, and are led by the Holy Spirit. Stay ready!

TODAY'S CHALLENGE:

Thank the Father for appointing you to represent Him to the world. Use the authority Jesus gave you as you choose to be led by the Spirit today.

Represent Him well.

Dive Deeper: Study Isaiah 6; 2 Corinthians 5:20

December 3

THE SEVEN SPIRITS OF GOD

Isaiah 11:2-3
"The Spirit of the Lord will rest on him — the Spirit of wisdom and of understanding, the Spirit of counsel and of might, the Spirit of the knowledge and fear of the Lord — ³ and he will delight in the fear of the Lord."

Have you ever noticed that the Bible says there are seven Spirits of God? No? It surprised me too.

Stop a minute and check out these scriptures: Revelation 1:9; Revelation 3:1; and, Revelation 4:5. I wondered specifically what these seven Spirits would be, and the Holy Spirit led me to today's passage in Isaiah 11:2-3.

So, are the seven Spirits of the Lord listed here by Isaiah? I believe they are. If so, they would be the Spirit of wisdom, the Spirit of understanding, the Spirit of counsel, the Spirit of might, the Spirit of knowledge, and the Spirit of the fear of the Lord. Wait. Isn't that only six?

I asked the Holy Spirit, what is the seventh? He had me focus on the first line, "the Spirit of the Lord…" That seems too general, but our Lord Jesus said, "I am the Truth." That's it, I thought, there must be a Spirit of Truth because the Lord told us He is Truth, and that is the one thing that is conspicuously absent from the list of the other six!

Now, I am not saying, "Thus says the Lord…", I am only sharing what I believe the Holy Spirit shared with me - truth, wisdom, understanding, counsel, might, knowledge and the fear of the Lord. I want more of all of the seven Spirits of God by and through the One Holy Spirit!

TODAY'S CHALLENGE:

Ask the Father to reveal more of each of His Seven Spirits to you through His One Holy Spirit.

Dive Deeper: Study Isaiah 11; Revelation 1:9, 3:1, 4:5.

December 4

THINGS PLANNED LONG AGO

Isaiah 25:1, 9
"Lord, you are my God; I will exalt you and praise your name, for in perfect faithfulness you have done wonderful things, things planned long ago...
⁹ In that day they will say, 'Surely this is our God; we trusted in him, and he saved us. This is the Lord, we trusted in him; let us rejoice and be glad in his salvation.'"

Matthew 25:34
"Then the King will say to those on his right, 'Come, you who are blessed by my Father; take your inheritance, the kingdom prepared for you since the creation of the world."

Could we just stop a few minutes to think about eternity in Heaven with our Lord and Savior?

As born-again children of our Father God, we have so very much to look forward to in eternity. God planned *"things long ago"* (Isaiah 25:1) concerning *"the kingdom prepared for you since the creation of the world."* (Matthew 25:34).

Just think about that. God always knew we would need a Savior from the day the Father, Son and Spirit said, *"Let us make man in our image."* (Genesis 1:26). Throughout the entire Bible, we can trace the scarlet thread of redemption all the way from the sacrifice required to cover Adam and Eve in the Garden (Genesis 3:21), to the Lamb in Revelation "who was slain from the creation of the world." (Revelation 13:8).

We who have trusted in Jesus can be assured with certainty we will inherit *"the city which has foundations, whose builder and maker is God."* (Hebrews 11:10). Oh, brothers and sisters in Christ, let us rejoice and be glad in His salvation!

TODAY'S CHALLENGE:

Thank the Father, Son and Holy Spirit for planning your inheritance from the creation of the world. Receive the Kingdom!

Dive Deeper: Study Isaiah 25; Matthew 25; Genesis 1:26, 3:21; Revelation 13:8; Hebrews 11:10.

December 5

PERFECT PEACE

Isaiah 26:3-4, 12
"You will keep in perfect peace those whose minds are steadfast, because they trust in you. ⁴ Trust in the Lord forever, for the Lord, the Lord himself, is the Rock eternal... ¹² Lord, you establish peace for us; all that we have accomplished you have done for us."

For many years I was searching for something to fill the emptiness within. In my school life, temporary fulfillment was found in popularity with others, academic achievement, and elected leadership roles. It mainly came from fickle "friends", and it was all fleeting. Nothing filled the hole inside.

In my professional life, I was certain the next raise, the early promotion, or another "good job" from the boss would satisfy the emptiness. The "top of the ladder" success on Park Avenue in New York City didn't cut it. Neither did the beautiful wife and adopted infant son.

Dissatisfaction with worldly success, and a mid-life crisis, led to searching for completion in drugs, alcohol, pornography and sexual immorality. The hole deep inside me only got deeper and wider. Nothing worked and I thought there was only one way to stop hurting – suicide. Couldn't do it.

Looking back, I praise God regularly for preventing my death and allowing me to go to prison. Alone, on my bunk, I cried out to God from the memories I had of Him growing up in the Baptist church, received His love and forgiveness, and asked Jesus to come into my heart.

Instantly I was filled with peace and sweet relief from the Holy Spirit of God. I haven't been lost, lonely, depressed, or empty since. Do you have His Peace?

TODAY'S CHALLENGE:

Reaffirm your trust in the Father, and thank Him for your Eternal Rock, Jesus. Rest in the Spirit.

Dive Deeper: Study Isaiah 26; Philippians 4:4-8; Romans 8:6; 2 Timothy 1:7; 1 John 4:18; Hebrews 13:5-6; John 14:27, 16:33; Isaiah 32:17, 48:17-18; Psalm 34:14, 119:65; 1 Peter 5:6-7; 2 Thessalonians 3:16; 1 Corinthians 14:33; Galatians 5:22-23.

December 6

STOP CONFRONTING US

Isaiah 30:9-11
"For these are rebellious people, deceitful children, children unwilling to listen to the Lord's instruction. ¹⁰ They say to the seers, 'See no more visions!' and to the prophets, 'Give us no more visions of what is right! Tell us pleasant things, prophesy illusions. ¹¹ Leave this way, get off this path, and stop confronting us with the Holy One of Israel!'"

In today's passage, God was speaking through Isaiah about His Israelite children. In fact, He begins chapter 30 by saying, *"Woe to the obstinate children... to those who carry out plans that are not mine..."* (verse 1). His children didn't listen, and they were eventually attacked by godless nations, carried off into captivity, and finally scattered among the nations.

They did not want to hear the truth prophesied over them. They did not want to be confronted about their sin. According to our passage today, they only wanted to hear encouraging, feel good messages from false Shepherds (see Ezekiel 34:1-10). They wanted to go their own way.

In the body of Christ, Paul warned that in the last days, *"For the time will come when people will not put up with sound doctrine. Instead, to suit their own desires, they will gather around them a great number of teachers to say what their itching ears want to hear."* (2 Timothy 4:3).

My heart breaks for so many in America who are sitting under false Shepherds eagerly hearing messages that tickle their ears and condone sin. America does not want to be confronted with Biblical truth because it is offensive to their sensibilities and lifestyles.

God punished His children before. How shall we escape?

TODAY'S CHALLENGE:

Pray that a spirit of repentance and revival will overcome our nation, and that everyone will relentlessly pursue truth and holiness before it is too late.

Dive Deeper: Study Isaiah 30; Ezekiel 34:1-10; 2 Timothy 4:3.

December 7

THIS IS THE WAY

Isaiah 30:19, 21
"People of Zion, who live in Jerusalem, you will weep no more. How gracious he will be when you cry for help! As soon as he hears, he will answer you... [21] *Whether you turn to the right or to the left, your ears will hear a voice behind you, saying, 'This is the way; walk in it.'"*

Isaiah is hearing from God and writing under the anointing of the Holy Spirit as he foresees the day when everyone will have ready access to the Holy Spirit. Perhaps he is looking ahead to the day when Jesus said He would send His disciples the Comforter, Teacher and Helper, the Holy Spirit:

"And I will ask the Father, and he will give you another advocate to help you and be with you forever— [17] *the Spirit of truth. The world cannot accept him, because it neither sees him nor knows him. But you know him, for he lives with you and will be in you."* (John 14:16-17)

Once the Holy Spirit came to live in us as Believers, we gained permanent access to the One Who wants to lead us all day every day. Romans 8:14, *"For those who are led by the Spirit of God are the children of God."* I believe this is the voice Isaiah was prophesying about in verse 21 above – the voice of the Holy Spirit.

His is the still, small voice, or gentle whisper, Elijah heard in 1 Kings 19:12, as the Lord instructed him. For me, He speaks quietly from the middle of my spirit. I do my best to listen and obey Him.

TODAY'S CHALLENGE:

Tell the Father you desire to better hear the voice of His Holy Spirit directing your life daily.

This is the way, walk in it.

Dive Deeper: Study Isaiah 30; John 14:16-17; Romans 8:14; 1 Kings 19:11-13.

December 8

THE FRUIT OF RIGHTEOUSNESS

Isaiah 32:17-18
"The fruit of that righteousness will be peace; its effect will be quietness and confidence forever. [18] My people will live in peaceful dwelling places, in secure homes, in undisturbed places of rest."

Romans 14:17
"For the kingdom of God is not a matter of eating and drinking, but of righteousness, peace and joy in the Holy Spirit..."

What wonderful truths are disclosed in these two passages! Before I was saved I never dreamed peace and fulfillment was so readily and easily available to me (see December 5 devotional). Yet, I have been so richly blessed to be experiencing it for years.

I realize I have no righteousness of my own, but in Christ I have the righteousness of God (1 Corinthians 5:21). Before I was born again, I thought it must be pretty boring to be a Christian always trying to do the right thing, and probably impossible to achieve anyway.

Jesus said to, *"...seek first his kingdom and his righteousness, and all these things will be given to you as well."* Isaiah, in verse 18 above, says, *"My people will live in peaceful dwelling places, in secure homes, in undisturbed places of rest."* Paul assures us, *"the kingdom of God is not a matter of eating and drinking, but of righteousness, peace and joy in the Holy Spirit..."*

Can I just tell you, in my experience, this is a wonderful, Kingdom of God way of abundant life!?! Before I gave my life to Jesus, I never really knew peace, joy and righteousness. Do you have it?

TODAY'S CHALLENGE:

Tell the Father you want to experience all of the fruit of the Kingdom that He has made available to you in the righteousness of His Son, Jesus, by His Holy Spirit.

Dive Deeper: Study Isaiah 32; Romans 14:17; 1 Corinthians 5:21; John 10:10.

December 9

ANCIENT PATHS

Jeremiah 6:16
This is what the Lord says: "Stand at the crossroads and look; ask for the ancient paths, ask where the good way is, and walk in it, and you will find rest for your souls. But you said, 'We will not walk in it.'"

When we are faced with a crossroads we are forced to make a decision. Which way should I go? God says for us to take these choices seriously. Stand, look, and examine the options. Talk to the Father about the best way. What have people who have stood here before discovered? Which way did they go that led to success? Ask God which is the good way. Which way is in His perfect will?

Robert Frost wrote a poem, "The Road Not Taken", which finishes with this stanza:

"I shall be telling this with a sigh
Somewhere ages and ages hence:
Two roads diverged in a wood, and I—
I took the one less traveled by,
And that has made all the difference."

All of us can think of opportunities in the past to choose between two different paths, and generally, we chose the easier one – the one with the most pleasure or immediate gratification. It was well worn. Most of the time, we could probably agree, it didn't work out too well. Usually we saw "the good way", but we deliberately said, "We will not walk in it."

The good path is narrow, and less traveled, but leads to abundant rest and peace. It is the ancient path that our spiritual fathers chose. Take it. It is much more rewarding.

TODAY'S CHALLENGE:

Talk to the Father about your choices today. Ask for wisdom and discernment to choose correctly.

Dive Deeper: Study Jeremiah 6; Matthew 11:28-30; John 14:6; Isaiah 30:21.

December 10

TRUTH HAS PERISHED

Jeremiah 7:28-29
"Therefore say to them, 'This is the nation that has not obeyed the Lord its God or responded to correction. Truth has perished; it has vanished from their lips. ²⁹ Cut off your hair and throw it away; take up a lament on the barren heights, for the Lord has rejected and abandoned this generation that is under his wrath.'"

This passage could easily apply to our world today, although it was written about 2,600 years ago and applied to Israel. The most striking phrase to me, *"Truth has perished; it has vanished from their lips."* Consider the current state of society. Doesn't this describe us?

I often hear phrases like, "He has his own truth", or, "She is living her truth her way". Society treats truth as "subjective" and "relative", meaning that it is determined by one's own mind, or is related to the circumstances at the time. We should actually say, "He has his perception of the truth", or, "She is living based on her interpretation of the truth".

Truth is "objective". That is, it exists outside and independent of one's own mind. It deals with actual facts without the distortion of personal feelings or prejudices.

Truth is a person, and His Name is Jesus Christ of Nazareth! He is the Living Word of God, and we have the Bible as the standard of truth determined independently from man by God Himself. Deep inside people know right from wrong, but when it interferes with their desires, they justify why it should be different for them.

Let's decide to seek objective truth from the Word of God, receive it as our standard, and obey it.

TODAY'S CHALLENGE:

Tell the Father you want to better know the Person Who is the Truth, Jesus; and, that you will live according to His instruction by the Holy Spirit.

Dive Deeper: Study Jeremiah 7; John 14:6.

December 11

BOAST ABOUT THIS

Jeremiah 9:23-24
"This is what the Lord says: 'Let not the wise boast of their wisdom or the strong boast of their strength or the rich boast of their riches, [24] but let the one who boasts boast about this: that they have the understanding to know me, that I am the Lord, who exercises kindness, justice and righteousness on earth, for in these I delight,' declares the Lord."

For most of us, the majority of our life is consumed with learning, doing things to support or strengthen our physical body, and working to pay bills and accumulate wealth. In and of themselves, there is nothing wrong with any of this; in fact, we deem these things to be evidence of living a responsible life.

Yet, our natural tendency is to take great pride in our intelligence, physical strength, and possessions. We may not always brag about them openly, but inside, to ourselves, we do.

But, all these things are temporary. Our intelligence and physical strength deteriorate over time; and, are totally gone with our physical death. Similarly, we cannot take our possessions into eternity with us. Someone said, "There is never a U-Haul trailer hooked up to a hearse."

I would much rather talk about who I am in Christ now than who I once was before I was saved. The success and money of my earlier life did not last; but what I have now in Christ will last for all of eternity. My life has never been fuller or possessed more meaning.

I didn't create it or earn it. It all flows from my growing knowledge, love and appreciation of God.

TODAY'S CHALLENGE:

Tell the Father you want to set good priorities; and, above all, you want to know Him better.

Dive Deeper: Study Jeremiah 9.

December 12

GOD SEARCHES THE HEART

Jeremiah 17:9-10
"The heart is deceitful above all things and beyond cure. Who can understand it? ¹⁰ "I the Lord search the heart and examine the mind, to reward each person according to their conduct, according to what their deeds deserve."

Joseph Conrad's, Heart of Darkness, is a literary classic. It explores the symbolic darkness of man's heart as two men experience the depths of literal darkness in the Congo in Africa. The dying last words of one of the main characters were, "The horror! The horror!"

Surely, most of the troubles of mankind throughout history can be traced to the misunderstanding, or misreading, of the true intentions or condition of a human heart. I can think of Hitler or Stalin, for example. Closer to home, men have always had trouble understanding the heart of the opposite sex. Do I have a witness?

When Samuel was sent to the house of Jesse to find the next King of Israel, God said, *"People look at the outward appearance, but the LORD looks at the heart."* (1 Samuel 16:7). Only God is capable of seeing, understanding and judging the human heart. Our scripture today says God searches the heart and examines the mind for the purpose of rewarding each person according to what their deeds deserve.

That should get our attention. When I was not living for the Lord I justified my sinful actions by saying, "God knows my heart." That's the problem! God saw my heart, and truthfully evaluated it which, thankfully, finally led to the conviction that I needed salvation.

It is only a heart that has been regenerated in the new birth that even comes close to properly representing God, and is therefore subject to receiving good rewards.

TODAY'S CHALLENGE:

Ask the Father to help you examine your heart today and purge it of anything that's not like Jesus.

Dive Deeper: Study Jeremiah 17; 1 Samuel 16:7; Matthew 12:34; Proverbs 4:23; Philippians 4:4-9.

December 13

GREAT IS HIS FAITHFULNESS

Lamentations 3:19-23
"I remember my affliction and my wandering, the bitterness and the gall.
²⁰ I well remember them, and my soul is downcast within me. ²¹ Yet this
I call to mind and therefore I have hope: ²² Because of the Lord's great
love we are not consumed, for his compassions never fail. ²³ They are new
every morning; great is your faithfulness."

In the past, if I let my mind dwell on the days before I was born again at age 57, my heart would sink into regret, remorse, shame and embarrassment. I could remember the hopelessness and despair leading to suicidal thoughts and attempts. I couldn't help but be reminded of the helplessness of my addictions, and the darkness of evil in the places I went to pursue pleasure. Does this ever happen to you?

Today, when the enemy reminds me just how sinful I really was, I stop right then and take those thoughts captive to the obedience of Christ. Out of my own mouth, I declare thankfulness to God that I am not that old person anymore. I thank God verbally that my old man is dead, and that I am a totally new man in Christ Jesus. I thank God that He did not let me die in my sin, and that He kept loving me in spite of myself.

In the years that have passed since 2009 when I was saved, I have seen God be ever so faithful, patient and kind with me. We are all still works in progress and we can be sincerely thankful for the complete and consistent faithfulness of God. Amen?

TODAY'S CHALLENGE:

Tell the Father how grateful you are for His love, patience, kindness and faithfulness towards you. Thank Him for making you a new creation in Christ Jesus.

Dive Deeper: Study Lamentations 3; Deuteronomy 7:9; Psalm 89:8, 98:3; Joel 2:23; 1 Corinthians 1:9.

December 14

KEEP ON KEEPING ON

Daniel 6:10
"Now when Daniel learned that the decree had been published, he went home to his upstairs room where the windows opened toward Jerusalem. Three times a day he got down on his knees and prayed, giving thanks to his God, just as he had done before."

Daniel's honesty, integrity and obvious favor with God made those around him uncomfortable and envious. They couldn't find anything he was doing wrong, so they created a "religious" law designed to entrap, persecute and eliminate him. They persuaded King Darius to pass a law that required people to pray to no god or man except the king for thirty days, else the offender would be thrown to the lions.

Certainly this was somewhat disguised, but it was outright persecution for Daniel's faith in God. Daniel stood firm for his convictions, kept putting God first in his life as he had always done, was arrested, and thrown in with the lions. Rather than deny God, Daniel quietly and bravely faced death. I am certain you know what happened, but the exciting story in fully contained in Daniel chapter 6.

Persecution of Christians worldwide has been a very serious problem for years, and America is just beginning to see its own examples, although they are not yet anywhere near as severe. The international ministry, Open Door, reported that 1 in 9 Christians worldwide already face high levels of persecution. In 2018, there were 4,136 Christians killed for faith-related reasons worldwide; and, 1,266 churches or other Christian buildings were attacked.

When we are faced with similar persecution, I pray we will all re-double our efforts to keep on faithfully serving God.

TODAY'S CHALLENGE:

Ask the Father for the same type of courageous spirit Daniel possessed. Keep on keeping on!

Dive Deeper: Study Daniel 6; Daniel 3:13-30; Acts 4:13-20.

December 15

SHINE LIKE A STAR

Daniel 12:3
"Those who are wise will shine like the brightness of the heavens, and those who lead many to righteousness, like the stars for ever and ever."

James 5:19-20
"My brothers and sisters, if one of you should wander from the truth and someone should bring that person back, [20] remember this: Whoever turns a sinner from the error of their way will save them from death and cover over a multitude of sins."

God calls all men everywhere to repent (Acts 17:30), and we know He is not willing that any should perish (2 Peter 3:9). No man can come to Christ unless the Spirit draws him (John 6:44). However, God gives us the opportunity to be involved with Him in the salvation of souls. I am sure He could do it all on His own, but I imagine He takes great pleasure in rewarding His children!

In 1 Corinthians 3:8, Paul says, *"The one who plants and the one who waters have one purpose, and they will each be rewarded according to their own labor."* Often times, we may think we cannot help with someone's salvation, but even the smallest efforts can be used by God as an act of planting or watering seed.

Some have the ministry gift of evangelism, but I would suggest most of the preparatory work to make a heart ready is really accomplished by others. Anyone can pray for the lost, leave a tract in a strategic place, give someone a Bible, or encourage someone with a verse of scripture.

God will reward you for helping in any way to bring someone to Him. Get involved.

TODAY'S CHALLENGE:

Ask the Father to help you stay alert for ways to encourage others to come to Christ.

Dive Deeper: Study Daniel 12; Acts 17:20; 2 Peter 3:9; John 6:44; 1 Corinthians 3:8; James 5:19-20.

December 16

SOW RIGHTEOUSNESS

Hosea 10:12
"Sow righteousness for yourselves, reap the fruit of unfailing love, and break up your unplowed ground; for it is time to seek the LORD, until he comes and showers his righteousness on you."

Galatians 6:7
"Do not be deceived: God cannot be mocked. A man reaps what he sows."

What does it mean to "sow righteousness"? To me, one way of looking at it would be when I am faced with a decision between two actions, I would always want to choose to "do the right thing". Also, since righteousness means "to be in right standing", I would want to be intentional about doing things with which God is pleased.

God's unconditional love is always extended towards us, but I believe if we are proactive about remaining in right standing with God, we would be positioned to more fully experience His unfailing love. Of course, doing good things for others with the right motivation will eventually result in more love being sent our way from others.

Since today's verse encourages us to "break up your unplowed ground", this might mean to examine those areas of my life where no righteousness is being produced, and then take action to surrender that part of my life to God. That is, "unplowed ground" could be parts of my life that I haven't yet fully committed to God.

Let's don't deceive ourselves, we are always sowing and reaping. What is happening in our lives today is a result of what we sowed sometime in the past. Choose to sow righteousness.

TODAY'S CHALLENGE:

Tell the Father you want to always be in right standing with Him. Ask the Holy Spirit to identify any unplowed ground and teach you how to make it productive.

Dive Deeper: Study Hosea 10; Galatians 6.

December 17

BE WISE AND DISCERNING

Hosea 14:9
"Who is wise? Let them realize these things. Who is discerning? Let them understand. The ways of the Lord are right; the righteous walk in them, but the rebellious stumble in them."

Before I was saved in 2009, I would not have referred to myself as "wise" or "discerning". I had a lot of book knowledge, and a fair amount of common sense, but I did not usually exercise wisdom or discernment. The proof was one poor decision after another resulting in a trail of destruction; and, generally, I was an easy "mark" because I was often so trusting. I was actually quite gullible, especially when it came to a sad story.

Of course, at the time I was in no way pursuing God or His ways, so I really had no idea what was right in His eyes. Occasionally, I would try to do good, or be good, but that never lasted very long because deep down I wanted to do things my way in my timing. That is the sure sign of a rebellious spirit. Consequently, it was never long before I was back to my old ways.

Paul tells us in 1 Corinthians 1:30, that Jesus Christ *"has become for us wisdom from God—that is, our righteousness, holiness and redemption."* After I gave my life to Jesus, the Holy Spirit has been making the wisdom and righteousness of Christ increasingly more real and available to me. The Holy Spirit also brings discernment the longer one walks in Christ.

Do you stumble in His ways? Are you rebellious in any area of your life?

TODAY'S CHALLENGE:

Ask the Father to reveal any areas in your life where you are not exercising wisdom and discernment. Ask the Holy Spirit to help you choose the ways of the Lord.

Dive Deeper: Study Hosea 14; 1 Corinthians 1:30.

December 18

GOD WILL REPAY YOU

Joel 2:25-26
"I will repay you for the years the locusts have eaten— the great locust and the young locust, the other locusts and the locust swarm— my great army that I sent among you. ²⁶ You will have plenty to eat, until you are full, and you will praise the name of the Lord your God, who has worked wonders for you; never again will my people be shamed."

Jesus told us that the devil came to steal, kill and destroy (John 10:10), but many of us pretty much cooperated with him and gave him everything because we were intentionally participating in sin. I doubt if I am the only one. Right?

Yet, today's verse also says God Himself sends a "great army" of destructive locusts into our lives. I believe God allows His law of cause and effect (or sowing and reaping) to do a natural boomerang on us due to our sin and other bad decisions. In this way, perhaps, He could finally get our attention and we could choose to turn to Him and be saved (Isaiah 45:22).

It is truly amazing how many real life examples I personally know of, including my own, where God has incredibly and richly blessed those who turned their lives back to Him. In every way that matters, I have so much more spiritually, emotionally, and materially, than I ever had when I was serving the devil.

God truly "has worked wonders" for us and taken away our shame. Our cup runs over (Psalm 23)!

Maybe you haven't seen it yet? Serve Him with your whole heart. He will absolutely amaze you.

TODAY'S CHALLENGE:

Thank the Father for His everlasting goodness and grace towards you. Count your blessings today and praise God.

Dive Deeper: Study Joel 2; John 10:10; Isaiah 45:22; Psalm 23.

December 19

GOD REVEALS HIS PLANS

Amos 3:7
"Surely the Sovereign Lord does nothing without revealing his plan to his servants the prophets."

It seems God gives us plenty of warning before He does something really significant. This includes, of course, the coming of the Messiah, Jesus; bringing judgment on the land; setting His people free from Egypt, restoring the land after a period of captivity, etc.

Bible teacher, Jack Kelley, believes at least 25-30% of the scriptures were actually prophetic when they were written:

"When you include the parts of the Bible that were prophecy when they were first written but have subsequently been fulfilled (such as the prophecies of the Babylonian captivity, the Lord's first coming, and the destruction of Jerusalem) with the parts that were prophecy when they were first written and have not been fulfilled yet (such as the prophecies of the end times judgments, the Lord's second coming, and the millennium) most experts agree with the 25-30% estimate I used. Some even place it higher."

The value of studying prophecies that have already been fulfilled is that they validate God's promise that prophecies of events still in our future will also be fulfilled. They also confirm that He is who He claims to be; the One who knows the end from the beginning."[1]

As you continue to study the Bible, and read the best research by the world's foremost Christian apologists, your appreciation for the beauty and accuracy of the Word will only keep growing.

TODAY'S CHALLENGE:

Thank the Father for the magnificence of His Word, and its accuracy and relevance over time.

Dive Deeper: Study Amos 3; Revelation 19:10.

[1] https://gracethrufaith.com/ask-a-bible-teacher/much-bible-prophecy-2/ (as of 6/9/19)

December 20

CALL URGENTLY ON GOD

Jonah 3:8-10
"'But let people and animals be covered with sackcloth. Let everyone call urgently on God. Let them give up their evil ways and their violence. ⁹ Who knows? God may yet relent and with compassion turn from his fierce anger so that we will not perish.' ¹⁰ When God saw what they did and how they turned from their evil ways, he relented and did not bring on them the destruction he had threatened."

When God first called Jonah to go to Nineveh with a warning of soon coming judgment, Jonah ran the opposite direction. I identify with Jonah's story because I ran from God for years. Have you?

There are always ramifications of refusing to serve God, but Jonah's were especially extreme and quick (Jonah 1). It didn't take too long for God to get Jonah's attention, and he called out to God in true repentance (Jonah 2). I think we make things a lot worse on ourselves the longer we wait to repent and obey.

God told Jonah a second time to go to Nineveh and this time he went. As Jonah entered the very large city which reportedly took three days to cross through, he sounded the warning God gave him, "Forty more days and Nineveh will be overturned." The Ninevites believed God and the King sent out an urgent message of national mourning and fasting as we see in today's passage.

God relented, withdrew His Hand of Judgment and Nineveh was spared at that time. The mercy and compassion of God in response to the urgent call on Him by truly repentant people leaves me with a measure of hope for our country and world. Will we repent in time?

TODAY'S CHALLENGE:

Cry urgently out to God on behalf of yourself, your family and our world. Repent. Time is short.

Dive Deeper: Study Jonah 1:1 – 4:11.

December 21

GOD ASSEMBLES THE EXILES

Micah 4:6-7
"In that day, declares the Lord, I will gather the lame; I will assemble the exiles and those I have brought to grief. [7] I will make the lame my remnant, those driven away a strong nation. The Lord will rule over them in Mount Zion from that day and forever."

Jesus makes the point in Luke 7:41-50, that those who have been forgiven much, love much; but those who have been forgiven little, love little. That really touches my heart, because I know how very much I have been forgiven, and I am radically in love with my Savior.

I can also relate to Matthew 25:31-40, where Jesus tells of a last days' judgment that will be based on how "the least of these" were treated. The "least of these" includes prisoners, the hungry, the needy and the sick. Having once been a starving, homeless person who eventually went to prison, my heart is now very tender towards those who suffer in these ways.

Since I suffered for years with bipolar illness and suicidal depression, I identify with those who are mentioned above as having been "brought to grief". Having been labeled a sex offender for the crime of solicitation of a minor, I sympathize with those who have been figuratively crippled by society; and certainly, also with those who are actually physically challenged.

Therefore, today's passage makes me love the Lord all the more. One day He will raise an army of those who have been marginalized, discouraged, exiled, and physically or emotionally challenged. I see Him doing it now in the prisons.

Those who are forgotten by the world are a glorious, loved, remnant nation to the Lord!

TODAY'S CHALLENGE:

Think about how much you are loved by the Lord. Receive it, and share it with someone.

Dive Deeper: Study Micah 4; Luke 7:41-50; Matthew 25:31-40.

December 22

WALK HUMBLY WITH YOUR GOD

Micah 6:8
"He has shown you, O mortal, what is good. And what does the Lord require of you? To act justly and to love mercy and to walk humbly with your God."

"He has shown you, O mortal, what is good." How has God done this? He has shown us in His Son, Jesus. He came from Heaven, and took on our fleshly body to live among us so He could show us the way to the Father.

He came to set us free from the power of sin so we can "act justly". In and of our own selves we are incapable of the righteousness required for us to act justly towards others. Yet, in Christ we are the righteousness of God (2 Corinthians 5:21). He was just.

Jesus loved mercy. One of many examples would be the woman caught in the act of adultery (John 8:1-11). Legally, He could have agreed with the Pharisees that her crime was punishable by death. Instead, He wisely convinced her accusers to be merciful, though they did so begrudgingly; and, He tenderly showed her God's pure love, forgiveness and mercy. He was even loving when He told her to stop sinning.

There is not a better example of humility for us to model than Jesus Himself. Here was the King of Kings, yet He humbled Himself to wash the feet of His disciples. He could have entered Jerusalem victoriously on a white stallion; instead, he rode unceremoniously on the foal of a donkey. There are many other examples.

It is not really hard to meet the Lord's requirement of us if we will just do the best we can to live every day like Jesus.

TODAY'S CHALLENGE:

Ask the Father, by His Spirit, to teach you how you can better imitate Jesus today.

Dive Deeper: Study Micah 6; 2 Corinthians 5:21; John 8:1-11; Philippians 2:1-13.

December 23

A JEALOUS AND AVENGING GOD

Nahum 1:2-3
"The Lord is a jealous and avenging God; the Lord takes vengeance and is filled with wrath. The Lord takes vengeance on his foes and vents his wrath against his enemies. ³ The Lord is slow to anger but great in power; the Lord will not leave the guilty unpunished. His way is in the whirlwind and the storm, and clouds are the dust of his feet."

The people of Nineveh urgently called out to God and repented after Jonah warned them of impending judgment (see devotional for December 20).

Unfortunately for them, within a relatively short time they returned to their old ways of idolatry and rampant sinfulness. In our passage today, God is speaking to them through another prophet, Nahum, one hundred years later. This time they did not repent and were utterly destroyed.

Nineveh was the capital of Assyria, and the Assyrian empire had only grown more wicked since the time of their earlier reprieve from God. They were known as the most brutal and violent conquerors of their day, and some historians say, there has never been an empire since then that surpassed their cruelty. They were the conquerors of the northern kingdom of Israel.

There is One God and He allows no room for idols. The Assyrians viewed Jehovah as just another of the many gods they worshiped. Surely the Lord is slow to anger, and merciful, but eventually His justice must be exercised. God is safety for those who take refuge in Him but danger to those who disregard Him. And because the Assyrians disregard Him they cannot be safe.[1]

God does not change. Pray for our nation and this world to repent and turn to the One True God.

TODAY'S CHALLENGE:

Pray to the Father for a spirit of repentance to reign on this earth.

Dive Deeper: Study Nahum 1.

[1] https://overviewbible.com/nahum/ (as of 6/10/19)

December 24

BE UTTERLY AMAZED

Habakkuk 1:5
"Look at the nations and watch— and be utterly amazed. For I am going to do something in your days that you would not believe, even if you were told."

From the time I gave my heart to Jesus in 2009, I have not ceased to be amazed at what God has done – utterly amazed! Not just in my own life, but in the lives of our prison ministry volunteers, many of whom are former offenders like me. Additionally, He continues to move dramatically in all the ministries with which we are associated, not just our own.

God is no respecter of persons, what He does for one He will do for all! Check out these scriptures: Deuteronomy 10:17; Psalms 36:7-8; Matthew 22:16; Acts 10:34; Romans 2:11; Ephesians 6:9; James 2:1-3; and, 1 Peter 1:17. God is able to do exceedingly more than you can even ask or imagine (Ephesians 3:20)!

He is able to restore children to you, repair broken marriages, provide employment opportunities, improve housing, increase finances, and reveal His perfect will for your life. He restores hope, purpose and passion for living. He reveals His love and longing for intimate relationship with you.

When you are totally committed to serving God as obediently as you know how, in spite of your circumstances, tests and trails, God honors your wholehearted devotion. Jesus said, in John 15:7-8, *"If you remain in me and my words remain in you, ask whatever you wish, and it will be done for you. This is to my Father's glory, that you bear much fruit, showing yourselves to be my disciples."* You will be utterly amazed!

TODAY'S CHALLENGE:

Talk to the Father about your hopes and dreams for your life. Serve Him wholeheartedly today.

Dive Deeper: Study Habakkuk 1; Deuteronomy 10:17; Psalms 36:7-8; Matthew 22:16; Acts 10:34; Romans 2:11; Ephesians 6:9; James 2:1-3; 1 Peter 1:17; Ephesians 3:20; John 15:7-8.

December 25

WONDERFUL COUNSELOR

Isaiah 9:6-7
"For to us a child is born, to us a son is given, and the government will be on his shoulders. And he will be called Wonderful Counselor, Mighty God, Everlasting Father, Prince of Peace. ⁷ Of the greatness of his government and peace there will be no end. He will reign on David's throne and over his kingdom, establishing and upholding it with justice and righteousness from that time on and forever. The zeal of the Lord Almighty will accomplish this."

Over 700 years before the birth of our Lord Jesus, Isaiah wrote this prophecy. Today is the day that has been designated as the celebration of His birth although no-one knows for sure when His actual birth date was. Frankly, we ought to celebrate His birth every day!

Jesus has been given to us to restore us to relationship with our "Everlasting Father" through the forgiveness of sin. He is the "Mighty God" and "Prince of Peace". His justice and righteousness know no bounds; and, His love for us is eternal, unlimited, and unconditional. He is the King of kings, and Lord of lords.

Today, I am especially thankful that He is "Wonderful Counselor"; and, I am reminded the angel announced to Mary that His Name would be "Immanuel", which means "God With Us" (Matthew 1:23). To me, "God With Us", foretold of the gift the Father and Son would send us in the form of their Spirit, the Holy Spirit (Acts 1:4), who would never leave us (Matthew 28:20).

Jesus said it was better for Him to go away because He would send the Counselor, the Holy Spirt (John 16:7). Today I am especially thankful He did!

TODAY'S CHALLENGE:

Thank the Father for sending the Son, and for the two of them sending the Holy Spirit.

Dive Deeper: Study Isaiah 9; Matthew 1:23; Matthew 28:30; Acts 1:4; John 16:7.

December 26

GOD REJOICES OVER YOU

Zephaniah 3:17
"The Lord your God is with you, the Mighty Warrior who saves. He will take great delight in you; in his love he will no longer rebuke you, but will rejoice over you with singing."

"The Lord your God is with you!" Yesterday, we celebrated the One Who is Immanuel, "God With Us", and the Holy Spirit Who was given to us when Jesus ascended to the Father. The Holy Spirit is always with us, and He is our Counselor, Teacher, Friend, Helper and Guide.

"The Mighty Warrior who saves." Our God is the Lord of Heavenly Hosts in that He commands innumerable angels to war in the spiritual realm. He never loses. Jesus forever defeated death, hell and the grave! *"If God is for us, who can be against us"* (Romans 8:31).

"He will take great delight in you." From the creation of the world God has loved you and wrote your name in His book (Revelation 17:8). His plan has always been to offer to you an intimate relationship because He enjoys His Creatures and only wants us to choose to be with Him forever.

"In His love He will no longer rebuke you." All the wrath of God towards sinners was poured out on His Son, Jesus. As believers, we do not incur His wrath (1 Thessalonians 5:9).

God *"will rejoice over you with singing."* This is a magnificent picture of His joy and love for us. Can you imagine Him holding you, smiling lovingly in your eyes, and singing over you like a proud Papa?

Imagine that, God rejoices over you!

TODAY'S CHALLENGE:

Tell the Father how much you love Him, and talk to him about today's verse from your heart.

Dive Deeper: Study Zephaniah 3; Romans 8:31; Revelation 17:8; 1 Thessalonians 5:9.

December 27

GIVE CAREFUL THOUGHT TO YOUR WAYS

Haggai 1:5-7
"Now this is what the Lord Almighty says: "Give careful thought to your ways. ⁶ You have planted much, but harvested little. You eat, but never have enough. You drink, but never have your fill. You put on clothes, but are not warm. You earn wages, only to put them in a purse with holes in it." ⁷ This is what the Lord Almighty says: "Give careful thought to your ways."

My first thought as I read this passage today is about my life before age 57 when I finally got saved. Think about your life before Christ. Can you relate?

In my early professional life, I was a "work-aholic". All my focus was on getting ahead, being the best, and climbing to the top of the ladder of success. Joyce Meyers once said, "Sometimes you can spend your whole life getting to the top of the ladder only to realize once you're there that your ladder was leaning against the wrong building!" That was me.

Material possessions never satisfied for very long. There was always something newer, or something better, to covet and possess. Whether it was intentional or not, trying to "keep up a good front" was expensive and never-ending. It didn't matter how much money I made, it always seemed like there was "still more month at the end of the money". Having anything saved back for "a rainy day" seemed impossible.

With Christ Jesus, I now experience true joy, fulfillment, peace, and satisfaction. Since I learned to generously give tithes and offerings I have more money put back than I ever had before.

If you're "saved", but not experiencing something similar, *"give careful thought to your ways."*

TODAY'S CHALLENGE:

Ask the Father to show you any of your ways that are not pleasing to Him.

Dive Deeper: Study Haggai 1.

December 28

ENEMIES OF THE CROSS

Philippians 3:18-19
"For, as I have often told you before and now tell you again even with tears, many live as enemies of the cross of Christ. [19] Their destiny is destruction, their god is their stomach, and their glory is in their shame. Their mind is set on earthly things."

My heart breaks for so many lost souls who are even now as I once was before Christ. Paul could have been describing me. Thank you, Jesus, it is no longer true of me, and I pray you too can say the same.

We are called to be ambassadors of Christ (see devotional for December 2), and as such, it is our duty to tell as many as possible about the love and forgiveness of God. We must pray diligently for those who are lost, and we should also pray for boldness and confidence to share the Good News with them.

Especially in these last days, our daily lives ought to bear witness of the reality of the power of God to truly transform a life from the kind of person we once were as described in today's passage. One of the fathers of our faith once said, "Preach the Gospel at all times, and only if necessary, use words." People should see something in us that attracts them to Christ.

People who have not truly repented and turned from their sin to obediently follow Jesus are, in fact, headed for destruction. If I had not turned around to receive love and forgiveness in Christ, I surely would have ended up where I was headed – to Hell.

Nobody has to end up there. Let's do everything we can to encourage them to turn around.

TODAY'S CHALLENGE:

Ask the Father for courage and boldness to tell someone about Jesus today.

Dive Deeper: Study Philippians 3.

December 29

TAKE HOLD OF TODAY

Philippians 3:12-14
"Not that I have already obtained all this, or have already arrived at my goal, but I press on to take hold of that for which Christ Jesus took hold of me. [13]Brothers and sisters, I do not consider myself yet to have taken hold of it. But one thing I do: Forgetting what is behind and straining toward what is ahead, [14] I press on toward the goal to win the prize for which God has called me heavenward in Christ Jesus."

"Forgetting what is behind" ... for me, this may be the biggest revelation that set me free. God has forgiven me for all of my past. He is not holding my past against me, so why should I? I used to say "I can't forgive myself"; but, God showed me that the Blood of Jesus was good enough for Him to forgive me, so who am I to say I can't forgive me? That would mean I am better than God?

Stop letting your past impact today or ruin your future. Let your tombstones be stepping stones. You must live today and look forward to tomorrow. Memory allows you to re-live your past, but it can become your jailer! Don't hold on to what God has let go!

God is an omnipresent God which means He is everywhere present all the time. You can only have a relationship with the Father in the present. He was in your past. He will be in your future. But, He is always only available to you in the ever present now.

If the enemy keeps you living in the guilt, shame, regret and remorse of your past, you cannot enjoy God in the present. Put the past in the past and let it stay there.

TODAY'S CHALLENGE:

Tell the Father you want to take hold of today. Thank Him for forgiving your past.

Dive Deeper: Study Philippians 3; Isaiah 42:9, 43:18; Genesis 19:26; Luke 9:60-62.

December 30

COMPLETING THE TASK

Acts 20:24
"However, I consider my life worth nothing to me; my only aim is to finish the race and complete the task the Lord Jesus has given me—the task of testifying to the good news of God's grace."

None of us is promised tomorrow. We do not know when we will take our last breath on Earth and our first breath in eternity. Life is so fragile, and time is very short. Compared to our life in eternity, our short time here on Earth is as the blink of an eye.

So, what is our life really worth? Perhaps God measures it by whether we impacted souls for eternity in Heaven. Jesus said the value of one soul is worth more than everything in the world (see Matthew 16:26). Jesus also said all of Heaven rejoices over just one soul who repents (Luke 15:7). Will I positively influence at least one soul for eternity in Heaven? Will you?

God has impressed upon me the lateness of the hour. I believe Jesus could return any day now. The Holy Spirit tells me to focus on today. Whatever He has told me to do today, I should do it the with a sense of excellence and urgency. Tomorrow, He will give me new marching orders.

Perhaps that is the main reason today's passage resonates so deeply inside me. Nothing else really matters if I can't help make eternity matter to one more person. My purpose and my passion – my whole reason for being here right now – is to testify to what the Blood of Jesus has done in my life. That is my task.

I want to finish strong. How about you?

TODAY'S CHALLENGE:

Tell the Father you want to serve Him today with a sense of excellence and urgency.

Dive Deeper: Study Acts 20; Matthew 16:26; Luke 15:7.

December 31

PRAY FOR PRISON MINISTRY VOLUNTEERS

Ephesians 6:19-20
"Pray also for me, that whenever I speak, words may be given me so that I will fearlessly make known the mystery of the gospel, [20] for which I am an ambassador in chains. Pray that I may declare it fearlessly, as I should."

As we close out the year, let's pray for every person who is a prison ministry volunteer, or prison Chaplain. There is a great revival happening all across America in the prisons. Many prophecies have gone forth that America's great revival will start there. I believe we are seeing it now.

God is raising up a mighty army of former offenders who are not ashamed of the Gospel of Jesus Christ. Before they were saved they were not afraid to serve the devil; and today, they are boldly serving Jesus! To my incarcerated brothers and sisters in Christ, please know you are crucial to this revival.

There is no-one more important to prison ministry than believers still behind razor wire. You are in the best position to see what needs to be done, and who needs help, in the ongoing battle to bind the strongman and carry off his possessions!

True, committed believers in prison may be considered as being behind enemy lines! You are God's special forces operating secretly in small numbers to spoil the enemy's plans and organize resistance to his evil schemes. Like the Navy SEALS, or the Army's Airborne Rangers, Christian prisoners are at the very tip of the spear, the leading edge of our attack on Satan and his forces. Be ready. Be vigilant. Be strong and very courageous (Joshua 1:5-9). Be strong in the Lord and in His mighty power (Eph. 6:10).

TODAY'S CHALLENGE:

Please pray often for me, Stephen Canup, and Freedom in Jesus Prison Ministries. God bless you!

Dive Deeper: Study Ephesians 6; Joshua 1:5-9; Jeremiah 29:11-14.

Take Action

YOU CAN HAVE "THE REAL THING"

"The Real Thing" has nothing to do with "religion."

Rather, it is an intimate personal relationship with our Heavenly Father, because of the finished work of Jesus at the Cross. The Holy Spirit comes and seals us as His very own, and begins an ongoing work in us to conform us to the image of Christ Jesus.

You can begin this exciting and abundant life today. It will continue throughout all eternity.

First, acknowledge and confess that you have sinned against God.

Second, renounce your sins – determine that you are not going back to them. Turn away from sin. Turn to God.

Third, by faith receive Christ into your heart. Surrender your life completely to Him. He will come to live in your heart by the Holy Spirit.

You can do this right now.

Start by simply talking to God. You can pray a prayer like this:

"Oh God, I am a sinner. I'm sorry for my sin. I want to turn from my sin. Please forgive me. I believe Jesus Christ is Your Son; I believe He died on the Cross for my sin and You raised Him to life. I want to trust Him as my Savior and follow Him as my Lord from this day forward, forevermore. Lord Jesus, I put my trust in You and surrender my life to You. Please come into my life and fill me with your Holy Spirit. In Jesus' Name. Amen."

If you just said this prayer, and you meant it with all your heart, we believe you just got Saved and are now Born Again in Christ Jesus as a totally new person.

"Therefore, if anyone is in Christ, he is a new creation; the old has gone, the new has come!" (II Corinthians 5:17)

We urge you to go "all in and all out for the All in All"! (Pastor Mark Batterson, All In)

We suggest you follow the Lord in water baptism at your earliest opportunity. Water baptism is an outward symbol of the inward change that follows your salvation and re-birth.

The grace of God Himself gives you the desire and ability to surrender completely to the Holy Spirit's work in and through you (Philippians 2:13).

The Baptism in the Holy Spirit is His empowerment for you.

YOU CAN RECEIVE THE BAPTISM IN THE HOLY SPIRIT

The Baptism in the Holy Spirit is a separate experience and a Holy privilege granted to those who ask. This is God's own power to enable you to live an abundant, overcoming life. The Bible says it is the same power that raised Jesus from the dead (Romans 1:4; 8:11; II Cor. 4:13-14; 1 Peter 3:18).

Have you asked the Father for Jesus to baptize you (immerse you) in the Holy Spirit (Luke 3:16)? If you ask the Father, He will give Him to you (Luke 11:13). Have you allowed the "rivers of living water" to flow from within you (John 7:38-39)? Our Father desires for us to walk in all His fullness by His Holy Spirit.

The power to witness, and live your life the way Jesus did in intimate relationship with the Father, comes from asking Jesus to baptize you in the Holy Spirit. To receive this baptism, pray along these lines:

Abba Father and my Lord Jesus,
Thank you for giving me your Spirit to live inside me. I am saved by grace through faith in Jesus. I ask you now to baptize me in the Holy Ghost with Your fire and power. I fully receive it through faith just like I did my salvation. Now, Holy Spirit, come and rise up within me as I praise God! Fill me up Jesus! I fully expect to receive my prayer language as You give me utterance. In Jesus' Name. Amen.

Now, out loud, begin to praise and glorify JESUS, because He is the baptizer of the Holy Spirit! From deep in your spirit, tell Him, "I love you, I thank you, I praise you, Jesus."

Repeat this as you feel joy and gratefulness bubble up from deep inside you. Speak those words and syllables you receive – not in your own language, but the heavenly language given to you by the Holy Spirit. Allow this joy to come out of you in syllables of a language your own mind does not already know. That will be your prayer language the Spirit will use through you when you don't know how to pray (Romans 8:26-28). It is not the "gift of tongues" for public use, therefore it does not require a public interpretation.

You have to surrender and use your own vocal chords to verbally express your new prayer language. The Holy Spirit is a gentleman. He will not force you to speak. Don't be concerned with how it sounds. It is a heavenly language!

Worship Him! Praise Him! Use your heavenly language by praying in the Spirit every day! Paul urges us to "pray in the Spirit on all occasions with all kinds of prayers and requests." (Ephesians 6:18)

CONTACT US

We would love to hear your feedback or answer your questions.

- We would especially like to know if you made a decision to receive Jesus into your heart and prayed the prayer of Salvation on page 379. Or maybe you had prayed a similar prayer before, but this is the first time you really meant it from your heart. Tell us about your decision.

- Perhaps you made a decision to rededicate your life to Christ – to go "all in and all out" for Jesus! If so, we would like to know so we can encourage you. Please write to us.

- If you prayed the prayer to ask Jesus to baptize you in the Holy Spirit, please tell us. When you do, we will send you more material on the Holy Spirit.

- As a further aid and encouragement, we would like to teach you more about how to follow Jesus – how to be a true disciple. A disciple is a "disciplined learner" and we want to share many truths with you about how to have an intimate relationship with God the Father, by the Holy Spirit. Jesus came to reconcile us to the Father. We want to help you develop a meaningful relationship with Him.

  Please ask for us to include you in our Discipleship Program whereby you will receive an encouraging teaching every three months or so. This is not the kind of lesson you are required to fill in and send back to us. You must only desire to be encouraged regularly in the Lord, and be willing to prayerfully study the materials. That's all.

Please send your comments, questions and feedback to:

Freedom in Jesus Prison Ministries
Attn: Stephen – DD
P.O. Box 939
Levelland, TX 79336

Ask your loved ones to check out our ministry website: **www.fijm.org**

We pray you are blessed abundantly by our Father every day, in every way, in Christ Jesus as you seek Him daily in and by the Holy Spirit!

I CHALLENGE YOU!!

God is able to transform your life in the same way He did mine.

But you must understand that He rewards those who diligently and earnestly seek Him (Hebrews 11:6); and, that you are transformed by renewing your mind through applying the principles in His Word to your daily life (Romans 12:1-2).

I challenge you to:

- Start every day with the Word and the Spirit. Ask the Holy Spirit to help you apply His Truth to your life. Focus on the scripture passage intently. Let the Spirit use the Word to transform you.

- Look up every scripture reference in this book. Mark the verses in your own Bible. Memorize the ones that mean the most to you.

- Study the scriptural principles in this book in small groups. Sharing concepts from the Word with others helps you learn and apply them to your life.

- Share your own testimony with others. You "overcome" when you personally testify to yourself and others what the Blood of Jesus has done in your own life (see Revelation 12:11).

- Loan this book to at least three others if your facility permits you to do so. As an ambassador for Christ (see II Corinthians 5:18-20), please use this book as a tool to reach the lost. After sharing it with them, tell them then to write to me and request their own copy of the book so they can study it and loan it to others. Each person who wants one must write me individually because I can only send one book to each person.

- Pray daily for me and for our ministry. We need your prayers. At your first opportunity, begin a program of regular giving to us so we can better minister to others who want to be free from every form of bondage.

INFORMATION FOR FURTHER STUDY AND APPLICATION

PRAYERS OF SUBMISSION

Daily Prayer of Surrender and Submission

Father God, I humbly surrender and submit myself fully to You and your leadership by Your Holy Spirit.

Lord, please forgive me for both my willful and my unintentional sins. Help me to freely and fully forgive others as You forgive me.

Father, I submit willingly and completely to your Hand as The Potter. Re-make me into the person You want me to be for the plan You have for me in Your perfect will. As You do, conform me to the image of Jesus by the sanctifying work of Your Holy Spirit.

Father, by Your grace help me to always be a grateful, humble heir of all Your promises; an obedient, faithful servant of all Your commands; a persistent, bold witness of Your salvation through Jesus; and, a loving, trusting child full of Your love. I surrender to Your Holy Spirit's leadership.

Let me be patient and persevering in prayer, ever watchful and responsive for opportunities to bless others as You have blessed me. Empower me Father with Your grace, through the Spirit of Jesus in me, to diligently seek You and Your eternal Kingdom, so that I will not be distracted and overcome with the temptations and temporary pleasures of this alien world. In everything I think, say and do today, Father, let me continually glorify and honor You.

I love You, Jesus. I praise You and adore You for first loving me. Thank You for being made sin for me so that I am made righteous in You. Please love and bless others through me today as I seek to know and do Your perfect will for my life. I want to be led today by Your Holy Spirit in me.

In the power of the blood of Jesus, and the authority of His Name I pray. Amen.

Prayer of Submissive Obedience in a Particular Area

Father, You are worthy of all praise, honor, and glory. I adore You. I worship You. I praise Your Holy Name.

Lord, You have been so patient with me, and I thank You. I also recognize Your still, small voice, speaking to me about an area of my life that needs resolution. You have been reminding me of my need to move ahead in this certain area, and I confess that I have not yet obeyed You. Please forgive me for my hesitation.

Today, I declare that I will take the step of faith You have spoken to me about. Lord, in regard to this step that I have been hesitant to take, I put away all my reluctance now, and I pledge to You that I will obey You.

And Lord, in those matters where I have been doing what You would prefer that I not do, I lay them aside, so that I can make room to do what You want me to do.

This is the way I choose to walk with you from now on. Laying aside my hesitancy and stubbornness, I step boldly, choosing You and Your purposes for my life. I declare that I will follow You in obedience.

Thank You, Lord! In Jesus' Name I pray. Amen.

Note: The prayer above was taken from a teaching by Derek Prince, www.derekprince.org

CONFESSIONS FOR EVERY DAY

Loved One in Christ - Build your faith and claim God's promises for yourself by reading these confessions of God's Word aloud (thoughtfully and prayerfully – with conviction) every day. Keep doing it until they are your thoughts so that you can use the Word against Satan to "take every thought captive" when he attacks your mind! To "confess" is to say the same thing as God, so that as the Word transforms your mind, His thoughts become your thoughts! Confess these daily at least once – early morning is best so you are "armed and dangerous" when Satan attacks during the day! Before bedtime is good too so you are protected as you rest.

- I am not just an ordinary man/woman. I'm a child of the living God.

- I am not just a person; I'm an heir of God, and a joint heir with Jesus Christ. I'm not "just an old sinner", I am a new creation in Jesus, my Lord. I'm part of a chosen generation, a Royal Priesthood, a Holy Nation. I'm one of God's people. I am His. I am a living witness of His grace, mercy and love!

- I have been crucified with Christ and I no longer live, but Christ lives in me! The life I live in the body, I live by the faith of the Son of God, who loved me, and gave Himself for me. When the devil tries to resurrect the "old man", I will rebuke him and remind him sternly that I am aware of his tricks, lures, lies and deception. The "old man" is dead. My "new man" knows all old things are passed away - all things have become new!

- I'm not under guilt or condemnation. I refuse discouragement, for it is not of God. God is the God of all encouragement. There is therefore now no condemnation for those in Christ Jesus. Satan is a liar. I will not listen to his accusations.

- I gird up my loins of my mind. I am cleansed in the Blood. No weapon formed against me shall prosper, and I shall condemn every tongue rising against me in judgment. I am accepted in the beloved. If God be for me, who can be against me?

- My mind is being renewed by the Word of God. I pull down strongholds; I cast down imaginations; I bring every thought captive to the obedience of Christ.

- As the Father loves Jesus, so Jesus loves me. I'm the righteousness of

God in Christ. I'm not slave of sin; I am a slave of God and a slave of righteousness. I continue in His Word; I know the truth and I practice it, so the truth sets me free.

- Because the Son sets me free, I am free indeed. He who is born of God keeps me, therefore the evil one does not touch me. I've been delivered out of the kingdom of darkness. I am now part of the Kingdom of Light, the Kingdom of God. I don't serve sin any longer. Sin has no dominion over me.

- I will not believe the enemy's lies. He will not intimidate me. He is a liar and the father of lies. Satan is defeated. For this purpose, the Son of God came into this world – to destroy the works of the devil. No longer will he oppress me. Surely, oppression makes a wise person mad. I will get mad at the devil. I defeat him by the Blood of the Lamb, by the word of my testimony as to what He has done for me, not loving my life, even to death.

- I will submit to God. I will resist the devil and he will flee. No temptation will overtake me that is not common to man. God is Faithful and True; He will not let me be tempted beyond my strength, but with the temptation He will also provide the way of escape (Jesus) that I may be able to endure.

- I will stand fast in the liberty with which Christ has made me free. Where the Spirit of the Lord is, there is liberty – not liberty to do what I "want", but freedom to do as I "ought". The law of the Spirit of Life in Christ Jesus has set me free from the law of sin and death.

- Nothing can separate me from the love of God that is in Christ Jesus, my Lord. His Holy Spirit is my guide, comforter, teacher and best friend! Jesus is my Protector, my Deliverer, my Rewarder, my Refuge, my Strong Tower, my Shepherd, my Light, my Life, my Counselor, my Rock, my Freedom! He is everything to me!

- Christ causes me to triumph. I will reign as a king in life through Christ Jesus. As a young man/woman I am strong. The Word of God abides in me, and I have overcome the evil one. I am more than a conqueror through Christ who loves me. I am an overcomer. I am invincible. I can do all things through Christ who strengthens me. Thanks be to God who gives me the victory through Jesus Christ, my Lord!

WISDOM AND GUIDANCE CONFESSIONS

- The Spirit of Truth abides in me and teaches me all things, and He guides me into all truths. Therefore, I confess I have perfect knowledge of every situation and circumstance I come up against, for I have the wisdom of God. (John 16:13; James 1:5)

- I trust in the Lord with all my heart and I do not lean or rely on my own understanding. In all my ways I acknowledge Him, and He directs my path. (Proverbs 3:5-6)

- The Lord will perfect that which concerns me, and fulfill His purpose for me. (Psalm 138:8)

- I let the Word of Christ dwell in me richly in all wisdom. (Colossians 3:16)

- I do follow the Good Shepherd, and I know His voice. The voice of a stranger I will not follow. (John 10:4-5)

- Jesus is made unto me wisdom, righteousness, sanctification, and redemption. Therefore, I confess I have the wisdom of God, and I am the righteousness of God in Christ Jesus. (I Cor. 1:30; II Cor. 5:21)

- I am filled with the knowledge of the Lord's will in all wisdom and spiritual understanding. (Colossians 1:9)

- I am a new creation in Christ. I am His workmanship created in Christ Jesus. Therefore, I have the mind of Christ and the wisdom of God is formed within me. (II Cor. 5:17; Ephesians 2:10; I Cor. 2:16)

- I receive the Spirit of wisdom and revelation in the knowledge of Him, the eyes of my understanding being enlightened. I am not conformed to this world but I am transformed by the renewing of my mind. My mind is renewed by the Word of God. (Ephesians 1:17-18; Romans 12:2)

I AM...

- I am forgiven. (Col. 1:13-14)
- I am saved by grace through faith. (Eph. 2:8)
- I am delivered from the powers of darkness. (Col. 1:13)
- I am led by the Spirit of God. (Rom. 8:14)
- I am kept in safety wherever I go. (Psalm 91:11-12)
- I am getting all my needs met by Jesus. (Phil. 4:19)
- I am casting all my cares on Jesus. (I Peter 5:7)
- I am not anxious or worried about anything. (Phil. 4:6)
- I am strong in the Lord and in the power of His might. (Eph. 6:10)
- I am doing all things through Christ who strengthens me. (Phil. 4:13)
- I am observing and doing the Lord's commandments. (Deut. 28:13)
- I am blessed going in and blessed going out. (Deut. 28:6)
- I am above only and not beneath. (Deut. 28:13)
- I am blessed with all spiritual blessings. (Eph. 1:3)
- I am healed by His stripes. (I Peter 2:24)
- I am more than a conqueror. (Romans 8:37)
- I am an overcomer by the Blood of the Lamb and the word of my testimony. (Rev. 12:11)
- I am not moved by what I see. (II Cor. 4:8-9)
- I am walking by faith and not by sight. (II Cor. 5:7)
- I am daily overcoming the Devil. (I John 4:4)
- I am casting down vain imaginations. (II Cor. 10:4)
- I am bringing every thought into captivity. (II Cor.10:5)
- I am not conformed to this world, but I am being transformed by renewing my mind. (Romans 12:1-2)
- I am blessing the Lord at all times and continually praising the Lord with my mouth. (Psalm 34:1)
- I am a child of God. (Romans 8:16)

PERSONALIZED DAILY PRAYERS

Loved one in Christ: These passages of scripture from Paul, David, and Isaiah have been personalized for you. They are powerful prayers, by powerful men, to the Most Powerful! As you pray God's Word back to Him, He is pleased, for He has told us to put Him in remembrance of His Word. Do you think He needs to be reminded? Like He forgot? No, we are the ones who need to be reminded. We claim these awesome promises for ourselves. Pray these daily as the Spirit leads you. You will be richly blessed in doing so.

In the name of Jesus,

I praise you Lord from my soul. From my inmost being I praise your Holy name. I praise you Lord from my soul. I will not forget all your benefits – you forgive all my sins and heal all my diseases. You redeemed my life from the pit and crowned me with your love and compassion. You satisfy my desires with good things so that my youth is renewed like an eagle's. Amen. (Psalm 103:1-5)

In the name of Jesus,

As I dwell in the shelter of the Most High I will rest in the shadow of the Almighty. I will say of you Lord, "You are my refuge and my fortress. You are my God and I will trust in you." Surely you will save me from the fowler's snare and from the deadly pestilence. You will cover me with your feathers, and under your wings I will find refuge; your faithfulness will be my shield and rampart.

I will not fear the terror of night nor the arrow that flies by day, nor the pestilence that stalks in the darkness, nor the plague that destroys at midday. A thousand may fall at my side, ten thousand by my right hand, but it will not come near me.

I will observe with my eyes and see the punishment of the wicked. I will make the Most High my dwelling – the Lord is my refuge – so that no harm will befall me, no disaster will come near my tent. God, you will command your angels concerning me to guard me in all my ways; they will lift me up in their hands, so that I will not strike my foot against a stone. I will tread upon the lion and the cobra; I will trample the great lion and the serpent.

Lord, you said because I love you, you will rescue me. You will protect me, for I acknowledge your name. I will call upon you and you will answer me; you will be with me in trouble, you will deliver me and honor me. With long life will you satisfy me and show me your salvation. Amen. (Psalm 91)

In the name of Jesus,

No weapon forged against me will prevail and I will refute every tongue that accuses me. This is my heritage as a servant of the Lord, and this is my vindication from you. Amen. (Isaiah 54:17)

In the name of Jesus,

I keep asking that you, God of my Lord Jesus Christ, my glorious Father, may give me the Spirit of wisdom and revelation that I may know you better. I pray also that the eyes of my heart may be enlightened in order that I may know the hope to which you have called me, the riches of your glorious inheritance in the saints, and your incomparably great power for us who believe. That power is like the working of your mighty strength, which you exerted in Christ when you raised Him from the dead and seated Him at your right hand in heavenly realms, far above all rule and authority, power and dominion, and every title that can be given, not only in the present age but also in the one to come. And you, God, placed all things under His feet and appointed Him to be over everything for the church, which is His body, the fullness of Him who fills everything in every way. Amen. (Ephesians 1:17-23)

In the name of Jesus,

I pray that out of your glorious riches you may strengthen me with power through your Spirit in my inner being, so that Christ may dwell in my heart through faith. And I pray that as I am rooted and established in love, I may have power, together with all the saints, to grasp how wide and long and high and deep is the love of Christ, and that I may know this love that surpasses knowledge – that I may be filled to the measure of all your fullness.

Now to you, God, who is able to do immeasurably more than all I ask or imagine, according to your power that is at work within me, to you be glory in the church and in Christ Jesus throughout all generations, forever and ever! Amen. (Ephesians 3:16-21)

In the name of Jesus,

This also is my prayer: that my love may abound more and more in knowledge and depth of insight, so that I may be able to discern what is best and may be pure and blameless until the day of Christ, filled with the fruit of righteousness that comes through Jesus Christ – to the glory and praise of you, God. Amen. (Philippians 1:9-11)

In the name of Jesus,

I pray that you fill me with the knowledge of your will through all spiritual wisdom and understanding. I pray this in order that I may live a life worthy of the Lord Jesus and please Him in every way: bearing fruit in every good work, growing in the knowledge of you, God, so that I may be strengthened with all power according to your glorious might so that I may have great endurance and patience and joyfully give you thanks. Amen. (Colossians 1:9b-11)

TEN POWERFUL PRAYERS FOR PRISONERS
BASED ON SPECIFIC SCRIPTURES

Praying the Word of God can be among the most powerfully effective prayers. Shonda Whitworth, Fortress of Hope Ministries, compiled and adapted these prayers from Scripture, and gave her permission to share them. Her website is www.fortressofhopeministries.com.

Favor

Lord, just as you were with Joseph & showed him mercy and gave him favor with the prison warden, I ask You to show me mercy & give me favor with the prison warden and C.O.'s. In Jesus name, Amen.
(Adapted from Genesis 39:21)

Prosperity of Prison Unit

Lord, I lift up this prison unit (name the unit) where I have been exiled. I pray for the peace and prosperity of the unit. As it prospers, so then shall I live in peace and prosper. In Jesus name, Amen.
(Adapted from Jeremiah 29:7)

Mercy

Lord, have mercy on me, according to Your unfailing love; and according to Your great compassion blot out my transgressions. Wash away all my iniquity and cleanse me of all my sin. In Jesus name, Amen.
(Adapted from Psalm 51:1-2)

Protection

Lord, keep me out of the hands of the wicked and protect me from those who are violent. The Lord is a fortress & a refuge in my day of distress. Lord, may Your love and faithfulness always protect me. In Jesus name, Amen.
(Adapted from Ps 140:4; 59:16; 40:11)

Healing

Lord, thank You that Jesus Himself bore my sins in His body for me on the cross, so that I might die to sin and live in righteousness, for by His wounds I am healed. In Jesus name, Amen.
(Adapted from 1 Peter 2:24)

Fear

Lord, I cast all my burdens on You, for You shall sustain me. For You shall never permit the righteous to be moved. Lord, You have not given me a spirit of fear, but of power, of love, and of a sound mind. In Jesus name, Amen.
(Adapted from Psalm 55:22; 2 Tim 1:7)

Peace with Enemies

Lord, I pray I live in a way that is pleasing to You. For when I live in a manner that is pleasing to You, then all my enemies will live at peace with me.
(Adapted from Proverbs 16:7)

Plans and Purpose

For You have thoughts that You think toward me, thoughts of peace and not of evil, to give me a future and a hope. For I am Your workmanship, created in Christ Jesus for good works, which You, God, prepared beforehand that I should walk in them.
(Adapted from Jeremiah 29:11; Ephesians 2:10)

Help

Lord, I lift my eyes upon the hills; where does my help come from? My help comes from the Lord, the maker of heaven and earth. The Lord is my helper. I will not fear. What can man do to me? The Lord is my strength and my shield; My heart trusts in in Him and I am helped. My heart rejoices and I sing songs or praise to Him.
(Adapted from Psalm 121:1-2; Hebrews 13:6; Psalm 28:7)

Pray for those in Authority

Lord, I thank You for Your Word that teaches me how to live. Lord, I come before You today as instructed by You to lift up supplications, prayers, intercession, and give thanks for the correction officers and wardens who are in authority over me. I ask You to have mercy upon them and I thank You for all You will do for them. Lord, I ask that You guide them in Your knowledge and understanding, giving them wisdom for each situation they face. I ask You to protect them from the evil one and meet all of heir needs according to Your glorious riches. I pray that they serve You with integrity and honesty. Lord, as I pray for those who are in authority over me, I ask that I be able to live with peace and quietness so I can spend my time inside living a godly life and serving You wholeheartedly. In Jesus name I pray, Amen.
(Adapted from 2 Tim 3:16; 1 Tim 2:1-2; Luke 6:36; Proverbs 2:6-8; Matt 6:13; Phil 4:19)

Diving Deeper
Scripture Passage Index

Acts 1:4-5; Feb. 20, Mar. 24

Acts 1:4-5, 8; May 22

Acts 1:5; Feb. 15; June 4

Acts 1:8; Feb. 18; June 5

Acts 1:14; May 23

Acts 2:1-4; Mar. 25, Apr. 13, May 24

Acts 2:3; June 22

Acts 2:15; June 16

Acts 4:12; July 22

Acts 5:3-4; April 2

Acts 7:51; Apr. 16

Acts 8:14-17; Mar. 27; June 6

Acts 8:15-16; Feb. 16

Acts 8:29; Apr. 11

Acts 8:39-40; June 21

Acts 9:17-18; June 7

Acts 9:31; June 1

Acts 10:38; Mar. 19, Sept. 15

Acts 10:44-47; June 8

Acts 13:2; Mar. 29, Apr. 11, May 9

Acts 19:1-2; June 9

Acts 19:1-6; Mar. 28

Acts 19:4-6; Feb. 17

Acts 20:24; Dec. 30

Romans 1:4; Apr. 26; May 19

Romans 1:21-22; July 2

Romans 1:24-25; July 3

Romans 1:24, 26, 28; July 5

Romans 5:8; Jan. 21

Romans 5:9; Jan. 22

Romans 6:6-7; July 17

Romans 6:23; June 23

Romans 8:11; Apr. 26, May 31

Romans 8:14; Aug. 31

Romans 8:26; May 6

Romans 8:27; May 7

Romans 8:28; May 8, Oct. 8

Romans 8:29; Aug. 11

Romans 8:35, 37; Sept. 8

Romans 9:20; Jan. 11

Romans 10:16-17; July 20

Romans 12:1; Jan. 14

Romans 12:2; Jan. 7, Jan. 15, Feb. 22; Aug. 29

Romans 14:17; June 17; Dec. 8

Romans 15:17-19; Aug. 7

Romans 15:30; Apr. 10, May 1

1 Corinthians 1:18; Apr. 1

1 Corinthians 1:30; Aug. 26

1 Corinthians 2:9-10; Apr. 4

1 Corinthians 2:15-16; Aug. 28

1 Corinthians 3:16; Apr. 5

1 Corinthians 4:10; Apr. 1

Ephesians 6:10; Sept. 4

Ephesians 6:19-20; Dec. 31

Philippians 1:9-10; Sept. 12

Philippians 2:13; May 28

Philippians 2:14-16; Oct. 1

Philippians 3:12-14; Dec. 29

Philippians 3:13-14; Jan. 24; July 15

Philippians 3:18-19; Dec. 28

Philippians 4:6; Sept. 3

Philippians 4:8-9; Jan. 17

Philippians 4:9; Sept. 17

Philippians 4:12-13; Aug. 6

Philippians 4:13; Sept. 4

Philippians 4:19; Sept. 2

Colossians 1:9-10; Aug. 27

Colossians 1:9-11; Sept. 14

Colossians 1:13-14; Aug. 30

Colossians 1:28-29; Aug. 9

Colossians 3:2-3; Jan. 18

Colossians 3:13; Jan. 30

Colossians 3:16; Sept. 11

1 Thessalonians 5:1-3; July 25

1 Thessalonians 5:3; Aug. 2

1 Thessalonians 5:16-19; Apr. 19

1 Thessalonians 5:19-22; June 13

2 Thessalonians 2:1-3; July 26

2 Thessalonians 2:3-4; July 27

2 Thessalonians 2:7-8; July 28

1 Timothy 1:12; Mar. 11; Aug. 17

1 Timothy 1:13-14; Mar. 12, Aug. 18

1 Timothy 1:15-16; Mar. 13, Aug. 19

1 Timothy 4:1-2; July 30

2 Timothy 1:6-7; June 11

2 Timothy 2:15; Feb. 24

2 Timothy 3:1-5; July 31

2 Timothy 3:16; May 12

2 Timothy 4:2; Feb. 26

Hebrews 4:12; Feb. 8

Hebrews 5:7: June 20

Hebrews 6:10; Sept. 21

Hebrews 6:17; May 25

Hebrews 9:14; Apr. 7, May 16

Hebrews 10:15; May 30

Hebrews 10:24-25; Mar. 2

Hebrews 10:29; Apr. 17

Hebrews 11:6; July 10

Hebrews 12:28-29; Mar. 6

Hebrews 12:29; June 22

Hebrews 13:8; May 27

James 1:5; Aug. 21

James 1:22; Sept. 17

James 3:9-10; Aug. 20

Diving Deeper

Subject Index

Holy Spirit:

Holy Spirit (continued):

Holy Spirit (continued):

Notes